PASSOVER HAGGADAH: THE COMPLETE SEDER

Step-by-Step Directions, Halakhic References, Reasons, and Sources for the Customs of the Seder

By
Arthur M. Silver

MENORAH PUBLISHING COMPANY, INC.
NEW YORK, N.Y.

First edition
Library of Congress Catalog Card Number: 79-92726
ISBN 0-932232-06-x
Manufactured in the United States of America

CONTENTS

To my parents
Harry and Sarah Silver
Their dedication to Jewish learning
has been my inspiration

FOREWORD

In the vast treasury of Jewish *halakhic* and liturgical literature, it has been the Passover *Haggadah* that has attracted the most attention throughout the ages. From about the 13th century, when the *Haggadah* began to appear as a book on its own, and especially since the advent of the printing press, the *Haggadah* has been published more often than any other Jewish work—more than 2,700 different editions. Why, one may ask, publish yet another? Because there is a need for a *Haggadah* that brings together all the details of the rituals and customs pertaining to the Seder. This is what I have attempted to do.

This *Haggadah* is written on several levels. For the novice, or one who has some knowledge of a Seder but is confused by the various rites, detailed step-by-step directions are given in the body of the *Haggadah.* Written in plain and non-technical language, every single detail of how to conduct a traditional Seder is explained, including: the preferred size of the wine goblet, when to stand, when to lift the Seder plate, when to cover the matzot, when to raise the wine glass, when to recline on the left, the proper foods for the Seder plate, the correct positioning of the foods on the Seder plate, how much of these foods should be prepared and kept in the kitchen, how much and the proper way to eat these foods, how to ritually lave the hands, the proper way to make the blessing over the *Havdalah* lights when necessary, all about the *kittel,* all about the Cup of Elijah, all about the "stealing" of the *afikoman,* as well as what to serve for the Seder meal. It will take everyone through an entire Seder without a hitch.

For those who know how to conduct a Seder but would like to know more, the reasons for and the meaning behind every action, custom, and rite are given in the explanatory section at the back of the *Haggadah,* in addition to a description of how each of these customs has come down to us through the ages. For the scholar, the source of each custom, a complete bibliography, footnotes, and an index are presented.

Many questions occur to anyone conducting a Seder. Why must the matzot be placed together with the other foods on the Seder plate? Why is there a broken plate on the table? Why is lettuce, not horseradish, preferred as the vegetable to be used for the bitter herbs? Why should all the foods on the Seder plate be eaten? Why do we "steal" the *afikoman?* Why does the youngest ask the four questions? Why do we remain seated throughout the Seder? Why do we have a Cup of Elijah? Why are eggs, cucumbers, zucchini, fennel, leeks, onions, melons, fish, and tongue among the foods that should be served as part of the Seder meal? These are but a few of the questions answered in this *Haggadah.*

The answers to these and other questions provide some surprises. Many of the customs are comparatively new. Thus, while the prayers and liturgical poems of the *Haggadah* have been established and unchanged for approximately 500 years, the customs and rites surrounding them have not. Many of our most cherished practices were established relatively recently, and many are still not firmly rooted.

It is the changing customs and the changing reasons for these customs that reflect the social upheavals and the history of our people, not only during the Exodus but throughout the ages. They have helped keep the Seder alive and made it today the most beloved and universally admired ceremony among all of Jewry: Orthodox, Conservative, Reform, and non-affiliated.

For almost 2,000 years it was tradition for the Leader of the Seder, as a sign of aristocracy and freedom, to have his wine goblet filled by his Jewish servant or, if he had none, by his wife. About 80 years ago, a great Sage recommended that this practice be abandoned because it proved nothing, as all Jews, including servants and women, are equal. The Talmud recommends the use of red wine for the four cups, since red wine is generally of a finer quality than white. However, during the 15th and 16th centuries our Sages recommended white wine because non-Jews were led to believe that the red wine used at the Seder was the blood of Christian children slaughtered for the Seder (the "blood libels"). This belief was used as an excuse for pogroms. Since the blood libels no longer pose any threats today, we again use red wine. The use of horseradish instead of lettuce for the *maror,* the bitter herbs, was based on the fact that in Eastern Europe it was too cold to grow lettuce in March and April; today there is a return to the original *maror* because of the universal availability of lettuce. The Talmudic custom that important women must recline on the left (*heseba*) was abolished from the Middle Ages onward, reflecting, in part, the position of the women of that age. Will this *minhag*, or custom, undergo another reversal to reflect the changing position of women in our society? The Cup of Elijah was instituted in the 16th century, a period of deepest depression for Jewry, as a symbol of a dream for the future, and today it represents the beginning of the fulfillment of that dream.

Finally, this is the first *Haggadah* which has included a proper and traditional menu for the Seder meal. There can be no traditional Seder without a traditional meal; such an inclusion is vital and should have been done long ago. Complete and detailed menus for Seder meals, including a menu for those who do not eat *gebroks*, are given in the section on *Shulḥan Arukh* (The Meal).

For the last-mentioned section, my thanks to Greta, my devoted wife, not for only preparing these delicious dishes on Passover nights, but for granting me permission to use these recipes from her forthcoming book.

Arthur M. Silver

New York, N.Y.
Kislev 27, 5740
December 19, 1979

PREFACE

A work of this nature, which is familiar to readers with a knowledge of Rabbinics, rarely appears in English. The general reader may therefore find the following explanations useful.

In the period of the Mishnah and the Talmud, our Sages were generally called by a single name, e.g., Rabbi Judah, Rabbi Meir, Rabbi Akiba. During the Middle Ages, the great Rabbis were generally referred to by their acronyms, e.g., Rashi (Rabbi Solomon ben Isaac), Rambam (Rabbi Moses ben Maimon), Rosh (Rabbi Asher ben Jehiel), Maharil (Morenu ha-Rav Jacob ha-Levi). From about the 14th century on, while not completely abandoning the use of acronyms, a great Sage was called by the title of his work, e.g. the *Tur* (Rabbi Jacob ben Asher), the *Shulḥan Arukh* (Rabbi Joseph Caro), the *Mishnah Berurah* (Rabbi Israel Meir Kagan), the *Arukh ha-Shulḥan* (Rabbi Jehiel Epstein). It is considered a mark of great distinction to be known by the title of one's most famous work. Although the title refers to a person, italics are used because, after all, it was originally the title of a book. Purely as a matter of style, the past tense is used for people, even where their name derives from their work, e.g., the *Tur* explained, the *Roke'aḥ* noted; the present tense is used for books alone, e.g., the Mishnah states, the Talmud rules.

Throughout, the *Encyclopedia Judaica*'s transliteration from Hebrew into English has been adopted except for the *tz* consonant where it was decided that the more familiar form should be used, e.g., matzah, *motzi*. All Hebrew words are italicized; however, those Hebrew words which have come into English usage are given as English words and therefore are not italicized, i.e., Seder, matzah.

Often multiple sources are cited. These represent the thinking of very important authorities at different periods of time and are meant to convey a feeling of historical development. The bibliography contains somewhat more information than is usual. It lists all names, both of books and of persons cited in this work and the dates when they lived.

TABLE PREPARATION

The Bible in Exodus (10:2, 12:26) tells us that one of the primary reasons for conducting a Seder is to teach our children about the origin of the Jewish people, the value of freedom, and the lessons and principles of Judaism. The *rishonim,* scholars from the middle of the 11th century to the 16th century, therefore, ruled that the table should be set before evening, without delay, lest the children fall asleep and miss the Seder.[1] However, when Passover eve falls on Saturday night, one may not prepare the table on Saturday for use on Passover[2] as the holiness of the Sabbath takes precedence over any other Festival in the Jewish calendar save Yom Kippur. Accordingly, one sets the table immediately after nightfall. Similarly, for the second Seder in the Diaspora the table is not set until after nightfall, because on the first day of a Festival one is not permitted to prepare for the second day of the Festival.[3]

The table is covered with a fine tablecloth, preferably white, suggested Rabbi Jacob Emden, as white symbolizes purity, happiness, and freedom.[4] The table is set, wrote the *Tur,* with the finest dishes, silverware, and other table appointments[5] even though throughout the year we tend to diminish the use of beautiful utensils as a remembrance of the destruction of the Holy Temple.[6] We surround ourselves with attractive and rich objects to mark this joyous occasion and to make us feel that on this night we are not slaves but free and unafraid, no matter what the true circumstances may be. An unblemished and clean wine cup or goblet that holds a *revi'it,*[7] which, according to *Siddur Minhat Yerushalaym,* is a minimum of 86.4 milliliters or 3.1 fluid ounces,[8] is required for each person. R. Emden[9] recommended a silver wine cup as the best way to follow the rule of using exquisite vessels on Seder night. Even small children old enough to be educated,[10] about five or six years of age,[11] should have their own wine cup. This is not obligatory,[12] however, and their cup need not be the proper size.[13] The Talmud relates that it is customary to give younger children nuts and sweets instead of wine in order to arouse their interest in the Seder.[14]

The question of *heseba,* or reclining on the left side during the Seder, has drawn the attention of our Sages since the Middle Ages. Historically it is known that the free and aristocratic ancients, through Roman times, used to eat while reclining on couches, each individual having his own small table. Since Passover is the festival of freedom, the Mishnah and Talmud[15] decree that one must recline during the Seder.

During the Middle Ages the style of eating changed so that everyone ate at large tables and were seated on benches or chairs, as we do today. Accordingly, some *rishonim*, among them the Ravon[16] and the Ravyah,[17] felt that since free people do not eat while reclining on couches anymore, this rule should be abolished. Although this is true, it remains incumbent on the participants in the Seder to view themselves as if they had come out of Egypt (Deuteronomy 6:23), and therefore most of our Sages ruled that we should recline as the Israelites did.[18] In addition, some Sages felt that this unusual position would attract the children's attention and prompt them to ask questions, a primary function of the Seder. Further, if we did not recline, one of the four questions of the *Mah Nishtannah* would be rendered meaningless.[19] Accordingly, it is normative practice[20] today for all adult males to recline on the left side[21] (even left-handed ones) during the Seder at the appropriate specified times.

As for women, the Talmud[22] has ruled that most women are not required to recline; however, the Talmud continues, an "important" woman is obligated to perform this act. Our Sages have discussed this question in detail, especially why most women were exempt from this requirement and what constitutes an "important" woman. One answer may be that since the woman is busy with the foods and dishes, preparing, serving, clearing, etc., the Rabbis did not require her to recline, but an "important" woman, one who has servants, does not have these duties and therefore she must recline as men do.[23] Today we follow the ruling of the Rema that although all women are considered "important," they themselves, relying on the Ravon and the Ravyah, decided they need not recline. The style of dress may have played some part in this decision. With corsets, hoops, multi-layered garments, stiff collars, and tight-fitting clothes, reclining would be not only very uncomfortable but downright painful. Today the *minhag*, or custom, is that women do not recline during the Seder.[24]

The *kittel*, sometimes called the *sargenes*, is a white linen garment resembling a surplice and consisting of a long loose gown with flowing sleeves and collar laced in front. It is accompanied by a belt of the same material and a skullcap to match. The words *kittel* and *sargenes* are of unknown origin. It is believed that the latter comes either from the French word *serge* (wool), or the Latin word *sericum* (silk), or from the German word *sarg* (coffin).

This garment, which incidentally is unknown among the Sephardim, was first mentioned in the 13th century in the *Roke'aḥ*[25] and in the *Haggahot Maimuniyyot*, a work written as a supplement to Maimonides' *Mishneh Torah* which cites the rulings of the scholars of Germany and France where they differ from those of Maimonides, who was of Spanish descent. According to the *Haggahot Maimuniyyot*,[26] in the time of his teacher, Rabbi Meir (Maharam) of Rothenburg, the *kittel* was worn every Sabbath and *Yom Tov* and served to satisfy the requirement of the Talmud[27] that, in honor of the Sabbath, everyday clothes should be changed and clean garments worn. He also felt that this garment, which was and still is also used as a shroud, would remind man of the day of death and so would prevent any undue excesses on what is usually a very happy and joyous occasion.[26] Thus, as early as the 13th century and possibly even earlier, the *kittel* was worn by the Ashkenazim every Sabbath and *Yom Tov* over their regular clothes.[28] Eventually the *kittel*'s use as a shroud overshadowed all its other functions and it became synonymous with death and mourning; its use on the Sabbath and Festivals was largely discontinued, possibly because the Jews were now, on the whole, financially better off and could afford a change of clothing for these festive occasions.

It appears that during the 15th or early 16th century Ashkenazic Jews instituted the *minhag* of wearing the *kittel* on Yom Kippur. According to the Rema,[29] the *kittel* served a dual purpose. It made the Jews appear before the Almighty pure and white as angels; and since it was also used as a shroud it served as a reminder of the temporary and fragile nature of life and therefore made the heart contrite and led to repentance. At first, women also wore the *kittel*;[30] however, the tradition gradually evolved that only men wear it on Yom Kippur.[31] Today in most synagogues it is worn without the special matching skullcap.

At about the same time, the 15th or early 16th century, it became the custom among Ashkenazic Jews for a bride to wear a *kittel* during the marriage ceremony as a reminder of the day of death,[32] as on Yom Kippur and for similar reasons. By the 17th century, however, it was the groom who wore the *kittel* at the marriage ceremony,[33] as many do today.

Some time later in the 16th century, Ashkenazic Jews began wearing the *kittel* for the Seder service[34] because its ultimate use as a shroud served as a reminder that curbed excessive exhuberance. Later, other reasons were added to explain the custom: white symbolized freedom; white was also the color of the robes that the Temple priests wore for the paschal sacrifice.[35] While at first all males, possibly even females, wore the *kittel* at the Seder,[34] the custom has gradually changed so that today only the person leading the Seder wears a *kittel*.[36]

An interesting question arises as to why, of all the Sabbaths and all the Festivals, i.e., Sukkot, Shevuot, it was only on Seder night that our Sages thought a *kittel* should be worn to dampen possible excess enthusiasm. It could be that since Passover is a festival of freedom, a festival on which a substantial amount of wine is drunk, it would be easy for the Jews, on that day, to forget their status, that they were living in exile with the ever-present danger of expulsion, blood libel accusations, and pogroms, the latter two especially reserved for Seder night.

The present practice of placing the Seder plate on the table before *Kiddush* is recited follows the Abudarham,[37] the *Peri Megadim*,[38] and the Prague *Haggadah*. However, some of our Sages, particularly the *Tur* and the *Shulḥan Arukh*,[39] placed the plate on the table after Kiddush, while the Gaon of Vilna[40] had the Seder plate brought to the table after *karpas*.

Originally when people ate at their own small tables and reclined on couches, Roman style, the Seder plate had to be brought in after *Kiddush*. With the advent of the large table, it could just as well be placed on the table before *Kiddush*. In fact, seeing it on the table would immediately arouse the curiosity of the children. Though either of the first two *minhagim* may be followed, we have adopted the custom of the Abudarham, and most people today have the Seder plate on the table before *Kiddush* is intoned.

Surprisingly, the Seder plate is not mentioned by the Mishnah, the Talmud, or the *geonim*.[41] In fact, there was no such thing; the various items were brought in as needed. It is, however, found in early *rishonic* literature,[42] the illuminated manuscript *Haggadahs*, the *Tur*, and the *Shulḥan Arukh*,[43] and is today a firmly established custom among both Ashkenazic and Sephardic Jews. This plate or basket should be large enough to contain those foods that commemorate and are used during the Seder ceremony: the three matzot, the *maror,* the *ḥaroset,* the *karpas,* the *ḥazeret,* and the two cooked foods. The question then arose as to how to place these items on the plate. Rabbi Isaac Luria had one method, others presented another.[44] All of them agreed, however, that all the foods should be put on the plate. Most people today follow the order advocated by R. Luria, known as the Ari (see the diagrams, p. 7), the founder of Jewish mysticism called *Kabbalah.* He saw the Seder plate as having special mystical significance, and of special importance was the unity formed by the plate and all the foods on it.[45]

At first, most people used a very large plate or basket as the Seder plate and placed all the items on one plane according to their custom, as illustrated in many illuminated manuscript *Haggadahs* and still practiced by the Sephardim today (see diagram B, p. 7). Some placed the matzot on the bottom of the plate, covered them with a heavy cloth, and then put the other foods atop the cloth.[46] With this method one had to be extremely careful not to break the matzot. Later, in the 19th century, someone devised a method whereby the matzot would be protected. The tiered seder plate[47] was invented (see diagram A, p. 7). Either plate is acceptable.

The two cooked foods are mentioned in the Mishnah.[48] The Talmud tells us that they represent, or are in memory of, the *korban pesaḥ,* the paschal lamb sacrifice, and the *korban ḥagigah,*[49] the sacrifice that was eaten in conjunction with the paschal lamb.[50] However, there was a dispute in the Talmud as to which two foods should be used. One Sage recommended beets and rice, another opted for fish with egg on it, a third suggested two kinds of meat, while another said that even a bone with its broth is enough. Although Maimonides and many other *rishonim*[51] ruled that we should use two meats, the *minhag* since the 14th century[52] has been to use one meat, a lamb shankbone with a little meat on it (although any bone with some meat on it would suffice[52]) and an egg.[53]

A shankbone is preferred because in Hebrew it is called *ziroa* and the Bible in one of the phrases of redemption uses the term *ziroa netuyah:* "I will redeem you with an *outstretched arm*"[54] (Exodus 6:6). Since this food is in memory of the paschal lamb, the custom is to roast it,[55] although many boil it.[56] Those who roast the shankbone save it for use at the second Seder in the Diaspora and then put it away until the next day, as no roasted meats may be eaten on Seder nights.[57] Care should be taken not to throw it away after its use, for this is a degradation of a *mitzvah*, but to save it to eat during lunch on the second day of *Yom Tov*.[58] When the *ziroa* is boiled, it is always eaten as part of the Seder meal. In the Diaspora where there are two Seders, one may save the boiled *ziroa* for the second Seder or prepare two boiled shankbones and eat one each evening.

The use of an egg as the second cooked food on the Seder plate, according to the *Kol Bo*, follows a statement in the Jerusalem Talmud not extant in our edition. This passage explains that egg in Aramaic is *beah*, which also means "to be willing," alluding to the thought "the Almighty *be willing* to redeem us."[59] It has also been suggested that the egg is a sign of mourning because we no longer can offer the *korban ḥagigah* in the Temple.[60] The Gra,[61] however, objected strongly to this last suggestion. While some may question whether the egg on the Seder plate is a symbol of mourning, all agree that hard-boiled eggs as the first course of the Seder meal represents our sorrow over the loss of the Temple.[62] Another suggestion connecting the egg with the *korban ḥagigah* is the fact that *Betzah* (Hebrew for egg) or *Beah* (Aramaic for egg) is the title of a tractate of the Mishnah and Talmud dealing with *ḥag* (Hebrew for Festival). Thus, the egg on the Seder plate is a fitting reminder of the *korban ḥagigah*, the Festival sacrifice brought on Passover.[63]

There has been a wide divergence of opinion among our Sages as to whether the egg should be boiled or roasted. Some roasted it and saved it for the second Seder.[64] Many roasted it and ate it during the meal, as only roasted meat is prohibited during the Seder,[65] while an equal number of Sages boiled the egg and ate it during the Seder meal.[66]

The Talmud is unclear as to whether we should eat these two cooked foods, the *ziroa* and the egg, during the Seder as we do the other items on the plate. Rabbi Jacob Weil said we do not,[67] while the Rashal stated that both items must be eaten during the Seder meal.[68] The *Hok Ya'akov* ruled that we eat the egg but not the *ziroa*.[69] All these *minhagim* are valid today, but because it is difficult to save the egg and *ziroa* for use at lunch on the second day of Passover,[70] it might be best to follow the *Arukh ha-Shulḥan*[71] and Rabbi Solomon

Zevin[72] and boil both the egg and *ziroa* and eat them during the Seder.

The remaining foods on the Seder plate as well as the lighting of the candles and the Cup of Elijah are discussed under their own headings. The need for at least three adult males at the Seder is discussed under *Barekh* (p. 67).

A

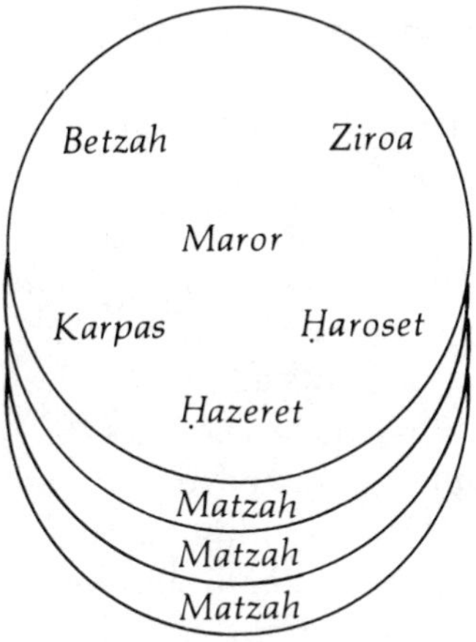

B

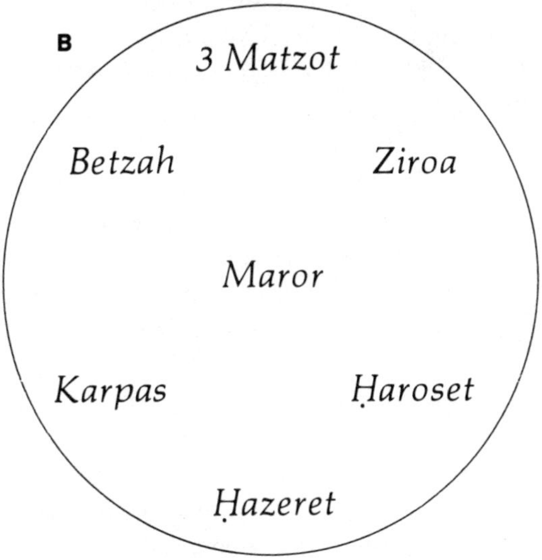

LIGHTING THE CANDLES

The Mishnah[1] relates that one of the three commandments that a woman should be careful to fulfill is the kindling of lights on Sabbath eve. According to Maimonides,[2] woman was given preference over man[3] in the performance of this act because she usually attends to household affairs. The Midrash[4] gives a homiletical explanation. Eve, the first woman, caused Adam to sin and thereby forfeit immortality. Metaphorically, she darkened his soul. Adam's soul is referred to in Proverbs (20:27) as the "Light of G-d." Therefore, to make amends woman was given the duty of kindling lights in honor of the Sabbath.

Kindling lights on the Festivals is not mentioned in the Babylonian Talmud. It was first quoted by the *Haggahot Maimuniyyot*[5] and the *Or Zaru'a*[6] in the name of the Jerusalem Talmud. It was reasoned that just as the lights add to the enjoyment of the Sabbath, so they will add to the joy of the Festivals.[7]

The *Ḥayyei Adam* recommended that candles be lighted approximately one hour before nightfall on the Sabbath and that the woman be dressed in her Sabbath and holiday clothes.[8] She must also have her head covered as she would in synagogue. The wife of the *Derishah* followed this same procedure when lighting the festival candles,[9] a procedure followed by most women today.

The *Kol Bo*[10] and the *Tur* stated that for the Sabbath a minimum of two candles must be lit. This is explained by the two terms "Remember" and "Observe" which introduce the Sabbath commandment in the two versions of the Decalogue found in Exodus (20:8) and Deuteronomy (5:12). The Rema noted[11] that it was the usual practice for many women to light more than two candles. Today, each woman makes her own choice as to how many Sabbath candles she lights. On *Yom Tov* the custom is the same as on the Sabbath.

As a general rule, the blessing relating to a *mitzvah* is said before the precept is performed. However, for the Sabbath some *rishonim*[12] felt that the candles should be lighted first inasmuch as by saying the blessing the woman assumes the holiness of the Sabbath and would then be prohibited from lighting them. Rabbi Weil and the Maharil suggested a method whereby candles may be lighted before pronouncing the blessing while still adhering to the general rule. If the woman spreads her hands over the candles immediately after she lights them so as not to see them, pronounces the blessing, and then takes her hands away so that she can see and enjoy the candlelight, it is considered, they reasoned, as if she had said the blessing before, for she has derived no use from the light until after the blessing.[12]

This problem, lighting candles before the blessing, does not apply on the Festivals since we are permitted the use of fire on *Yom Tov*. Nevertheless, the *Magen Avraham*[13] advised that in order not to create confusion we follow the same procedure as that followed on the Sabbath. The son of the *Derishah*,[14] however, citing his mother, wrote that on the Festivals the custom is to recite the blessing first and then to light the candles; every woman knows that while kindling a fire is prohibited on the Sabbath, it is permitted on the Festivals. Later Sages[15] were divided over this issue, and each woman may follow her own tradition in this matter.

Most Sages agreed that the principal candlelighting must be at the table or in the room where one will partake of the Sabbath or Festival meal.[16] As Rashi explained, there can be no festive meal without light.[17]

THE SEDER PROGRAM

This list is one of several mnemonic devices found in early manuscripts of the *Haggadah* which describe the order of the Seder. Formerly attributed to Rashi, the list more probably was composed in the 13th century by one of his students, Rabbi Samuel of Falaise,[1] a member of a group of scholars known as the tosafists. There were other lists composed even earlier[2] but this was the one adopted by the first printed illustrated *Haggadah*, the Prague *Haggadah* of 1526, and it has been universally used ever since.

The Prague printed the Seder Program only at the beginning of its *Haggadah*. The Amsterdam *Haggadah* of 1712, which had the greatest impact on all subsequent editions, inserted each of the terms of the Program as the title of the particular section it described.[3] Today virtually all *Haggadahs* follow this example. These headings, when read aloud and explained by the Leader, the person who conducts the Seder service, provide the participants with an excellent explanation of the ritual they are about to perform.

KADDESH: Recite the Kiddush

On Passover, *Kiddush* may not be recited before the stars appear, even though on the Sabbath and other Festivals one may start earlier. Normally it is permitted to add to the holy from the profane; the Passover *Kiddush* is different because the wine cup of the *Kiddush* is one of the required four cups of wine on this night, and just as the paschal lamb, the matzah, and the *maror* have to be eaten after the stars appear,[1] so, ruled the *Terumat ha-Deshen,* did the four cups of wine have to be drunk only at night.[2]

According to the Talmud, when *Kiddush* is recited on Seder night the matzot must be covered, just as the two challahs on Sabbath and *Yom Tov* are covered during the *Kiddush.*[3] One reason for this, explained the *Tur* quoting the Jerusalem Talmud, is that we do not want to "shame" the bread; since bread is mentioned in the Bible before wine in the second section of the *Shema* (Deuteronomy 11:14), it would only be proper to make a blessing over it before the wine.[4] Another reason, probably of *gaonic* origin,[5] is that we remember the time our forefathers in the desert ate the manna, which had a covering of dew both beneath and above. The tablecloth or challah plate serves as the covering below, while a napkin or challah cloth serves as the one above. Because the manna was covered with dew until it was eaten, our Sages said that the top covering of the challah used on the Sabbath and *Yom Tov* should be removed only after the *motzi*[6] (blessing over bread).

The Talmud states that the wine goblets must be spotlessly clean and should be filled to the brim[7] with the finest red wine available, because the Jerusalem Talmud,[8] basing itself on a verse in Proverbs (23:3), considers that red wine on the whole is of a finer quality than white wine. Some 17th century commentators[9] added that the specific use of red wine on Passover commemorates the innocent blood of our ancestors spilled by the Egyptian Pharaoh. Nevertheless, advised the *Roke'aḥ,* where a white wine is superior to the red, it should be used for the four cups that are obligatory on Passover.[10] On a more somber note, while all our Sages of the 16th and 17th centuries agreed that for the Seder red wine is preferred, they all recommended the use of white wine because of the danger from vicious "blood libels" spread by the various anti-Semitic governments and prelates.[11] The "blood libels," false accusations leveled against the Jews throughout history, claimed that before Passover the Jews killed a Christian child and mixed his blood with the red wine that was used on Seder night. These libels became an excuse for a *pogrom* or attack on Jewish communities. Rumblings of these falsehoods are, unfortunately, still heard today in some parts of the civilized world.

The wine should be poured, according to the Mishnah[12] and most of our Sages,[13] by someone other than the Leader, as a sign of freedom. The *Arukh ha-Shulḥan,* however, strongly objected to this practice.[14] He stated that to request a wife or guest to pour the wine does not solve the problem or prove anything as they are no less commanded to be free than the Leader. He suggested that anyone can pour the wine, and one should not make an issue of it.

The Leader begins the Seder by announcing *Kaddesh,*[15] the first of the mnemonic devices recorded at the beginning of the *Haggadah* in the Seder Program. Some Sages[16] recommended reciting the *hinne memuḥan,* a kabbalistic incantation, intended, among other things, to explain to everyone the nature of the *mitzvah* about to be performed. This custom, probably started by R. Emden, is not universally used, and if the Leader gives a short explanation of what is about to be performed and the reason for and meaning of the ceremony that is to follow, it is sufficient.

The law that each person must drink four cups of wine at the Seder is found in the Mishnah.[17] The Jerusalem Talmud[18] gives several reasons why there are four cups and our Rabbis have added other reasons.[19] The first reason offered by the Jerusalem Talmud, and the most familiar, is that the four cups are suggestive of the four expressions of redemption used by the Bible in connection with Israel's liberation from Egypt (Exodus 6:6–7): "I shall *bring you out*"; "I shall *save*"; "I shall *redeem*"; and "I shall *take.*" Another reason is that the four cups of the Seder parallel the four times a wine cup is mentioned in the dream of the chief wine steward in the story of Joseph (Genesis 40:11–13). This is elaborated upon by the *Midrash ha-Gadol.*[20] The chief butler's dream contained, in addition to a prophecy about his own future, a prophecy regarding the future of Israel. Joseph divined this as well but, of course, kept this part to himself. The three branches are the three Fathers, Abraham, Isaac, and Jacob, whose descendants in Egypt were to be redeemed by three leaders, Moses, Aaron, and Miriam. The cup given into the hand of Pharaoh is the cup of wrath that he would have to drain in the end.

The wine cup is lifted with both hands in order to show complete acceptance of and love for this *mitzvah.* When the performance of the *mitzvah* is about to begin, the wine cup is held with the right hand alone so that it does not appear to be a burden.[21] The right hand is used because it is considered the more important of the two hands. If, however, one is left-handed, observed the *Shibbolei ha-Leket,* the wine cup should be held in the left hand.[22] While the *Magen Avraham*[23] felt that even a left-handed person should hold the wine cup in the right hand, the *Maḥazit ha-Shekel* and the *Arukh ha-Shulḥan* agreed with the *Shulḥan Arukh:* a left-handed person should use his left hand, as is done when putting on *tefillin* (phylacteries).[24] The wine goblet must be raised at least a *tefaḥ* (about four inches) higher than the table so that all present may see it. All these laws are based on the Talmud[25] and apply to any occasion where wine is used as part of the ritual, i.e., *Kiddush, Havdalah,* Grace, etc.

There is a question among our Sages as to whether *Kiddush* should be recited standing or sitting, but neither the Talmud, the *Tur,* nor the *Shulḥan Arukh* ruled on this matter. The Rambam, the Ravyah, and the *Tosafot* recited *Kiddush* seated, while later Sages, notably the Ari, performed this rite standing.[26] Today, one may stand or sit, as both are acceptable, although most people do stand while *Kiddush* is being recited.

The Leader recites the *Kiddush* in a loud voice, and although we fulfill our obligation by paying attention to the words, it is far better to follow the Leader and repeat the *Kiddush* quietly with him, word by word.[27]

At the conclusion of the *Kiddush,* all are seated and the males drink their wine while reclining on the left side.[28] The drinking of the four cups of wine is one of the parts of the Seder where reclining is required. There are authorities who maintain that if the men drink without reclining, they have not performed the *mitzvah* and must drink another cup in its stead.[29]

The Talmud states that the cup must hold at least a *revi'it*[30] of wine. Today, a *revi'it* is 3.1 fluid ounces or 86.4 milliliters, according to the *Siddur Minhat Yerushalaym;* 3.3 fluid ounces (on the Sabbath

4.42 fluid ounces) according to Rabbi Moshe Feinstein,[31] a leading Rabbinical decisor; and somewhat more according to the Ḥazon Ish, another Rabbinical authority.[32] While one should try to drink the entire *revi'it*,[33] one must, at a minimum, according to the Talmud,[34] drink most of it. The *Roke'aḥ*[35] stated that the wine should be drunk fairly quickly, without lengthy pauses between sips, and one should take no longer than four minutes (some authorities allow up to nine minutes) to finish.[36]

A question arises if the goblet is larger than a *revi'it*. Does one have to drink most of a *revi'it* or most of the wine in the goblet, no matter how large the goblet is? This problem has been widely discussed and disputed by the *rishonim*[37] and *aḥaronim*, all our scholars since the 16th century.[38] The *Arukh ha-Shulḥan*[39] was of the opinion that one must drink most of the wine in the cup, no matter how large it is. The *Mishnah Berurah*,[40] on the other hand, ruled that most of a *revi'it*, even in a large goblet, is sufficient. However, continued the *Mishnah Berurah*, it is best to use a goblet that is not too large so one may drink most of the wine in the cup and thus avoid this entire problem.

As the *Haggadah* itself tells us,[41] it is a cherished tradition to discuss on this night the laws, the history, and the customs, and to give homilies concerning Passover and the Seder in as much detail as possible. This is accomplished by allowing anyone present to offer, between paragraphs or after the performance of a ritual, a saying of our Sages, a reconciliation of a difficulty, a *halakhic, aggadic,* or historical insight, anything appropriate to the *Haggadah* section just completed.

Kiddush for Saturday Night

Every Saturday evening, the *Havdalah*, a special prayer closing out the Sabbath and ushering in the weekdays, is recited. This prayer must be said even when the following day is a holiday. Therefore, when this occurs the *Havdalah* is incorporated into the holiday *Kiddush* but is slightly different from that offered on a regular Saturday night.

The commandment to perform the *Havdalah* service, according to Maimonides,[1] is Biblical, while the form of the prayer, says the *Gemara*,[2] was composed by the Men of the Great Assembly. At first there was only prayer, then a cup of wine was added, and by the *tannaitic* period[3] the spices and candlelight were incorporated.

Spices are not used for the *Havdalah* service when Saturday night ushers in a Festival. Tosafoth[4] explained the reason for the inclusion of spices in the regular *Havdalah* service: on the Sabbath, as the Talmud[5] tells us, we are endowed with an extra soul which departs on Saturday night and makes us sad; the pleasant smelling spices revive our sense of good feeling. On a holiday eve, *Tosafoth* pointed out, the holiday cheer and good food perform the same function as the spices.

The blessing over light in the *Havdalah* service on Saturday night is in remembrance of the fire created for the first man, Adam, on Saturday night. As the Talmud[6] relates, fire was one of the things the Almighty left uncreated when the Sabbath set in, but after the close of the Sabbath, the Almighty endowed man with divine wisdom. Man then took two stones and by grinding them together produced fire, after which he recited the blessing, "Blessed be He who created the blaze of the fire." This is elaborated further in the Midrash,[7] which explains that there was no night on the sixth day of creation and when darkness set in at the conclusion of the seventh day, Adam, who had not yet experienced night, became frightened that the Serpent would overwhelm him. The Almighty furnished him with two stones which he rubbed together until fire was produced, whereupon he offered a benediction over the fire.

In the *Havdalah* service on a regular Saturday night, according to the *Otzar ha-Tefillot*,[8] after the blessing over the wine, the wine cup is shifted to the left hand or placed on the table and the spices are taken in the right hand. After the blessing over the spices, they are either passed around or shifted to the left hand while the right is readied for the blessing over the lights. As there are no spices on this holiday eve, the wine cup may either be placed on the table or shifted to the left hand.

The *minhag* of looking at the fingernails stems from *Pirkei De-Rabbi Eliezer*,[9] which states that the palm of the hand is spread out facing the light of the candle and the nails, which are whiter than the flesh, are viewed. The blessing is then pronounced. The custom of looking at the fingernails and the palm of the hand at the same time derives from Rabbi Natronai Gaon.[10]

Why should both the palm and fingernails be viewed together? First, to comply with the Talmudic[11] precept which prohibits the pronunciation of a benediction over light unless some use is derived from it; one can see the lines of his palm or the difference between nail and flesh. Second, looking at the lines of the palm is considered a good sign;[12] and the fingernails, in their unceasing growth, are a symbol of prosperity which, it is hoped, the coming week will bring.[13] Other reasons are cited by the *Mordecai*.[14]

The entire procedure—bending the fingers over the thumb, looking at the nails and the palm at the same time, then spreading them out and looking at them from the back—is taken from R. Emden.[15] It is based on the practices of the *geonim*,[16] the Rema[17] and the *Magen Avraham*.[18] Each action has a reason and a meaning. The four fingers are bent over the thumb so that the nails and the palm are seen together.[19] The fingers are spread so that light enters the palm, echoing the theme of light instead of darkness as recited in the *Havdalah* prayer.[20] The action of turning the palm away from the face and the staring at the fingernails from the back side of the hand is from the *Zohar*,[21] which states that one should not look at the fingers from the inside but only at the fingernails from the back, as indicated by the verse: "Thou shalt see My back; but My face shall not be seen" (Exodus 33:23).

Quoting other *aḥaronim*, the *Arukh ha-Shulḥan*[22] said that this rite should be performed with the right hand only.

U'REḤATZ: Lave the Hands

The ritual washing of the hands before eating the *karpas* is a custom that has been extensively discussed by our Sages.[1] The *halakhah* in the time of the Mishnah and the Talmud[2] stated that one had to wash and pronounce a blessing over this laving before eating vegetables dipped in a liquid. The *geonim,* Rashi, and the Rambam continued this tradition. However, the Maharam of Rothenburg ruled that since this law concerns only ritual cleanliness, a law that does not affect us today, we do not have to wash before eating vegetables dipped in a liquid. This ruling was not conclusive, however, and later Sages continued to dispute the question. As a compromise, the *Shulḥan Arukh*[3] suggested that before eating vegetables to be dipped in a liquid, one should wash without the accompanying blessing. Although the Gaon of Vilna demanded that we revert to the original practice,[4] we follow the *Arukh ha-Shulḥan*[5] who ruled that today there is no obligation to wash before eating vegetables dipped in a liquid.

Why does this custom persist at the Seder? The *Ḥok Ya'akov* suggested that because washing the hands before eating vegetables dipped in a liquid is so unusual the children would ask questions.[6] In addition, explained the Netziv,[7] it is a remembrance of Passover in the time of the Temple.

Who has to perform this symbolic ritual washing? To most *rishonim* there is no problem, as this is not *minhag* but *halakhah* and everyone must do it. However, the *Leket Yosher,*[8] a student of the *Terumat ha-Deshen,* and many manuscript *Haggadahs*[9] indicated that only the Leader need perform the ritual washing since it is only a symbolic gesture; either is acceptable.

The method of laving the hands in a ritual manner is found in the *Shulḥan Arukh*[10] and applies all year round for divers occasions, particularly before eating bread. These laws are very old, dating from Mishnaic times. The only point of difference today is whether one pours alternately once over the right, once over the left, again over the right and again over the left,[11] or follows the *Arukh ha-Shulḥan*[12] and pours twice over the right and twice over the left. Either method is acceptable.[13]

KARPAS: Eat the Karpas

Karpas is a word found in Talmudic literature to denote celery or a type of parsley.[1] In fact, the Mishnah and Talmud in *Pesaḥim*,[2] in describing this part of the service, speak of green vegetables in general and not of any vegetable in particular. Any vegetable, preferably one over which one makes the blessing *boreh pri ha-adamah*, may serve as the *karpas*.[3]

The use of the vegetable *karpas* and the use of the term *Karpas* to describe this ceremony were unknown by the Talmud, Rashi, the Rambam, and early tosafists. The *geonim* were the first to mention *karpas* as one of several vegetables used in this rite.[4] It was the *Shibbolei ha-Leket*[5] in the 13th century who first recommended *karpas* as the vegetable to be dipped; and a contemporary of his, the author of the Seder Progam at the beginning of the *Haggadah*,[6] gave this section of the *Haggadah* its universally accepted name.

Why was the *karpas* adopted as the preferred green vegetable to be used in the first dipping at the Seder? The Abudarham[7] explained that if the word is read backwards in Hebrew it can be divided into *sameḥ-peraḥ*, an illusion to the "sixty" myriads of Israelites who were oppressed with "back-breaking work."

What is the reason for this ceremony? Rashi[8] answered that it is unusual to dip vegetables and eat them before the meal. By so doing, adults and particularly the children will be stimulated to ask questions. Another reason may be that this is a reminder of ancient customs when free man began a banquet with vegetable dips.

Why is only a small piece of *karpas*, less than a *kezayit*, or one ounce, eaten? The Maharil[9] explained that it is to avoid the problem of a final blessing. Generally when more than a *kezayit* of any food is eaten, two blessings are recited, one before and one after. Since there is a dispute among our Sages about whether a final blessing should be recited at the Seder if more than a *kezayit* of *karpas* is eaten, the Maharil suggested that less than a *kezayit* be eaten in order to avoid the problem[10]—and this is the custom today. However, if one happens to eat more than a kezayit, one still does not have to pronounce a final blessing.[11]

In what should the *karpas* be dipped? This question has drawn the attention of our Sages throughout the ages. From the Mishnah and Talmud in *Pesaḥim*,[2] it would seem that the *karpas* should be dipped in the *ḥaroset;* so ruled the Rambam, the *geonim*, and the Maharam of Rothenburg, and so it is written in many manuscript *Haggadahs.*[12] However, Rabbenu Tam, the Rashbam, and other tosafists ruled that the *karpas* should be dipped in either wine vinegar or salt water. Although all later decisors and *Haggadahs* allow dipping in either salt water or vinegar,[13] it has become the modern custom to use only salt water.[14]

R. Emden[15] recommended that when making the blessing *boreh pri ha-adamah*, the leader explain that it will also apply to the *maror* and *korekh* which comes later in the Seder. *Halakhically*, without this reminder the *maror* and *korekh* would still not need another *boreh pri ha-adamah* as they are part of the meal, everyone having made a *motzi* over the matzot. However, our Sages[16] felt that there was a legal possibility that since the *maror* comes not as a course of the meal but as a special *mitzvah*, it would not be exempt by the *motzi* and therefore it would be best to exempt the *maror* from the *boreh pri ha-adamah* by this reminder.

Since the *karpas* and the salt water are no longer needed, they may be removed from the table.[17] The remaining *karpas* should not be thrown out but eaten during the meal or on the next day, applying to it the same rule as we do to the *ziroa.*[18]

YAḤATZ: Divide the Middle Matzah

We know from the *Gemara* in *Berakoth*[1] that during the Seder one of the matzot over which the *motzi* is recited has to be a broken one. Does that mean that, where normally on the Sabbath and Festivals we make the *motzi* over two whole loaves of bread or two whole matzot, on Passover we make the *motzi* over a whole matzah and a broken one, the position adopted by the Rambam, the Rif, and many other Sages? Or does it mean that, in addition to the two whole matzot required on every Sabbath and *Yom Tov* in memory of the double portion of manna given on these days during the 40 years of wandering in the desert, on Passover we must add an additional broken matzah to make the total of two and a half matzot, the position adopted by the tosafists and the Rosh?[2] This question was discussed extensively in *gaonic* times. We follow the custom of the tosafists, hence the three matzot on the Seder plate.[3]

Why is the middle matzah broken into two unequal pieces and the smaller part then replaced in its original position? The Rosh[4] and the *Tur*[5] observed that when the matzot are used later in the Seder service, they will be in the proper sequence. The whole top one will receive the *motzi*, while the second broken one is in place for the second blessing of *al aḥilat matzah*. However, the Mordecai ruled that it is the top matzah that should be broken, with the smaller part replaced on top, because of the principle that one must take the first that comes to hand when performing a *mitzvah*. The *Semag* recommended that we should break the top one, in line with the Mordecai's reasoning, but it should be placed in the middle following the Rosh's custom.[6] Our *minhag* follows the Rosh.[7]

Why is the matzah broken in two, the smaller part replaced, and the larger part, the *afikoman*, hidden at this stage of the Seder? According to the *Kol Bo*,[8] it is because of the *Ha Laḥma Anya* that follows; this prayer should be recited over a *leḥem oni*, which the Talmud[9] explains is a piece of broken matzah. The *afikoman* is put away now, continued the *Kol Bo*, so that the children will be puzzled and ask why matzah is being hidden before any of it is eaten. In addition, if the Leader does not put away some matzah now, all the matzah on the Seder plate may be eaten during the meal and none would be left for the *afikoman*. The Ran,[10] however, explained that this ceremony, the *Yaḥatz,* is just a procedural convenience so that the matzah does not have to be broken later in the Seder. It is interesting to note that the Rambam[11] broke the matzah right before the *motzi.*

Why is it broken into two uneven parts, with the larger part saved for the *afikoman?* The Maharil[12] explained that it is for love of a *mitzvah:* to the special *mitzvah* of *afikoman* is allotted the larger piece of matzah. The *Baḥ*[13] said that since two *kezaytim* must be eaten for the *afikoman,* the larger of the two pieces is put away.[14]

The *Roke'aḥ* recommended that the *afikoman* be given to someone seated at the table who places it under the tablecloth. This act is a reminder of the time the Jews left Egypt and bound up their unleavened dough "in their clothes upon their shoulders" (Exodus 12:34). That person to whose care it was entrusted also guarded it[15] so that it would not be eaten by accident[16], thereby ensuring its use for the final course of the meal.[17] The Rashal,[18] however, suggested that the *afikoman* be wrapped in a napkin (one not starched with a substance that might contain *ḥametz*[16]) and placed between the pillows of the seat. Later, after the meal, the Leader should take the *afikoman* still wrapped in the napkin, place it on his shoulder, and walk a few feet to dramatize the verse in Exodus (12:34). R. Emden[19] recommended the "walk about" at this stage, during the *Yaḥatz,* before the matzah is hidden away between the pillows. Today most follow the Rashal. The Leader wraps the *afikoman* in a napkin or a special sack made for this purpose and hides it between the pillows of his seat, but dispenses with the custom of carrying it on the shoulders.[20]

Around this rite, the hiding of the *afikoman,* revolves what to most children is the highlight of the Seder: the "stealing" of the *afikoman* and witholding it until it is ransomed by the father for a special gift or prize. In many homes the children eye the Leader carefully for the right moment to pounce, grab the *afikoman,* and guard it carefully until it is ransomed. In many homes the father hides the *afikoman* himself somewhere in the room and the children dart around looking for it so as to "steal" it and hide it themselves. It all makes for an interesting and memorable time. However, no matter how wonderful this is for the children, it should not be overdone as this is but one phase of the Seder. It is best to allow this playful interlude after the meal immediately before the *afikoman* is eaten so as not to disrupt unduly the entire evening.

When and how did this custom arise? It is first mentioned in the *Hok Ya'akov*,[21], about the 17th century, which lists it as one of the customs in current vogue. It is safe to assume, then, that it was probably introduced some years previously. Its basis is the enigmatic phrase in the Talmud,[22] "*Ḥotfim et ha-matah,*" freely translated as "grabbing the matzah." Rashi interpreted this to mean that we should rush the meal for the sake of the children, while the Rashbam explained it as grabbing the matzah from the children so they will not overeat and fall asleep and miss the rest of the Seder. The Rambam[23] seemed to interpret the phrase as meaning that the people at the Seder should playfully grab the matzah one from another. Later it came to mean the "stealing" of the *afikoman* by the children, as explained above.

MAGGID: Recite the Haggadah

Ha Laḥma Anya: This Is the Bread of Affliction

The *Gemara Pesaḥim*[1] states that before the *Maggid* section is begun, the table in front of the Leader should be removed to arouse the children's curiosity, for when they see this action they will ask, "How is it that the table is being removed when we have not yet eaten?" As some *rishonim* have already pointed out, this was applicable only when each person ate at his own small table, Roman style. It cannot and does not apply when people eat together at one large table.[2] *Tosafoth* and others, therefore, recommended that the proper procedure is to shift the Seder plate to the end of the table. However, there were some in the 12th century who lifted the Seder plate for the recital of *Ha Laḥma Anya* but removed the *ziroa* and the egg. The Rashbam[3] took exception to both aspects of this practice. He claimed that the *ziroa* and egg do not have to be removed since no one will confuse them with actual sacrifices, and the entire lifting action is meaningless to the children anyway. He suggested, as did *Tosafoth*, placing the Seder plate at the other end of the table as though finished with it, thus causing the children to wonder why the plate is being moved away, nobody having yet eaten.

The Rosh[4] took a middle course. He recommended lifting the Seder plate, to indicate to everyone present that the *Ha Laḥma Anya* is said over the matzot, and leaving the *ziroa* and egg on the plate. This procedure was followed by the *Tur*,[5] *Shulḥan Arukh*,[6] and *Mishnah Berurah*.[7] The *Arukh ha-Shulḥan*,[8] however, advised lifting either the Seder plate or only the matzot.

In the past, there were many other customs at this point in the Seder service. The *Maḥzor Vitry*[9] ruled that the Leader had to lift only the matzot, while the *Shibbolei ha-Leket*[10] recommended filling the wine glass and taking it in the right hand while the Seder plate was held with the left hand and everyone sang the *Ha Laḥma Anya* together. Some illuminated manuscript *Haggadahs*, the Sarajevo and the Kaufmann in particular, follow the Rambam and advise removing the Seder plate from the table before saying *Ha Laḥma Anya*.[2] The early printed *Haggadahs*, the Prague and the Amsterdam, prescribe lifting the Seder plate and removing the *ziroa* and the egg, a practice to which the Rashbam objected. R. Emden[11] recommended that one hand lift the Seder plate while the other hold the broken matzah as the *Ha Laḥma Anya* is recited. Today, most people follow the Rosh and *Shulḥan Arukh* and lift the Seder plate with the matzah on it for the *Ha Laḥma Anya.*

Such wide differences occur because the *Ha Laḥma Anya* was added to the *Haggadah* in Babylonia during the Talmudic period or perhaps even much later. This is deduced by the *Maḥzor Vitry*[9] because the passage is written in Aramaic, the language spoken in Babylonia. Another reason for believing that it is of later origin than much of the *Haggadah* is that the *Ha Laḥma Anya* invites guests to partake of the Seder meal. During the Temple period, guests could not be invited to partake of the Seder after the slaughter of the paschal lamb, as all participants had to be included beforehand. Therefore, the Rosh probably thought that when the Talmud says the table is removed, it referred to an action taken before the four questions, as it is unlikely they would recommend the removal of the matzot before the recital of a prayer which refers to it. Since this passage was a new one, the Rosh recommended a new *minhag,* that the matzot be uncovered and the Seder plate be raised. This serves a dual purpose, for the first sentence, "This is the bread of affliction," refers to the matzot, while the second sentence, "All who wish come and eat," refers to the other foods on the plate.

Other *rishonim,* particularly the Rashbam and the Rambam, did not feel that a new *minhag* was needed. As the Abarbanel[12] explained, removing the plate and then saying *Ha Laḥma Anya* will certainly prompt the children to ask, "You are removing the food and inviting people to eat?"

In this section, the matzot should be uncovered as they are referred to in the *Ha Laḥma Anya.* R. Emden[13] pointed out that as a general rule during the recital of the *Haggadah* the matzot should be uncovered except where the wine is featured or even mentioned.

As the Rashal[14] noted, the Leader recites this passage aloud,[15] for it marks the start of the *Maggid* section of the *Haggadah.*[16] It is a positive Biblical commandment[17] that one recite the *Maggid* section of the *Haggadah* on Seder night, and most Rabbis agree that this commandment is incumbent on women as well.[18] Therefore, according to the Rema,[19] citing a 12th century authority, the Re of London, the Leader should translate the entire *Haggadah* for the women.

However, observed the *Arukh ha-Shulḥan*,[20] since our *Haggadahs* all have translations, the Leader does not have to translate everything said. Today, many women can read and understand Hebrew as well as the men, so they can and should recite the *Haggadah* in the original along with the Leader.

Mah Nishtannah: The Four Questions

Some *rishonim*, following the Talmud in *Pesaḥim*,[1] required the removal of the Seder plate from the table,[2] while others[3] said that it should be moved to the opposite end of the table. As for the later Sages, the *Tur*[4] and R. Emden[5] ruled that one should remove the plate entirely from the table, while the *Shulḥan Arukh*[6] and the *Mishnah Berurah*[7] stated that it can be placed at the opposite end of the table. The *Magen Avraham*[8] allowed the plate to remain in front of the Leader and the *Arukh ha-Shulḥan*[9] concurred, adding that the matzot should now be covered in lieu of all this moving and removing.

The Mishnah[10] states that the wine goblets for the second cup are filled before the four questions. The reason, explained the Rashbam,[11] is that the children will be prompted to wonder why we are drinking a second cup of wine and still have had no food.

One of the best known features of the Seder is the *Mah Nishtannah*, the four questions that are sung by the youngest present. Since the entire Seder revolves around and stimulates children to ask questions, it would seem that this particular custom is of ancient origin; nothing could be further from the truth. The universally accepted tradition that the youngest present pose the four questions is relatively recent.

The actions of the Seder till now are intended to prompt the children to ask questions. For example, why are the vegetables dipped? Why is the plate removed or the matzot covered? Why haven't we eaten yet? Why have the cups been filled a second time before any food has been served? In fact, the Mishnah[12] tells us that at this point the son usually asks the father about these inconsistencies which he has witnessed. The Mishnah instructs that if the children do not ask these questions, or do not as yet understand what to ask, then the father or the one leading the Seder should recite the *Mah Nishtannah* himself, as if to say, come and see why and how this night is different from all other nights. This was the practice in the time of the Talmud[13] and during the *gaonic* period. Even Rashi, the *Maḥzor Vitry*, the *Shibbolei ha-Leket*, the Maharil, the *Tur*, the *Shulḥan Arukh*, and Rema all had this *minhag*, and no mention was made of the youngest asking the four questions. The first reference to the youngest asking the four questions is found in the Ravyah and the *Semag.*[14] The custom gradually spread throughout Jewry, but by no means rapidly or to the exclusion of the original *minhag*. While R. Emden[15] had the youngest ask the four questions, Rabbi Solomon Ganzfried,[16] a late 19th century Sage, and the *Mishnah Berurah*,[17] one of our most recent decisors, followed the old tradition of the father or Leader asking the four questions. However, the *Arukh ha-Shulḥan*[18] stated that instead of the son asking questions based on what he has seen, the questions are formalized through the *Mah Nishtannah* which the child recites. Today, it is universally accepted that the youngest present asks the four questions as written in the *Mah Nishtannah*.

Avadim Hahyenu: We Were Slaves

The *Tur*[1] noted that the Seder plate should now be returned to the table because the *Haggadah* should be recited over the uncovered matzah. This is inferred from the Talmud[2] when it states that the reason matzah is called *leḥem oni* is that the *Haggadah* is recited (*onim*) over it. Furthermore, explained the *Tur*, the Seder plate is returned at this point in the service because it is needed later in the *Maggid* section for the prayers "This Matzah" and "This *Maror*." Expanding on this theme, the *Bah*[3] thought it best to bring the plate in now[4] as it may be completely forgotten in the intensity of the *Haggadah* recital. The custom of returning the Seder plate to the table now is followed by the *Shulḥan Arukh*[5] and the *Mishnah Berurah*.[6] The *Arukh ha-Shulḥan*,[7] however, in keeping with his *minhag*, merely uncovered the matzot.

Vehe Sheamdah: This Covenant Has Sustained

Raising the wine cup at this point is first mentioned by the *Shenei Luḥot ha-Berit*[1] in the name of the Ari, the famous 16th century kabbalist. It is also mentioned in the Amsterdam *Haggadah*,[2] one of the earliest printed *Haggadahs*, which also quotes the Ari as its source. This custom eventually spread throughout the entire Ashkenazic community.[3]

The *Arukh ha-Shulḥan*[4] gave several reasons for raising the wine cup at this point. This prayer refers to our joy that the Almighty has always granted salvation in time of our greatest need. As a general rule wherever prayers of thanksgiving and salvation are recited the wine cup is raised, an allusion to the passage in Psalms (116:13): "The cup of Salvation will I lift up and on the name of the G-d will I call." Another reason is that without wine, joy cannot be fully expressed. It is written in Psalms (104:15): "And wine will make the heart of man happy." A third reason, esoteric in nature, has to do with *gematria*, a homiletic interpretation based on the numerical value of letters. *Elohim* (the Almighty) in *gematria* is 86; *hatevah* (nature) in *gematria* is also 86. This proves that even nature and natural laws are under divine guidance. *Koth* (wine cup) in *gematria* is also 86. Therefore, when reciting this passage which speaks of Divine guidance and salvation in time of need, we raise the *koth*.

The matzot are covered so as not to shame the bread when the emphasis is placed on wine, just as we cover the challah all year round when we recite *Kiddush*.[5]

R. Ganzfried in his *Siddur*[6] recommended that the Leader recite this passage aloud. Today, it is usually sung by the Leader and the company to one of several well-known tunes.

Dam, Ve-Esh . . . B'aḥav: The Ten Plagues

Neither the *rishonim* nor the *Shulḥan Arukh* spoke of removing drops of wine from the cups at the mention of the ten plagues. This custom was first recorded by the Maharil,[1] repeated in his name by the Rema,[2] and accepted by the Ashkenazim from then onward.[3] There is, however, a dispute among the Rabbis as to the correct method of removing drops of wine from the goblet. Should the index finder be used, a reference to the verse in Exodus (8:15): "It is the finger (*etzbah* in Hebrew is usually the index finger) of the Almighty,"[2] the fourth finger, or the pinky,[4] or is the wine cup tilted?[5] However, as the *Arukh ha-Shulḥan*[6] observed, all these methods are correct and each person may follow his own tradition.

It is not clear from the writings of our Sages which hand should remove the drops of wine from the wine cup, or whether only the Leader or everyone performs this rite. Most people remove the drops with the right hand, although the Me'am Lo'ez[3] wrote that the left should be used. Based on the *Sefer Amrakhal,*[7] a recently discovered work of the 13th century, everyone removes the sixteen drops of wine at the mention of the plagues. These drops, stated R. Emden, are to be spilled onto a broken vessel placed under the table.[8] It might be more convenient to have several broken vessels near the table or brought to the table for this section. After the conclusion of *B'aḥav,* these vessels should be removed.

What does this custom symbolize? R. Emden[8] said it symbolizes our hope that G-d will save us from future plagues and visit them upon our enemies. Amplifying R. Emden's words, R. Ganzfried[9] explained that the broken vessel used to receive the drops symbolizes our enemies in kabbalistic lore. These drops are spilled from the wine cup which symbolizes the Almighty, as indicated in the verse in Psalms (116:13): "The cup of salvation will I lift up and on the name of the Lord will I call." A more recent interpretation, given by Rabbi Samson R. Hirsch,[10] is that we remove a drop of wine as we recite each plague to indicate that our cup of happiness is diminished because redemption came to us through the punishment and suffering of others; it is written in Proverbs (24:17): "Rejoice not when thine enemy falls."

The total number of drops spilled, sixteen, also has symbolic meaning. As the Darkei Moshe[11] pointed out, sixteen in Hebrew is written as *Yud Vav,* the first two letters of the word *Yoaḥ,* a mystical reference to the sword of the Almighty and the Angel of Revenge. The *Mishnah Berurah*[12] observed that the *Yud Vav* is part of the Almighty's name, He who smote the Egyptians with these plagues.

Since the volume of wine in the cups has been diminished by the removal of the sixteen drops, it is necessary to refill them, as now there may be less than a *revi'it.*[13]

Matza Zu and Maror Zeh: This Matzah and This Maror

The Talmud *Pesaḥim*[1] states that when reciting *Matzah Zu* the Leader must lift up the matzah, and when intoning *Maror Zeh* the Leader similarly must raise the *maror* to show all who are present the items being discussed. This action is taken, according to the Rashbam,[2] in order to endear these items to everyone. However, the Talmud says specifically that when reciting the previous passage, *Pesaḥ Zeh,* one must not lift up the *ziroa,* the food that signifies or represents the paschal lamb, as this might be taken to mean that one may eat sacrifices outside the Temple environs, something that is categorically prohibited. All the major decisors[3] followed the *minhag* that while reciting *Pesaḥ Zeh* the Leader should not lift the *ziroa* or even point to it, but while reciting *Matzah Zu* and *Maror Zeh* he lifts the matzah and *maror.* This practice is the one followed by most today.

However, there are some variations of this custom found in the writings of our Sages. Rabbi Weil[4] suggested that although we do not pick up the *ziroa* when reciting *Pesaḥ Zeh,* we nevertheless point to it on the Seder plate. There is an illuminated manuscript *Haggadah*[5] which shows the husband pointing to his wife while reciting *Maror Zeh;* in fact, the earliest printed *Haggadah,* the Prague *Haggadah,* states specifically that one points to one's wife while reciting *Maror Zeh* as an allusion to the passage in Ecclesiastes (7:26): "and I find more bitter (*mar*) than death the woman." Rabbi Menachem Kasher in his *Haggadah*[6] wrote that when reciting *Pesaḥ Zeh, Maror Zeh,* and *Matzah Zu,* we point to the object discussed in all three instances, and nothing is raised or lifted.

Which matzah does the Leader lift when he recites *Matzah Zu?* The Rema,[7] quoting R. Weil, said that one is to lift the broken one, as this is the one that is likened to *leḥem oni,* while the Maharil[8] recommended using the top one, the whole one. We follow the Rema[9] and display the broken one.

The Leader intones these prayers aloud[10] and everyone reads along with him in keeping with the usual practice of reciting the *Haggadah*.

Lefeḥaḥ . . . Go'al Yisrael: Therefore . . . Who Redeemed Israel

The custom of everyone at the Seder raising the wine cup when *Lefeḥaḥ* is recited comes from the *Midrash Shoḥer Tov,*[1] a work written during the Talmudic era. The Midrash explains that *shirah,* or hymn, song, or poetry, must be chanted over wine. The Abudarham[2] elaborated: until now we were reciting the prose section of the *Haggadah;* now we are beginning the *Hallel* Psalms, technically known as *shirah,* and *shirah* should be recited over wine.[3]

The *Haggahot Maimuniyyot,* in the name of the Maharam of Rothenburg, ruled,[4] as did the *Tur*[5] and the *Shulḥan Arukh,*[6] that the cup is held aloft from *Lefeḥaḥ* until the end of the blessing, *Go'al Yisrael.* The *Haggahot Maimuniyyot* and the Prague *Haggadah* also pointed out that this means keeping it raised until after the blessing over the second cup of wine, according to the Ashkenazic practice of pronouncing a blessing over each of the four wine cups. However, the custom had changed in the time of the Abudarham, a student of the *Tur.* He wrote[7] that in his country (Spain) the wine cup was raised only at the beginning of the blessing of *Go'al Yisrael.* R. Emden,[8] however, stated that the Ashkenazic *minhag* was to raise the wine cup at *Lefeḥaḥ,* put it down at the end of that particular prayer (at *halleluyah*), raise it again at the start of *Go'al Yisrael,* put it down at its conclusion if some comment is offered, and then raise it for the blessing over the second cup. The *Arukh ha-Shulḥan*[9] agreed with R. Emden, and this is the custom followed by most Ashkenazim.

There appears to be no explanation for the change in *minhag* as quoted by the *Midrash Shoḥer Tov* and the *Tur.* Why did it change? Possibly it may have proved impractical to keep the wine cup raised so long, during the recital of four prayers, two of which, the opening Psalms of *Hallel*, are usually sung to lengthy tunes. Therefore, a compromise evolved that the cup would be raised for the first and last prayers of this series and put down for the middle two, the *Hallel* Psalms, which usually took the longest to sing.

The custom of covering the matzah during the *Lefaḥah* is according to the ruling of the *Agur*, quoted by the *Beth Yosef*,[10] and followed by the Rema,[11] *Arukh ha-Shulḥan*,[12] and all *aḥaronim*. It is the practice today. The reason, as quoted by the *Agur*, is to avoid shaming the bread, for the same reason we cover the matzah during *Kiddush*.[13]

The Second Cup

There is a wide-ranging debate among the *geonim* and *rishonim*, our earliest and greatest Sages, over whether one makes blessings before and after drinking the second and fourth cups of wine. The Gaon Cohen Tzedek, the Rosh, the Rashba, the *Tur*, and the *Shulḥan Arukh* argued that a blessing is not required before the second and fourth cups and a concluding blessing is obligatory only after the fourth cup. The Rif demanded no prior blessing for the second and fourth cups, but a final blessing after each of them; Rav Sherira Gaon, Hai Gaon, *Tosafoth*, and the Rema ruled that each wine cup requires a prior blessing but only the fourth cup needs a concluding blessing. This dispute centers around the *halakhah* that when one recites a blessing, for example, over an apple, it need not be repeated if one eats another apple so long as there was no *heseḥ ha-da'at* (discarding from the mind). Similarly, since a blessing is recited over wine at *Kiddush*, there would be no need to pronounce the same blessing again over the second cup of wine; and as a blessing was said over the third cup at the Grace after the meal, the fourth cup would also be exempt. Opposing authorities, while conceding these facts, claimed that since each wine cup is a *mitzvah* in its own right, each one requires a separate blessing as well.[1]

Regarding the special concluding blessing after drinking wine, there is a law that anything one drinks or eats before the meal, as part of the main meal, is exempt from a special final blessing by the Grace after the meal. Thus, the Grace exempts the first two cups, while the special concluding blessing for drinking wine pronounced after the fourth cup exempts the third cup.

Ashkenazim follow the *minhag* cited by the Rema,[2] the illuminated manuscripts and early printed *Haggadahs* such as the Kaufmann, the Sarajevo, and the Prague, and later authorities such as R. Emden,[3] the *Mishnah Berurah*,[4] R. Zevin,[5] and the *Arukh ha-Shulḥan*[6] that a prior blessing is required over each of the four cups of wine but a concluding blessing is needed only after the fourth cup.

RAḤTZAH: Lave the Hands

Preparation of the matzah portions for each person before this ritual washing of the hands follows the *minhag* of the *Ḥatam Sofer,*[1] and the reasons for the sizes and type of matzah are explained in the following section.

The second ritual laving follows the *Gemara Pesaḥim*[2] which says that even though the hands were washed before eating the *karpas,* this action may have been forgotten (*heseḥ ha-da'at*) and the hands might have become defiled by touching something unclean. Thus, this ritual is performed a second time. Some later Sages[3] claimed that if one washed and blessed before the *karpas* and then was careful not to touch anything that would defile the hands during the recital of the *Haggadah,* one need not wash and bless again. Today, because we do not recite a blessing for the ritual washing before the *karpas,* there is no question that the hands must be washed a second time and the blessing pronounced.

The exact washing procedure is the same as that given in the *U'Reḥatz* section of the *Haggadah.*[4] This procedure and the added blessing, pronounced while the hands are still wet,[5] also applies all year round whenever there is a ritual washing of the hands.

In many illuminated manuscript *Haggadahs,* the *Raḥtzah* is portrayed as taking place at the table. This was a sign of freedom and wealth; servants brought the washbasin, pitcher, and laver to the table, to the master. Today, however, as in the case of pouring the wine, a wife, mother, or sister taking the place of the servant proves nothing about freedom.[6] In addition, since there was no modern plumbing or running water in those days and all ritual laving of the hands was done by bowl, laver, and ewer, this act of washing at the table has no special significance and one may wash at a sink.

The *Tur,* quoting his brother,[7] said that from the *Raḥtzah* until after the eating of the *korekh,* except when necessary to the performance of the various rites and ceremonies involved , there should be no talking. This is because all these blessings and rituals are interrelated, and one must not engage in unnecessary talk between pronouncing a blessing and performing a *mitzvah.*

MOTZI–MATZAH: Blessings over the Matzah

The three matzot used for the Seder plate[1] and all the matzah portions distributed to the participants for the blessings of *motzi* and *matzah* should be *shemurah* matzah; as the Talmud[2] tells us, on Seder night one must eat at least a *kezayit* of *shemurah* matzah. This law is derived from a passage in Exodus (12:17): "And you shall observe (*shemartem*) the unleavened bread." Therefore, on Seder night,[3] the first taste should be these specially prepared matzot made specifically to be used for the *mitzvah* of eating matzah. They are made from wheat guarded from the moment it was cut against conditions that could cause it to become *ḥametz;* that it is, it has not come into contact with water.[4]

Needless to say, until recently all matzot were hand-made round matzot, prepared by our forefathers in much the same way for centuries. The advent of machine-produced matzot raised a whole host of *halakhic* problems.[5] While machine-made matzot are permitted for Passover use, a point should be made that for the Seder, to avoid any doubts at all, hand-made round *shemurah* matzot should be used even though they are very expensive.[6] In addition to satisfying all *halakhic* requirements, *shemurah* matzot also serve as a reminder of the exact matzot our forefathers used, not only in talmudic, *tannaitic,* and Temple times, but even when they left Egypt.

The way to lift and bread the matzot during this part of the *Haggadah* service is first found in the *Gemara Berakoth:*[7] "R. Papa said: All admit that on Passover one puts the broken matzah under the whole one and breaks them. Why? Because Scripture speaks of 'Bread of Poverty' (Deuteronomy 16:3)." However, it is not clear from this *Gemara* exactly how one should pronounce the two blessings, the *motzi* and the *aḥilat matzah,* that have to be said on this occasion. Some *rishonim* ruled that the *motzi* should be pronounced over the whole matzah alone and the *aḥilat matzah* over the broken one.[8] Other *rishonim* felt that the opposite procedure was the proper one to follow.[9] Still others held that both blessings should be said only over the broken matzah.[10] The Ri[11] used to make both blessings over both matzot. A further dispute arose as to when each of the matzot is to be broken. To further complicate matters, we use three matzot. How does all of this fit together?

The *Tur*, the *Shulḥan Arukh*, and other Sages[12] indicated that we hold all three matzot during both blessings. However, the procedure followed today stems from Rabbi Shlomo Luria[13] who recommended that the Leader lift all three matzot during the *motzi* because the two whole ones are needed for *leḥem mishneh*, the two loaves required on all Sabbaths and Festivals. After the *motzi*, the top matzah is cracked but not separated; the third matzah is put back on the plate and the *aḥilat matzah* is recited over the two uppermost that remain in the hands. A *kezayit* is broken off from each matzah and the two pieces are eaten together. The Maharil[14] agreed with R. Luria but said it was not necessary to crack the top matzah after the *motzi*. The *Ba'er Heitev*, the *Ḥok Ya'akov*, the *Mishnah Berurah*, and R. Zevin[15] all followed the Maharil, as do most of us today.

In order to fulfill the *mitzvah* of eating matzah on Seder night, a minimum of a *kezayit* (the size of an olive), which according to the *Siddur Minhat Yerushalaym*[16] is 26 grams or about one ounce, a piece about 4″ x 7″, must be eaten. The question now arises, from which matzah is the *kezayit* to be taken, the whole matzah or the broken one? The *Tur*,[17] the *Shulḥan Arukh*,[18] and most of the later Sages, in order to avoid the question, suggested that two *kezaytim* be eaten, one from each matzah. This is the general practice today, although the *Mishnah Berurah*[19] seemed to feel that one *kezayit* combined from both matzot should be sufficient.

Those partaking of the Seder are equally commanded with the Leader to fulfill the *mitzvah* of eating matzah this night. Since the matzah on the Seder plate barely suffices for the Leader, it is necessary to prepare additional matzot, preferably hand-made *shemurah*, for everybody. The procedure we follow,[20] the one suggested by the *Ḥatam Sofer*, is to bring to the table and serve, after the *motzi*, pieces of matzah, each one approximately 4″ x 7″ which had been prepared immediately before *Raḥtzah*. In order that these pieces of matzah should resemble those of the Leader, one section should have been broken off from a whole matzah while the other section should have been broken off from a broken one. After the Leader finishes both blessings, he breaks off a *kezayit* from each matzah for himself and as a gesture distributes small pieces of the remaining two matzot to all. The company then place this small piece with their own portions which they eat at the same time as the Leader. Thus, everyone is eating matzah together.[21]

The Rambam and the *geonim* stated that the matzah must be dipped in *ḥaroset.*[22] However, the *Tur,* based on a passage in the Jerusalem Talmud not extant in our editions, recommended dipping the matzah in salt.[23] This *minhag* was followed by the *Shulḥan Arukh* and the Ari.[24] However, the Rema,[25] referring to the Talmud *Berakoth*[26] which states that bread baked from pure flour does not need salt at any time, ruled that on Seder night the matzah should not be salted. In a comment on this ruling, the Maharil[27] explained that the matzah is not salted because we do not want to alter the pure taste of the matzah and nothing should interfere with one's joy in fulfilling this *mitzvah.* The *Levush,*[28] in his comment on this ruling, explained that it would be inappropriate to enhance the matzah with salt as the matzah on Seder night represents "bread of affliction." R. Emden,[29] following the *Tur,* recommended dipping the matzah in salt, as did the *Arukh ha-Shulḥan*[30] and R. Kasher.[31] The *Ḥayyei Adam* and the *Mishnah Berurah*[32] agreed with the Rema and ruled that one should not dip the matzah in salt. Therefore, the use of salt on the matzah is optional.

The matzah must be eaten quickly, within a period called *keday aḥilat pras* (literally, the time it takes to eat a piece of bread), a period computed by the *Siddur Minhat Yerushalaym* to be four minutes. However, other estimates of the Sages range from two to nine minutes.[34] Since we have to eat two *kezaytim* of matzah, twice this length of time is allowed. More time than this is considered to be two time periods, like two snacks rather than one meal, and so the *mitzvah* would not be fulfilled.

Tosafoth[35] ruled that the matzah must be eaten in one mouthful and swallowed in one gulp. The *Tur*[36] and the *Shulḥan Arukh*[37] agreed that one should try to eat and swallow both *kezaytim* together. The Maharil,[38] however, allowed one to eat the matzah piece by piece, provided it is eaten within the allotted time. The *Mishnah Berurah*[39] conceded that while one must try to put both *kezaytim* of matzah in the mouth, one need swallow only one *kezayit* at a time. The *Arukh ha-Shulḥan*[40] tended to agree with the Maharil, that one may eat the matzah piece by piece. However, continued the *Arukh ha-Shulḥan,* one must try to follow the *Shulḥan Arukh* and eat the two *kezaytim* in one mouthful and swallow them in one swallow.

The *Gemara* in *Pesaḥim*[41] ruled that one must recline on the left side for this *mitzvah*. All our Sages have agreed and every male must be sure to recline on the left while eating the matzah over which he pronounced the blessings of the *motzi* and *aḥilat matzah*.

MAROR: Bitter Herb

The Mishnah[1] lists five vegetables that one may use for *maror: ḥazeret, tamḥah, ḥarḥevinah, ulshin,* and *maror.* We can identify only *ḥazeret* with certainty. As the Talmud explains in *Pesaḥim,*[2] *ḥazeret* is *ḥasa,* or lettuce. Because the lettuce grown then was romaine, that is the type usually used, although in fact any lettuce fulfills the requirement of *maror.*

Of the five vegetables enumerated, the Talmud[2] prefers that we use *ḥazeret* or lettuce for the *maror* on the Seder plate. The *Gemara* explains that the Aramaic word for lettuce, *ḥasa,* alludes to the pity (*ḥas*) that the Almighty had for the Israelites whom He therefore freed from their slavery. The lettuce also symbolizes the Egyptian behavior in another way. Just as the Egyptians were kind and soft to the Israelites at first, inviting them in as free men and honored settlers, and then became hard and cruel to them, enslaving them and persecuting them, so is the lettuce. Its leaves are soft and tender but its end or stem is hard, almost as hard as wood. This explanation answers a vexing question. How can the *mitzvah* of *maror,* the definition of the word itself being bitterness, be fulfilled best by lettuce? Lettuce is not bitter. The answer is, as the *Arukh ha-Shulḥan*[3] explained, that *maror* symbolizes two things: bitterness in taste and a similarity to Egyptian behavior. The Talmud considered the latter more important, hence the preference for lettuce.

Rabbi Culi[4] stated that only lettuce and no other bitter herb fulfills the true requirement of *maror.* He reasoned that the three foods about which the Seder revolves are: the paschal lamb, the matzah and the *maror.* Each one has a dual meaning, good and bad. The paschal lamb alludes to the death of the Egyptian first-born and to the Almighty passing over the houses of the Israelites, exempting them from a similar fate. The matzah is the *leḥem oni,* the bread of affliction, and alludes as well to the Exodus from Egypt. Similarly, the *maror* symbolizes the bitter life of slavery in Egypt and the redemption; the Almighty had pity (*ḥas*=lettuce) and redeemed the Israelites.

As for the other four vegetables, there are problems with their exact definitions. Some identify *tamḥa* as *marrubium vulgare* (a kind of mint), the *ḥarḥevinah* as erynago (sea holly, an herb), *ulshin* as endive or chicory, and *maror* as sonchus (a health herb).[5]

In the 14th and 15th centuries our Eastern European Sages[6] identified *tamḥa* as horseradish, and our later Sages accepted this interpretation.[7] This identification was possibly based on a misinterpretation of the words of the *Haggahot Maimuniyyot.*[8] Eastern European Jews were forced to use horseradish instead of lettuce for the *maror* by necessity. As explained by the *Arukh ha-Shulḥan,*[9] in Eastern Europe it was the only bitter vegetable available, and at this time of the year, lettuce was to be found only in the nobleman's conservatory.[10] Consequently, in the late 16th century, among Ashkenazic Jews, horseradish became the *maror* for the Seder.

The use of horseradish as *maror* led to a number of Rabbinic questions. May one eat it grated or only whole? If grating is permitted, how long before its use may one grate it? And what part of the horseradish is called the stem and what part the root? *Halakhically* roots are not permitted to be eaten for the *maror.*[11] In addition, there was the problem of being able to eat a *kezayit* of such a sharp and pungent vegetable. In view of these questions and the preference of the Talmud, the *Tur,* and the *Shulḥan Arukh* for lettuce as the *maror,* the latter is unquestionably the vegetable of choice as the *maror* for Seder night. However, it must be carefully and thoroughly washed lest any worms remain on it.[12]

What is *ḥaroset* (in Hebrew the word means clay) made of? The Talmud[13] says that *ḥaroset* should resemble mud and straw. The Jerusalem Talmud[14] adds that is should also contain a liquid, a reminder of the Jewish blood spilled by the Egyptians. *Tosafoth,*[15] quoting the *geonim,* therefore ruled that the *ḥaroset* should contain elements to resemble blood, straw, and mud. For the blood, *Tosafoth* suggested red wine or wine vinegar; for the straw the Talmud recommends spices, and those named by the *geonim* and *Tosafoth* are cinnamon and ginger. Since the cinnamon and/or ginger should resemble straw, they are not to be ground into powder but shreded into fine strips. To represent mud, the *geonim* suggested any combination of fruits to which Israel is compared in the Song of Songs: apples, pomegranates, figs, dates, nuts, and almonds. Today the *ḥaroset* is prepared from the same ingredients.[16] The *ḥaroset* is saved for use at the second Seder and may then be served to the children and adults for dessert. It should not be thrown away.

The Mishnah states that a minimum of a *kezayit*[17] of *maror* (a piece of lettuce weighing about one ounce or about 8″ x 10″ in size[18]) must be eaten in order to fulfill the *mitzvah* of *maror* on Seder night.

The *maror* must be dipped in the *ḥaroset*, which has several functions. It is said to negate any toxic effects of the *maror*,[20] and it will remove any worms[21] that might have been left in the lettuce after it was washed.

The *ḥaroset* is important in its own right, however. Each of its ingredients is a reminder of our slavery in Egypt. The apples remind us of the passage in the Song of Songs (8:5): "Under the apple tree I awakened thee; There thy mother was in travail with thee; There was she in travail and brought thee forth," a poetic allusion to the Jewish women in Egypt who, during the time of the evil decree that all males had to be killed, gave birth to their babies under the apple trees without a sound so that the Egyptians would not hear.[22] The wine or wine vinegar is a reminder of the Jewish blood spilled by the Egyptians and the cinnamon and ginger of the mud and straw that the Israelites used to make the bricks while in bondage.

All traces of the *ḥaroset* must be shaken off the *maror*, stated the *Tur*,[23] quoting Rabbi Yona, as one must taste only the *maror*. The Talmud[24] tells us that the *maror* must be chewed well and not swallowed so that the full taste of it is experienced.

Why is a special blessing not recited over the *ḥaroset*? The *Tur*[25] answered that it is subsidiary to the *maror*. R. Emden[26] suggested that we do not make a blessing over the *ḥaroset* because it is not eaten, or even tasted.

Must all of the *maror* be dipped in the *ḥaroset* or only a part of it? The *Roke'aḥ*, the *Tur*, the *Shulḥan Arukh*, and the *Arukh ha-Shulḥan*,[27] following the sense of the Talmud,[28] ruled that the *maror* must be dipped completely in the *ḥaroset*. However, the *Peri Ḥadash*[29] claimed that it is only necessary to dip part of the *maror* in the *ḥaroset*. The *Mishnah Berurah*[30] accepted either ruling.

When is the blessing of *aḥilat maror* said? The Maharil[31] felt that it should be recited before the *maror* is dipped into the *ḥaroset*. Similarly, he ruled that for *karpas* the blessing is said before dipping in salt water. Nevertheless, most of our Sages[32] ruled that the blessing of *aḥilat maror* is recited after the *ḥaroset* is shaken off the *maror*, and this is the practice today.

The Talmud[33] states that there is no *heseba* while the *maror* is eaten. Rashi[34] explained that since *maror* is a remembrance of slavery, it would be incongruous to recline on the left, an action that is symbolic of freedom.

KOREKH: Combine Matzah and Bitter Herb

The *Tur*,[1] based on *Tosafoth* and the Rosh, ruled that for the *Korekh* portion of the Seder program we should use the third and as yet unused matzah. This, explained the *Baḥ*,[2] is so that all matzot on the Seder plate will be involved in performance of a mitzvah.

Ḥazeret is the name given to the *maror* provided for the *Korekh* ceremony. As noted previously, *ḥazeret* means lettuce according to the Talmud, and it is the preferred vegetable for use as *maror*.[4] It was the Ari who in his arrangement of the Seder plate employed the term *ḥazeret* to denote the *maror* used for the *korekh*. Those who have adopted the Ari's arrangement of the Seder plate have also taken over this term. Some have mistakenly assumed that the *ḥazeret* should be a different vegetable from the one used for *maror*. The *Ḥayyei Adam*[5] derided this idea and claimed, correctly, that any vegetable proper for use as *maror* is also proper for *korekh*. Although lettuce is preferred, a combination of lettuce, endive, and chicory may serve as the *ḥazeret*.[6]

Is there a minimum amount of matzah and *maror* necessary for the *korekh*? Most of our earlier Sages were not specific on this point. The *Shibbolei ha-Leket*[7] indicated that a *kezayit* of matzah and a *kezayit* of *maror* were needed to fulfill the *Korekh* part of the Seder. However, the Rosh[8] seemed to indicate that no minimum requirement is necessary. Our major decisors are silent on this point. The question came to the fore in the 18th century when the *Sha'agot Aryeh*, R. Emden, the *Ḥayyei Adam*, and the *Ma'amar Mordecai* all stated that the necessary minimum is a *kezayit* of matzah and a *kezayit* of *maror* for the *korekh*.[9] The *Mishnah Berurah*[10] accepted their ruling, and today it is normative practice.

There is a long-standing dispute among the early *rishonim* as to whether one must dip the *maror* used for the *korekh* in the *ḥaroset*? The *Avi ha-Ezri*, the Ramban, the Mahari Trena, the Maharil, the Rema, and many other Ashkenazic Sages did not require dipping. However, Rashi, the Rambam, the *Or Zaru'a*, the *Maḥzor Vitry*, the Rosh, the *Tur*, and the *Shulḥan Arukh* all felt the *maror* must be dipped in the *ḥaroset* for the *korekh*[11] because Hillel dipped the *maror* for the *korekh*, and if we perform this ceremony in memory of Hillel we should also be required to dip. The opposing view is that one of the four questions asks about two dippings and not about three, which would be the case if we dipped here.[12] Those who favor dipping for *korekh* feel that it is an extension of the *maror*, and, therefore, both dippings are really counted as only one.[13] Some later Sages[14,15] ruled that either *minhag* is acceptable; however,the majority[16-19] preferred that the *ḥazeret* be dipped in *ḥaroset*.

There is complete agreement that all trace of *ḥaroset* must be shaken off for *Maror*. However, for the *Korekh*, the *Agur* in the name of the Maharil[20] ruled that one need not shake it off. However, reasoned the *Ma'amar Mordecai*[21] and the *Mishnah Berurah*,[22] since this *minhag* is in memory of Hillel, who definitely shook it off, we should do so also.

There is also a difference of opinion about whether the males must recline on the left while eating the *korekh*. The *Shibbolei ha-Leket* and the *Roke'aḥ* did not require *heseba*. The *Manhig*, the *Or Zaru'a*,[23] the *Shulḥan Arukh*,[24] the *Mishnah Berurah*,[25] the *Arukh ha-Shulḥan*,[26] and almost all the later Sages required *heseba* for the eating of the *korekh* because, as the *Beth Yosef*[27] explained, Hillel reclined on the left when he ate the *korekh*. The question arises, how could Hillel have reclined on the left, since the sandwich contains *maror* and one does not recline while eating *maror*? Reclining is a symbol of freedom while *maror* is a symbol of slavery. The answer is that while we need not recline when eating *maror*, if one does so, it does not negate the *mitzvah* and one does not have to perform the *mitzvah* again. But the matzah must be eaten with *heseba*, and so the *korekh*, which contains matzah, must be eaten while reclining on the left.[28]

The time allotted for the eating of the *korekh* is the same as that allowed for eating two *kezaytim*, eight minutes.[29]

SHULḤAN ARUKH: The Meal

The *minhag* of eating eggs on Seder night seems to have become widespread during the 16th century. There are many reasons for this custom. The Rema[1] observed that eggs are traditionally eaten as a symbol of mourning, they are served to a bereaved family as their first meal after a funeral. An egg has no opening or mouth, a fitting symbol for mourners struck dumb with grief. At the same time, the roundness of the egg offers encouragement, for the wheel of fortune is also round, and in its turning can bring joy and happiness.[2]

Since *Tishah be-Av* (the Ninth day of Av), the fast day commemorating the destruction of the Temple, always falls on the same day of the week as the first day of Passover, the egg reminds us of the destruction of the Temple where we used to sacrifice the paschal lamb. The *Peri Megadim*[3] believed that we eat the eggs in remembrance of the fact that Abraham died on the 15th of Nison, the first day of Passover. A more modern Sage[4] noted the similarity between the Jews in Egypt and an egg. Eggs get harder the longer they are boiled. Similarly, the more the Jews in Egypt were oppressed, the more they were tortured, the harder became their resolve to live and flourish.

The Gaon of Vilna tended to belittle this *minhag*. He stated[5] that we are only supposed to eat the egg that is on the Seder plate in remembrance of the *korban ḥagigah*, as the Talmud tells us, the sacrifice brought to the Temple together with the paschal lamb.[6] The eating of eggs as a course of the Seder meal is a mix-up of the original custom. The *Mishnah Berurah* and the *Ḥayyei Adam* agreed with the Gaon; in fact, the *Ḥayyei Adam* wanted to abolish this custom entirely, claiming that people fill up with eggs and are not able to eat the *afikoman*.[7] However, this *minhag* has been widely accepted, and today almost every Seder meal begins with hard-boiled eggs.

What is the proper way to eat the hard-boiled eggs? Most modern *Haggadahs* recommend dipping them in salt water. However, this does not seem proper. Many Sages prohibited the eating on Seder night of any foods that were dipped.[8] The correct way to eat the eggs is either by themselves, without any dipping, or chopped up and mixed with salt water, creating a hard-boiled egg soup.[9]

The custom of not eating any roasted meats or roasted fowl dates back to Mishnaic times.[10] Only boiled meats were eaten on Seder night because eating roasted meat might lead people to think the paschal lamb was being eaten outside the Temple precincts, a serious breach of *halakhah*. All later Ashkenazic Sages ruled that Ashkenazic Jews may not eat roasted meats or fowl on Seder night.[11] What exactly is meant by roasting? The *Arukh ha-Shulḥan*[12] stated that only a process similar to the spit roasting of the paschal lamb is prohibited; pan roasting, therefore, is permitted. However, the *Magen Avraham*, the *Ḥayyei Adam*, and the *Mishnah Berurah*[13] ruled that any cooking without a liquid is included in the ban on roasting. Ashkenazic Jews today do not eat any roasted or even braised or fried meat or fowl on Seder night.

The Maharil and the Rema[14] stated that some people do not eat any dipped foods on Seder night. Since the second of the four questions implies that we dip only twice, that question would become meaningless if we ate other dipped foods.

A rather recent *minhag*, of Hasidic origin, is not to eat any food prepared with matzah or matzah meal (*gebroks*) lest, through contact with liquid, the matzah ferment and cause leavening or *ḥametz*. Although this practice is unheard of in any of the *halakhic* literature, it has found acceptance among a large segment of orthodoxy.

Because there is so much confusion over what foods may be used, how they should be prepared, and which foods should traditionally be eaten, we have included detailed menus and recipes for Seder nights.[15]

The meal should be eaten in a festive mood, as we celebrate our liberation from the slavery of Egypt.[16] However, one must be careful not to drink too much or overeat during the meal. As the Maharil[17] explained, if one drinks too much wine he might become drunk and fall asleep and so fail to complete the Seder. One must not overeat, admonished the *Roke'aḥ*, because then the eating of the *afikoman* becomes a burden and thus negates the *mitzvah*. Our later Sages agreed with these injunctions.[19] Since the *afikoman* should be eaten before midnight,[20] the meal should conclude before then.

Menus and Recipes

The Seder Plate

1. 3 *shemurah* matzot.

2. Egg, preferably boiled. After it has been hard-boiled, however, it can be broiled quickly over a flame until slightly charred. If it is only boiled it may be used with the first course of the meal, either in egg soup or with the addition of a slight sprinkling of salt. If you do boil it, prepare another for the second evening.

3. *Ziroa.* Any shankbone with some meat on it or just a chicken bone with some chicken on it may represent the *ziroa.* It, too, may be boiled or roasted. If roasted, it may not be eaten at the Seder and should be used for the second Seder. It is preferable to boil the *ziroa* so that it can be eaten at the meal. Then there is no problem of deciding when it can be eaten. None of the food used as part of the Seder ritual may be thrown away. It is sinful and wasteful. If the meat bone is boiled, prepare two pieces, one for each Seder.

4. *Maror.* Romaine lettuce, the variety used by our ancestors, is preferred, but any lettuce, even iceberg, may be used. Wash carefully at least two large romaine lettuces. The leaves should be separated from the main stem and soaked for about five minutes to loosen the dirt and insects. Today, with the use of pesticides, the latter are not a problem. Each leaf is washed under cold running water. Shake well and store in a plastic bag in the refrigerator. Before they are used, the leaves should be thoroughly and gently dried with paper towels prepared for the purpose. Place four lettuce leaves on the plate, leaving the remainder in the refrigerator until needed. Two large lettuces are enough for 10 people for each Seder, assuming that each person will eat the required amounts. Note: A *kezayit* of lettuce is approximately one and a half large outer leaves or two medium-sized leaves, the equivalent weight of an olive, one ounce. Place at least two *kezaytim* on the plate.

5. *Ḥazeret.* This, too, is *maror.* Use romaine preferably, but any lettuce will do. Chicory or endive may be substituted. This lettuce is used for the "Hillel sandwich," the first ever recorded. Place at least one *kezayit* on the plate.

6. *Karpas.* In modern Hebrew this word means celery and that is the vegetable of choice, although any other vegetable may be used, including radishes, parsley, onions, and even boiled potatoes. One whole celery is enough for 10 persons for both Seder nights since only a small piece is given to each person. Enough celery for the entire company is placed on the plate: three or four stalks are sufficient for 10 people. A small bowl containing one cup of cold water and 3/4 teaspoon salt is placed beside the Seder plate.

7. *Ḥaroset.* This is a dip which represents mud, blood,and straw. Any fruit mentioned in the Song of Songs, to which Israel is compared, may be used: apples (preferred), almonds, nuts, pomegranates, dates, and figs. These are pounded together to represent the clay or mud which was used to make bricks. The spices represent the straw. Stick cinnamon or fresh ginger is usually chosen because it can be shredded to resemble the straw. Powdered spices should not be used. Wine represents the blood of the Children of Israel, spilled by the Egyptians. Quantities given below are sufficient for two nights.

Traditional Ashkenazic Recipe

2 apples, grated
½ cup almonds or walnuts, finely chopped or ground
1 tablespoon red wine
¼–½ teaspoon cinnamon stick, shaved, or fresh ginger, shredded
Prepare the cinnamon by inserting the stick in a small hand pencil sharpener used especially for this purpose, or shave it using a new razor blade, in the same way a pencil is sharpened. The shavings are then easly crushed to resemble straw. If using fresh ginger, shred it on the medium fine part of the standard hand grater. Mix all ingredients together and chill. Before the Seder begins, the mixture should be thinned with more red wine until it is the consistency of a thick batter that coats the back of a spoon but will not hold its own shape. Serve in a saucer or wide bowl since the whole lettuce leaf has to be dipped in it.

Sephardic Recipe

¼ cup dates, ground
¼ cup apple, grated
¼ cup almonds, ground
1 tablespoon red wine
¼ cup figs, ground
¼ teaspoon cinnamon stick, shaved
or ¼ teaspoon fresh ginger, shredded

Prepare as in Ashkenazic recipe.

Traditional Foods for the Seder

Fried, broiled, or roasted meats and poultry are not permitted to be eaten, only poached or boiled meat and fowl. However, meat or fowl that is first fried or roasted and then boiled with the addition of liquid, such as water, soup, or wine, is permitted. This prohibition does not apply to fish, even though fried fish is never part of a traditional menu. The third of the four questions mentions that on Seder night we dip twice only. Therefore, any food that is prepared by dipping in some sort of batter, such as fried fish, is not served. This rule also applies to the first course, the hard-boiled egg. It may be prepared as an egg soup or served whole with some accompaniment. It should not be dipped into salt water and then eaten. The meal traditionally begins with hard-boiled eggs in some form (see page 43).

Many other foods are traditionally served. R. Kasher in his *Haggadah* mentions that cucumbers should be eaten at the Seder, a custom based on the Biblical verse, (Numbers 11:5): "We remember the fish, which we were wont to eat in Egypt for nought; the cucumbers, and the melons, and the leeks, and the onions, and the garlic." Sephardic Jews always serve leeks in some form at the Seder, and it is proper to serve any or all of the foods mentioned.

The Ramban used to eat fennel on Seder night. In Hebrew, fennel is *shumor* and he noted its punning similarity to one of the names given to this night in the Book of Exodus, *leyl shimurim*, the night of watching. Similarly, *kishuim*, which in the Book of Numbers is translated as "cucumbers," in modern Hebrew means squash. R. Emden recommends fish and meat in addition to hard-boiled eggs.

The *Ḥatam Sofer* used to eat tongue with horseradish sauce for one of the Passover meals. He based his custom on the story told in Genesis 18. It is the story of the three angels who dined with our Father Abraham and then announced that Sarah and Abraham would become the parents of a son to be born the following year. Rashi commented that the meal which was served to the angels included, among other things, the choicest part of the tongue of the calf, served with mustard. The Midrash seems to indicate that this event occurred on Passover because in the following chapter of Genesis, the angels, after leaving Abraham and Sarah, continued on their journey to visit Lot, who served them matzot. Lot served the angels matzot because, Rashi explained, it was Passover. To commemorate these events, the *Ḥatam Sofer* ate tongue, but substituted horseradish sauce for the equally pungent mustard, which is not permitted on Passover. Referring to the same story, other Rabbis noted that Abraham instructed Sarah to use three measures of flour to bake cakes instead of two, and they fancifully claimed that the three matzot of the Seder plate represent the three measures of flour.

Most Rabbinic Sages suggest a very light meal for the Seder. One Rabbi commented that he could hardly eat more than a hard-boiled egg because of all the matzah, *maror,* and *afikoman* he had to eat. This holds true today. The Seder meal is one that emphasizes the eating of matzah. That is its main purpose, and the meal should be planned with this in mind. An enormous banquet that leaves one so stuffed that there is no room for the *afikoman* and the remaining two cups of wine is forbidden.

There is a custom among Ashkenazim, mainly of Hasidic origin, not to eat foods prepared and cooked on Passover that contain matzah or any derivative of matzah (*gebroks*) such as matzah flour or matzah farfel. These people fear that if a small particle of flour remains uncooked in the baking of the matzah and it is then mixed with water or some other liquid, it would become *ḥametz,* leaven. However, this custom is relaxed on the eighth day of Passover since the extra day is rabbinic and not Biblical. For those who do not eat *gebroks,* potato starch or boiled potatoes are substituted in cakes, stuffings, and gefulte fish.

Seder Menus

All ingredients used should have proper Passover certification where necessary. If in doubt, consult your rabbi. A dairy meal is inappropriate, since the Seder plate is by definition meat. Vegetarians should eat a *pareve* meal. Recipes marked with an asterisk are prepared with matzah products.

Menu No. 1

Egg soup
Gefulte fish with horseradish sauce
Beef and chicken broth with knaidlach* or egg noodles
Boiled chicken, flanken, and tongue
Braised leeks, or fennel
Cucumber salad
Zucchini kugel
Melon, fruit salad
Almond sponge cake, macaroons
Tea or black coffee

Menu No. 2

Hard-boiled egg with cucumber and fennel salad
Halibut or salmon trout with lemon sauce
Chicken, leek, and potato soup
Poached breast of veal and/or pickled tongue
Braised onions
Stewed apples and walnuts with wine sauce
Chocolate cream roll
Tea or black coffee

Recipes

Quantities given are for 10 people.

Egg Course

If the hard-boiled egg on the Seder plate has not been roasted, use it in one of the recipes below.

Egg Soup

6 hard-boiled eggs
2 cups cold water
1½ teaspoon salt (or to taste)
2 teaspoons parsley, finely chopped (optional)

Coarsely chop eggs in serving bowl. Add salt and water. Mix until soup appears pale yellow. Serve immediately in small bowls. Garnish with chopped parsely if desired.

Egg, Cucumber, and Fennel Salad

6 hard-boiled eggs (sliced or halved)
2 squat-shaped fennel
1 cucumber
salt and pepper
1 tablespoon olive oil
1 teaspoon lemon juice or wine vinegar

Cut off tops and leaves of fennel. Discard bruised and discolored stalks. Starting from base of fennel, remove and discard ¼-inch slice. Slice fennel as thinly as possible. Wash and pat dry. Peel and slice cucumber thinly. Add salt, pepper, and olive oil.Toss well. Add lemon juice or wine vinegar and toss again. Garnish with round slices of egg.

Fish Course

Gefulte Fish: Special Passover Recipe

3 pounds fish fillets of 1 large white fish, 1 yellow pike, piece of carp, salmon trout, cod, or halibut
1 large Bermuda onion
1–2 teaspoons salt (or more to taste)
1 tablespoon sugar
1 teaspoon white pepper
3 extra-large eggs
2 hard-boiled eggs
4 tablespoons water
3 tablespoons almonds, skinned and ground (optional)

Wash fillets and salt them lightly. Refrigerate about 2 hours. Fish stock (recipe below) can be prepared at this stage. Wash fillets to remove salt. Remove tendons and small bones, and cut into 2–inch pieces. Grind fish, onion, and hard-boiled eggs. Put through food chopper twice. Place mixture in large wooden bowl and with a hand chopper, blend in remaining ingredients. This blending takes 10–15 minutes. Chill for 2 hours (optional). The mixture should be just firm enough to be shaped. The hands should be wet when shaping the fish balls or the mixture will be sticky.

Fish Stock

Heads and large bones of the fish from which fillets were taken
1 large Bermuda onion
4 large carrots, sliced
2 stalks celery
½ parsley root
1 teaspoon salt
1 teaspoon sugar
cold water to cover

Put fish heads and bones into large broad-based pot. Add salt and sugar and cover with water. Bring to boil and skim carefully. Add sliced onion, celery, and carrots. Shape fish into ovals 3 inches by 1½ inches and place in boiling stock on top of vegetables. Bring to boil again; then reduce heat until liquid is barely simmering. Cover and poach for 2 hours. Remove fish to large bowl. Drain stock into a jar and chill thoroughly. Garnish each fish ball with a carrot slice. Serve with jellied fish stock and horseradish sauce.

Horseradish Sauce

1 large horseradish root
1 pound beets
salt to taste
1 teaspoon sugar
1 ounce cider or wine vinegar or lemon juice

Wash beets well. Cut off tops and boil in their skins until soft. Peel and wash horseradish. Grate it in the food processor using the coarse grater. Then, using the chopping blade, reduce it to a fine pulp. This method eliminates lumps. Peel and cube beets. Add to horseradish and blend. Add remaining ingredients and blend again. Adjust seasonings. Prepare several days ahead so that sauce has time to mellow.

Poached Jellied Fish

5 pounds fish, sliced (halibut, pike, whitefish, carp)
1 large onion
3 carrots
2 stalks celery
1 bay leaf (imported, not California)
½ cup dry white wine, or ½ cup wine vinegar, or 2 ounces lemon juice
6 peppercorns
2 teaspoons sugar
½ teaspoon salt
2 cups cold water (approx.)

Clean fish well. Remove blood along backbone of visceral cavity. Cut off heads and save for fish stock. Slice halibut and carp into

1-inch slices. Pike and whitefish should be at least 2 inches thick. Salt fish lightly and refrigerate for 1 hour.
Prepare fish stock: Put fish heads together with all other ingredients and salt into fish kettle. Add water to cover, bring to boil, skim and cook covered for 30 minutes, until vegetables are just soft. Wash off fish slices and place them gently into the boiling fish stock. Simmer gently with cover slightly tilted for about 25 minutes. Remove fish to platter. Strain stock; if there is more than 2 cups, reduce by boiling.

Lemon Sauce

2 eggs or 3 egg yolks
2 cups reduced fish stock
1½ teaspoons potato starch
lemon juice to taste

Heat 1½ cups fish stock. Add potato starch dissolved in remaining cold stock. Bring to boil, stirring constantly until it thickens. Add lemon juice. Remove from heat. Pour a small amount of stock over well-beaten eggs or egg yolks and stir vigorously. Return the egg mixture to the fish stock. Over very low flame, stirring continuously, cook sauce another 5 minutes. Chill.

Poached Whole Salmon or Salmon Trout

whole fish with or without head, approx. 6 pounds
1 large onion
1 large leek
4 peppercorns
1 small imported bay leaf, or 2 sprigs of fresh dill
lemon zest
juice of 1½ lemons
½ cup dry white wine (optional)

Wash fish well and clean visceral cavity, especially blood along the backbone. If possible, remove the small bones which line the visceral

cavity. This facilitates serving after the fish is cooked. There are two methods for preparing this recipe. The results are similar for both.
Oven method: Take a large piece of heavy aluminum foil. Grease with olive oil. Add cleaned, sliced vegetables and lay fish on top of them. Add remaining ingredients. Seal foil well and bake for approximately 1 hour at 350° F.
Stove burner method: Place thinly sliced onion diagonally over the bottom of a long (14 to 16 inches) roasting pan. Lay whole fish on top of slices. Add remaining ingredients around fish and add water to a depth of 1 inch. Place roasting pan over two burners on stove. Bring to a boil and reduce heat on both burners until liquid is just barely simmering. Cover with heavy foil shaped like a tent. Poach at least 40 minutes; it may take 1 hour depending on the thickness of the fish. It is unnecessary to prepare a court bouillon beforehand when poaching large fish as the stock develops flavor from the vegetables when cooked more than 30 minutes. Allow fish to cool for 15 minutes, then remove to a large platter using two spatulas. To serve, remove skin on top side of fish and the small bones that run along the top of the back and along the belly side near the tail. These peel away easily when fish is warm. Decorate with olives, lemon slices, cucumber, parsley, and cooked leek. Serve with horseradish or lemon sauce. If fish is to be served cold, cover with plastic wrap to prevent its drying out.

Soup Course

Chicken Soup with Matzah Balls or Egg Noodles

Prepare chicken soup using any recipe. The variations are endless.

Matzah Balls (Knaidlach)*

4 eggs
1 cup matzah meal (approx.)
1½ teaspoons salt, or 2 chicken soup cubes
3 tablespoons melted chicken fat
1 tablespoon water

Beat eggs well. With a fork, slowly stir into the eggs enough matzah meal to make a thick batter which just falls off a spoon. Stir in melted fat, a pinch of salt, and water. Cover batter with wax paper or plastic wrap and chill for at least 2 hours, preferably 6 hours. In 5-quart pot with tightly fitting lid, bring 3 quarts water to a boil. Add salt or chicken soup cubes. With wet hands, form small dumplings the size of large walnuts. Drop into rapidly boiling water. Bring water back to boil, cover pot, reduce flame and boil gently for 30–40 minutes. Drain and serve with clear chicken soup.

Egg Noodles

6 eggs
6 tablespoons cold water
3 tablespoons potato starch
pinch of salt

Beat eggs well. Add remaining ingredients. The batter is quite thin and must be stirred at intervals to prevent potato flour from sinking to bottom. Temper 8 to 10 inch frying pan by heating it and adding dry table salt. Rub salt around inside of hot pan with a paper towel. Pour out salt. Do not wash pan. Add a little oil to coat base and sides, and pour off excess. Stir batter and pour, in a thin stream, into fry pan, which is tilted so that batter coats base. Cook until bottom is lightly browned, then flip over so that browned side is on top. Remove to a tea towel. Repeat frying procedure until all batter is used up. Roll up each pancake, jelly-roll fashion, and cut to form thin strips. Drop into hot soup and serve immediately.

Chicken, Leek, and Potato Soup

1½ quarts chicken soup
6 leeks
6 medium-sized potatoes
2 eggs (optional)
2 tablespoons chicken fat
1 tablespoon potato starch
coarse salt to taste

Finely slice leeks and potatoes, and cook gently in chicken fat until just slightly brown. Add chicken broth and salt. Cook for 45 minutes. Purée potatoes and leeks. Add potato starch dissolved in a little cold water to thicken hot soup. Stir for 2–3 minutes. If a creamier color is desired, add 2 eggs. Beat eggs well. Pour a small amount of hot soup into eggs, beating continuously. Pour egg-soup mixture back into remaining soup. Cook very gently, stirring continuously, but do not allow to boil or eggs will curdle. Serve with chopped parsley.

Meat Course

Pickled Tongue

4 pounds fresh tongue
5 imported bay leaves
4 cloves fresh garlic
1 dried chili pepper
1½–2 cups kosher salt
½ ounce saltpeter
water to cover
a fresh egg

To prepare: Place tongue in large plastic or earthenware bowl. Add enough cold water so that tongue is covered by ½ inch when it is held under water with fingers. Remove tongue. Put fresh egg into the water and slowly add kosher salt in small amounts. Each increment of salt should dissolve before more is added. The brine is of adequate strength when egg floats to the surface. Remove egg. Add remaining ingredients. Put the tongue in the brine and weight it down with a heavy plate. Cover with cheesecloth or other loose cover that allows air to circulate. Store in refrigerator 10 days to 2 weeks. Turn tongue every 2 days.

To cook and serve: Place tongue in large stock pot; cover with cold water. Bring slowly to a boil and simmer for 1½ hours. Remove tongue and cool rapidly under cold water. Discard cooking liquid. Peel tongue and trim excess fat and gristle from the butt. Replace tongue in pot. Cover with cold water. Bring to a boil and simmer gently with cover slightly askew for approximately 2 hours, until tongue is tender when pierced with a fork. Remove tongue, cool, and then chill in refrigerator for 2 hours. Slice tongue thinly when thoroughly chilled and replace slices in same shape as whole tongue. Wrap securely and tightly in heavy aluminum foil. Heat until warm, not too hot. Transfer to large platter. If the tongue slices are not replaced in their original position, they lose their reddish color when reheated and turn brown.

Mixed Boiled Meats and Chicken

2 small chickens (4 pounds each)
1 small fresh tongue
4 pounds flanken
4 carrots
1 parsley root with tops
3 stalks celery
4–5 leeks
1 potato
2 cloves garlic
2–3 tablespoons coarse salt

Place tongue and flanken in a 10 to 12 quart pot. Cover with cold water. Add salt. Bring to a boil and skim carefully. Simmer for 1½ hours. Remove tongue from broth; peel it and remove excess fat from the butt. Return to hot broth and add chickens, whole or cut in halves. Skim broth again. Add vegetables and continue cooking for 1½ hours. Remove chicken and vegetables. Leave tongue and flanken in broth. The soup should be served with egg noodles or knaidlach. The meats should be sliced and served with a small amount of broth and the chicken and vegetables. Serve with horse-radish sauce.

Pan-Cooked Veal

5 pounds shoulder of veal, boned and rolled
5 small cloves fresh garlic, peeled and crushed
¼ teaspoon peppercorns, crushed
1 small bay leaf

Italian parsley
2 tablespoons olive oil or chicken fat
1 cup dry white wine
2 leeks
1 carrot
2 stalks celery
2 cups chicken bouillon

Insert garlic pieces and parsley into spaces in veal. In a heavy-bottomed pan or enamel casserole which just fits meat, heat olive oil or chicken fat, and brown meat well on all sides for about 20 minutes. Add pepper, vegetables, wine, and bouillon. Simmer with cover of pot slightly askew for 2–3 hours until tender. Add a little more water or bouillon if necessary. Turn meat from time to time so that it does not stick to pan.

Vegetables and Salad

Braised Onions

2½ pounds small white onions of uniform size
chicken fat or olive oil
1 teaspoon sugar
1 cup chicken soup

Peel onions. Heat fat or oil in large fry pan. Slowly sauté onions until slightly brown. Sprinkle sugar over onions; add chicken soup and cook gently until stock is almost evaporated and onions are soft.

Braised Leeks with Tomatoes

2 pounds leeks
1 pound tomatoes
1 tablespoon olive oil
salt
pepper
2 cloves garlic (optional)

Clean leeks throroughly. Trim half of dark green leaves, roots, and the outer skin of white part. Make a slit in green and greenish-yellow part of leek. Open out leaves and wash out sand. Let soak in large bowl of cold water for 10 minutes. Rinse off again. Peel tomatoes by pouring boiling water over them and leaving them for 2 minutes in hot water. The skin separates easily. Heat olive oil in pan. Add leeks and sauté until almost tender. Add chopped tomatoes and garlic and cook for 10 minutes. Add salt and pepper to taste.

Braised Fennel

4 fennels
1 pound tomatoes
1 tablespoon olive oil
salt
pepper

Use squat-shaped fennel if possible. Cut off stalks and leaves, and 1/8–inch slice from base. Wash thoroughly. Starting at base, slice fennels ¼ inch thick. Peel and seed tomatoes. Heat olive oil. Sauté slices of fennel lightly. Add chopped tomatoes, salt, and pepper. Cook until tender.

Zucchini Kugel

2 pounds zucchini
1 large onion
1 tablespoon chicken fat
2 extra-large eggs
salt
pepper

Wash, peel, and grate zucchini. Place in colander. Salt grated zucchini lightly and let drain. Peel and chop onion. Fry onion in chicken fat until transparent. Squeeze zucchini until most of the liquid is removed. Put zucchini into a bowl, add fried onion, eggs, and pepper to taste. The kugel may be cooked on top of the stove or baked in the oven. Grease a shallow Pyrex dish. Pour in zucchini mix. To steam, cover and tie foil over top of dish. Place on rack in a large roasting pan. Add water halfway up side. Cover with heavy foil and steam for 1½–2 hours, or bake uncovered at 350° F. for 40 minutes until browned.

Cucumber Salad

6 cucumbers
2 scallions
chopped fresh dill
salt
1 teaspoon sugar
2 ounces lemon juice or wine vinegar
1 tablespoon olive oil

Peel and slice cucumbers thinly. Salt cucumbers well. Let drain for at least 2 hours in colander weighted down with a heavy plate. Place cucumbers in bowl and add finely sliced circles of the white part of the scallion. Mix lemon juice or wine vinegar with a little cold water to dilute. Add dill, oil, and pepper. Pour over cucumbers and let them marinate. Serve with fish.

Dessert Course

Stewed Apples, Topped with Walnuts and Wine Sauce

3 pounds apples
½ cup orange juice
¼ teaspoon cinnamon
sugar to taste
4 ounces walnuts

Peel and slice apples thinly. Simmer gently in orange juice with cinnamon and sugar to taste until just soft. Peel walnuts, if possible, by boiling them for 2 minutes and then removing brown skins with a pointed paring knife. This is tedious but worth the effort. Toast them in the oven for 10 minutes. Sprinkle over apples just before serving.

Wine Sauce

½ cup cherry liqueur plus ½ cup water, or 1 cup wine
¾ cup sugar
3 eggs
grated rind of ½ orange

Beat eggs well. Gradually beat in sugar until eggs begin to foam. Heat wine, or liqueur and water, to almost boiling. Pour hot wine slowly into egg mixture, beating continuously. Cook sauce over hot water until it is thick, stirring continuously. Serve hot or cold with stewed apples.

Macaroons with Chocolate Cream

Macaroons
4 egg whites
pinch of salt
½ cup cocoa
2–3 tablespoons hot water
1½ cups sugar
1 cup blanched almonds or walnuts, finely ground

Egg whites must be at room temperature. Sift cocoa and mix with a small amount of hot water to make a thick paste. Beat egg whites with salt until they form soft peaks. Slowly add sugar and continue beating until whites are stiff and glossy. With rubber spatula, fold in ground nuts and cocoa paste. Line cookie sheet with lightly greased foil. Shape macaroons into circles 1–1½ inches in diameter using a tablespoon or pastry bag with a fluted nozzle. Bake in slow oven, 300° F., for about 45 minutes until firm. Allow to cool on foil; peel off foil when cold. If macaroons are slightly soft, return them to the oven. Turn off gas and let macaroons dry out with oven door slightly ajar. Sandwich flat sides of two macaroons together with chocolate cream.

Chocolate Cream
4 egg yolks
5 ounces bittersweet *pareve* chocolate
1 cup sugar
8 ounces margarine
1 teaspoon brandy
½ cup water

Boil sugar and water to 240° F. on candy thermometer. Melt chocolate over hot water or in oven. Beat egg yolks in a bowl over hot water until thick and pale yellow. Pour hot sugar syrup slowly into egg yolks and continue beating until mixture is a very thick pale cream. Remove bowl from hot water and beat in melted chocolate and brandy. When cream is lukewarm, beat in softened margarine. Chill for 3 hours. Spread cream on flat side of one macaroon and add another to make a sandwich. Store in freezer.

Passover Sponge Cake

9 eggs
1½ cups sugar
grated rind of 1 lemon or orange
juice of 1 lemon or ½ orange
¾ potato flour
½ cup almonds, finely ground

Separate eggs immediately after removing them from the refrigerator; then leave separated eggs at room temperature for 30 minutes. Beat egg yolks until light. Gradually add sugar and continue beating until yolks are a light creamy color and tripled in bulk. Add grated rind and juice. Beat egg whites with a pinch of salt until they form soft peaks and cling to sides of bowl when it is turned upside down. Stir potato flour and nuts into egg yolk mixture and then quickly and thoroughly fold yolks into whites using a rubber spatula. Pour into large ungreased tube pan and bake at 300° F. for 1 hour. Turn tube pan upside down after removing it from the oven. Cooling the cake this way reduces shrinkage. To frost a Passover sponge cake, freeze it first. It is much easier to handle a cold firm cake than a soft crumbly one at room temperature. Frost with chocolate cream.

Chocolate Cream Roll

4 eggs, separated
1¼ cups sugar
1 tablespoon orange rind
2 ounces orange juice
pinch of salt
½ cup cocoa, sifted
½ cup potato starch, or ¼ cup each potato starch and almonds, finely ground

Beat egg yolks until light. Gradually add 1 cup sugar and continue beating until pale and creamy. Beat in rind and juice. Whip whites with pinch of salt until they form soft peaks. Gradually add remaining ¼ cup sugar and continue beating until stiff and glossy. By hand, using a rubber spatula, fold sifted cocoa, potato starch, and ground nuts into yolk mixture. Pour cocoa mixture over egg whites and fold quickly and thoroughly until there are no more flecks of egg white. Pour into 12 x 16 x 1–inch cake pan previously lined with lightly oiled aluminum foil. Spread evenly over base of pan. Bake at 350° F. for 20 minutes. Remove from oven and turn cake upside down onto a damp cloth slightly larger than the cake pan. Gently remove foil from hot cake. Trim ends and sides of cake with a sharp knife and roll up cake and cloth together. Chill well in refrigerator for 2–3 hours. Unroll cake gently. If cake seems to be sticking to cloth, dampen the cloth a little. Spread with chocolate cream and roll up. This cake freezes well.

TZAFUN: The Hidden Matzah

This section of the Seder is called *Tzafun,* which in Hebrew means hidden, because the matzah about to be eaten as the *afikoman* was hidden at the beginning of the Seder. This term was first used by the author of the Seder Program,[1] and as all modern *Haggadahs* follow this program, it has been universally adopted to denote this section.

Afikoman is a term derived from a Greek word believed to mean dessert.[2] This word first appears in the Mishnah:[3] "One may not eat *afikoman* after eating the *korban pesaḥ* (the paschal lamb)." After the paschal lamb, together with the matzah and *maror,* had been eaten in the Temple, no other food was permitted, not even an *afikoman* (dessert).[4] After the destruction of the Temple, the Talmud[5] debated whether one may eat *afikoman* after the matzah with which the meal concludes, now called *tzafun.* The Rif, the Rambam, the Rosh, the *Tur,*[6] the *Shulḥan Arukh,* and all later Sages ruled that after *tzafun,* one may not have any dessert or any other food whatsoever. The meal must end with the taste of matzah in the mouth.[7]

Some *rishonim,* namely the *Or Zaru'a,* the *Shibbolei ha-Leket,* the *Manhig,* and the *Haggahot Maimuniyyot,*[8] began to call this piece of matzah *afikoman.* In time, everyone adopted their nomenclature and today in all *halakhic* literature the piece of matzah that concludes the meal is called *afikoman.*

The reason for eating two *kezaytim* of matzah for the *afikoman* goes back to a dispute among *rishonim* as to what the *afikoman* represents. Rashi and the Rashbam[9] claimed that it was in remembrance of the matzah eaten with the paschal lamb in the Temple, while the Rosh, the Ran, the Mordecai, and the *Tur*[10] all claimed that it commemorated the paschal lamb itself. All later Sages[11] recommended that one should try to eat two *kezaytim* to allow for both interpretations.

Rashi, the Rashbam,[12] the Rosh, the *Haggahot Maimuniyyot,* the *Tur,* and the *Shulḥan Arukh*[13] ruled that the eating of the *afikoman* requires *heseba.* The Rambam[14] disagreed. Later Sages[15] ruled that the *afikoman* should indeed be eaten while reclining on the left, and that is the custom today.

Is there a time limit for the eating of the paschal lamb and the *afikoman?* There is a dispute in the Talmud[16] as to whether one must finish before midnight or not, and it continued among the *rishonim.* The Rambam[17] and the Rif[18] ruled that there is no time limit, that one may eat the *afikoman* at any time throughout the night. However, the Rosh, Rabbenu Tam,[9] the Ran, the *Semag,* the Mordecai,[20] the *Tur,* the *Shulḥan Arukh,* and the Rema[21] all ruled that one must eat the *afikoman* before midnight. Among the later Sages, R. Emden and the *Ḥayyei Adam*[22] ruled that one must finish before midnight, while the *Mishnah Berurah* and the *Arukh ha-Shulḥan*[23] were not sure. Most people today try to eat the *afikoman* before midnight.

Is one permitted to drink after eating the *afikoman?* Some *rishonim*[24] permitted it. Drinking, they felt, would not spoil or remove the taste of the matzah in the mouth. However, most prohibited it, arguing that alcoholic beverages cause drowsiness which would prevent one from finishing the Seder, while drinking other liquids washes away the taste of the matzah.[25] The *Ḥayyei Adam*[26] recommended that one drink no liquid after the *afikoman.* Today most people are guided by the *Mishnah Berurah* and the *Arukh ha-Shulḥan*[27] who permitted water, seltzer, tea, and any liquid that is non-intoxicating and bland enough not to spoil the taste of the last piece of matzah.

In the past there have been a number of customs in connection with the *afikoman* to arouse the interest of the children. Some people used to put the *afikoman,* still wrapped in its napkin, over the shoulders, walk around the room and say, "So did our forefathers carry the matzah." Others made a hole in the *afikoman,* tied it around the neck with a piece of string, and walked around the room with it.[28] However, among the Ashkenazim none of these customs is in vogue today. The idea of "stealing"[29] the *afikoman* has been so successful in capturing the children's interest that nothing more is needed.

BAREKH: Grace

Concerning Grace after the meal throughout the rest of the year, there has been dispute among the *rishonim* and *aḥaronim* over whether one recites it over a cup of wine. Some Sages have said that even a person eating alone must say Grace over a cup of wine, while others said only three and of course, ten who eat together must say Grace over wine.[1] However, on Passover, the Mishnah[2] tells us, we say Grace over a cup of wine even if only one adult male is present. The reason, according to the Talmud,[2] is that we may perform a *mitzvah* with each of the four wine cups.

Where did the custom originate of having at least three adult males present for the Grace on Seder night? It is first mentioned in the *Midrash Tehillim*[3] in connection with the *Hallel* (see p. 74). Most laymen misunderstood the Midrash and assumed that it meant that a minimum of three adult males was necessary for the recital of the Grace on Seder night.[4] Eventually this incorrect assumption by laymen was given validity by R. Emden[5] and later authorities such as the Netziv.[6] R. Emden stated that the presence of at least three male guests for the entire Seder would enable the host to say the introductory lines of Grace (the *Zimun*) which would make him appear like a rich man, a man of means who could afford to entertain. The Netziv took a more legalistic position and claimed that according to the Talmud there should be a *mezuman* (three adult males) for Grace at the Seder.

The *Ḥayyei Adam* and the *Arukh ha-Shulḥan*[7] recommended having at least three male adults for the entire Seder, not because three are needed for the Grace but because three are needed later on in the Seder service, for the *Hallel*. The *Mishnah Berurah*[8] added, in the name of the *Zohar*, that it is a *mitzvah* to invite people in need to a meal on any holiday, and more so on Seder night as the Seder itself is introduced by the phrase, "All in need come and eat."

The Rema,[9] in the name of the *Aguddah*, wrote that on Seder night it is customary for the host to lead in the recitation of Grace after the meal, so that he would recite the blessings over all four wine cups. Another reason, added the Rema, is that he, by virtue of being host, has demonstrated kindness, hospitality, and graciousness, and only such a person should lead the Grace on Seder night. However, the *Aguddah*[10] continued, if the host wished a guest to lead the Grace, the latter might do so. The *Mishnah Berurah* and the *Arukh ha-Shulḥan*[11] both ruled that the host may give the honor of leading Grace to a distinguished guest. As the *Arukh ha-Shulḥan* explained, on all other occasions, according to the Talmud, a guest should lead Grace, for through the *Haraḥamons,* he can bless his host.

Before Grace is recited the table should be cleared. The food is returned to the kitchen because, the Talmud[12] tells us, since we wash after the meal we are afraid lest the water used for this washing fall on the food and spoil it, violating a prohibition against destroying food. On Passover, in addition to this prohibition, there is the problem of *ḥametz.* Water on pieces of matzah left on the table can produce *ḥametz,* leavening, a serious offense on Passover. Finally, as no food is allowed to be eaten after the *afikoman,* no food should be left on the table lest one forget and eat some of it. The *Kitzur Shulḥan Arukh*[13] suggested removing the dirty dishes from the table, as he no doubt felt that it is proper for Grace and the rest of the Seder service to be recited at a clean table.

The Talmud in *Hullin*[14] tells us that if the smallest crumbs of food are stepped on, it is deemed a degradation of food and carries the punishment of poverty for the person who left the crumbs. On Passover there is an additional compelling reason for removing crumbs from the table. These crumbs may become wet, either from the water used for washing before Grace or from any other liquid used for drinking during the recitation of the rest of the *Haggadah,* causing them, if they happened to be matzah crumbs, to ferment and become *ḥametz.*

However, a small piece of matzah is left on the table, conforming to the Talmud's[15] dictum that one who does not leave over a piece of bread on the table after eating will not see any good fortune. There are several sources in the Talmud for this. We know that the prophet Elisha (Kings II 4:43) said: "They shall eat and shall leave thereof." There are also indications of this dictum in the *Zohar* and in Job.[16] The reason, explained Rashi, is that bread would thus be available should a poor person come in unexpectedly. However, this would not apply on Seder night since everyone has a Seder. The *Levush* added two other reasons which would apply to Seder night as well. We give praise, via the Grace, to the Almighty for the bounty he has bestowed upon us, that we are satiated and there is still food left over. By having some food on the table, it becomes evident to all that we are blessing the Almighty for the food he has given us.[17]

Before Grace a psalm is recited, Psalm 137 on weekdays and Psalm 127 for the Sabbath and Festivals. The reason, explained the *Shenei Luḥot ha-Berit*,[18] is that even when we are satiated we should remember the destruction of Jerusalem. Since on the Sabbath and holidays we are not allowed to talk of destruction, we sing of our hope for Israel's complete redemption. Rabbi Adin Steinsaltz[19] added that the recital of a psalm before Grace is in the nature of a homily from the Torah, a *d'var Torah* at the meal. This custom is associated with a passage from the Ethics of our Fathers:[20] "Any meal that did not contain any conversation on Torah, it is as though they had eaten of sacrifices offered to the dead."

The question of washing the hands after the meal, before saying Grace, is one that has been extensively discussed by both the *rishonim* and *aḥaronim*. The Talmud[21] requires that one wash the first two joints of the hands after a meal because the hands might have picked up a certain salt whose chemical makeup would be injurious to the eyes if they were rubbed. Many Sages have stated that today, for various reasons, we do not have to wash the hands after the meal before Grace; many others, however, insist that the law is still incumbent upon us.[22] Each one may act according to his tradition.

The proper way to lift and hold a wine cup for the performance of a ritual is discussed on pp. 12–13.

When three adult males eat bread together, the Mishnah[23] states that a special introductory prayer called the *Zimun* must be said before Grace. The purpose of this prayer is to gather the individuals together into a single entity[24] for the purpose of saying Grace. It is in the form of a responsory, the Leader reciting certain passages to which the company responds.[25] The final form of the *Zimun* has been set since the 17th century[26] except for the last phrase, *Barukh who u-barukh shemo*, Blessed be He and blessed be His Name. The *Arukh ha-Shulḥan*[27] stated that since this phrase has no basis in the Mishnah or the Talmud, it should be omitted. However, the *Magen Avraham*, citing a number of *rishonim*,[28] stated that the *Barukh who u-barukh shemo* should be added to the *Zimun*. R. Emden, the *Sha'arei Teshuvah*, and the *Mishnah Berurah* explained that this phrase is to be said only by the Leader and not by the company.[29]

The *Shulḥan Arukh,* quoting the *Shibbolei ha-Leket,* advised that the person leading the Grace should recite each paragraph aloud while the company says it quietly with him; the Rema suggested that they should hasten to conclude each paragraph first so that they may respond Amen after the Leader says each blessing.[30] Later Sages recommended that the Leader recite only the first paragraph aloud, everyone following along quietly and responding Amen after the Leader concludes the first blessing and then reciting the remainder of the Grace quietly by themselves.[31] Modern custom calls for the Leader and company to sing together the entire Grace after the meal.

The words *al yeḥasreinu* conclude the *Berḥat hatov;* the following passages, the *Haraḥamons,* are later additions. To indicate this, many answer Amen after *al yeḥasreinu.* The Hakham Tzevi, however, put his wine cup down at this point, the custom adopted today, to differentiate between these two parts of the Grace.[32]

HALLEL: Praise

Shefokh Hamatkha: Pour Out Thy Wrath

The Mishnah[1] tells us to complete the recitation of *Hallel* over the fourth wine cup. Therefore, the fourth wine cup should be filled before Psalm 115, *low lanu,* that part of the *Hallel* that is chanted after Grace. This custom undoubtedly continued until the Middle Ages when the *Shefokh Hamatkha* was inserted.[2] Why was it added at this point in the *Haggadah?* The Maharal[3] explained that Psalm 115 refers to the War of Gag and Magag, the terrible conflagration in which Israel's enemies will be destroyed before Israel's final redemption. *Shefokh Hamatkha,* then, is a fitting introduction to this psalm as it announces the theme of the destruction of Israel's enemies. The Abudarham[4] described the four wine cups we drink during the Seder as representing the four destructions the Almighty will visit upon our enemies. When we fill the fourth cup we are, in effect, pleading with the Almighty: "See, we have fulfilled our part of the *mitzvah* of the four cups, now *Shefokh Hamatkha,* visit the four destructions promised, upon our enemies."[5]

Our Sages are divided over whether the fourth cup should be filled before Psalm 115 or before *Shefokh Hamatkha.* The *Tur,* the *Shulḥan Arukh,* R. Emden, the Amsterdam *Haggadah,* the *Ḥayyei Adam,* and the *Arukh ha-Shulḥan* all recommended filling the wine cup before Psalm 115.[6] The Kaufmann and Sarajevo illuminated manuscript *Haggadahs,* the Prague *Haggadah,* the Abudarham, the Maharal, and R. Kasher[7] prefered that the fourth cup be filled before *Shefokh Hamatkha.* Either *minhag* is acceptable.

We now fill the Cup of Elijah, the cup that has stood in the center of the table since the start of the Seder. Some fill the Elijah cup at the beginning of the Seder, but that really makes no sense. First, it might spill, especially during the meal or if removed. Second, it does not fit in with the reasons given for this *minhag.*[8]

Everyone at the Seder table looks with awe at this beautiful wine goblet and expects Elijah to visit their Seder and partake of his drink, albeit just the tiniest of sips. When did this custom arise and what meaning does it convey? For one thing, it is of relatively recent origin. There is no mention of it until the late 17th or early 18th century. It is first recorded by Rabbi Moses Hagiz[9] of Jerusalem, a Sage of Spanish origin, and Rabbi Jacob Reischer[10] and R. Emden, two Ashkenazic rabbis of great renown. We know that R. Hagiz traveled extensively in Germany and throughout Europe, and in fact met R. Emden, but it cannot be determined whether he brought the *minhag* of the Elijah cup to Europe from Jerusalem or back to Jerusalem from Europe.

None of the above Sages wrote very much about this custom. R. Reischer merely noted in his commentary that at this point in the Seder (*Shefokh Hamatkha*) "an extra cup called the Cup of Elijah is filled." R. Emden stated that before the Seder is to commence, a large goblet called the Cup of Elijah is to be placed on the table. "We pour the remains of the wine left over in our cups after each of the wine blessings into this cup and we use this wine for drinking with the Seder meal."[11] The tradition today is to fill the Elijah cup with unused wine.

R. Hagiz was the most expansive of the three. In his responsa he noted that on Seder night there is a custom to set an extra place at the table, with a special wine cup for Elijah the prophet. The reason for this setting is similar to that given for the Elijah chair at a circumcision ceremony. Elijah is the "Angel of Covenant (circumcision)," and can therefore testify that Israel has always kept this commandment faithfully. When Elijah visits the Seder, he can see that Israel has adhered to the Covenant, as on Passover only circumcised males may partake of the paschal lamb, and that they are keeping the Passover. He can now plead on Israel's behalf for a speedier redemption.[12]

R. Hagiz went on to state that those who use the Cup of Elijah as a receptacle for the wine left over in each cup after each of the blessings, alluding to the custom recited by R. Emden, are in error and are denigrating the name of Elijah the prophet. He concluded that the correct procedure, the one he used, is to have two extra wine cups, one for use as a receptacle for the unused wine, and another for Elijah. Just as the four required wine cups represent the redemption from Egypt, so does this cup represent the final redemption, the redemption that will be heralded by Elijah the prophet.[13]

Today most tend toward the Vilna Gaon's explanation.[14] He noted that there is a long-standing dispute among our Sages as to whether one should or may drink five cups of wine on Seder night instead of four. Scholars, therefore, were wont to leave an extra cup of wine on the table as an expression of the idea that this question will be decided when Elijah the prophet comes; it is he who, according to tradition, will resolve all pending *halakhic* difficulties. The general population adopted this custom and embellished it with thoughts of Elijah's arriving to herald Israel's redemption.

Another reason for this *minhag* can possibly be found in the history of the period in which it was established. The 17th–18th century was the time of the Shabbetai Tzevi movement, the movement started by the infamous false messiah that split Judaism apart in its time. R. Hagiz and R. Emden were the most ardent fighters against this heresy. The custom of the Cup of Elijah was instituted at the point in the Seder where the discussion becomes eschatological in nature, the coming of the Messiah and the redemption of Israel. Tradition has it that Elijah the prophet will herald the appearance of the Messiah, and the point made by R. Hagiz and R. Emden is that Shabbetai Tzevi was not the Messiah, and we raise the wine cup in welcome to the prophet Elijah who will herald the coming of the true Messiah. This wine cup, as the fifth cup, is an allusion to the *vehayveisi:* "And *I will bring you* in unto the Land, concerning which I lifted up My hand to give it to Abraham, to Isaac and to Jacob," the fifth statement of redemption mentioned by the Bible (Exodus 6:8).[15]

The Cup of Elijah did not spread rapidly, and the great majority of the *Haggadahs* until quite recently do not mention it. However, since the late 19th century and particularly since the early part of the 20th century, this *minhag* has become universally accepted, and today both the Ashkenazim and the Sephardim feature the Cup of Elijah on their tables and perform the ceremony as outlined above during this part of the Seder.

The wine in the Cup of Elijah may not be thrown out after the Seder. This would degrade a religious rite and violate the prohibition against wasting food.[16] A commendable procedure to follow is that of the *Ḥatam Sofer.*[17] After the Seder, he covered the Cup of Elijah and used it for *Kiddush* the following afternoon.

The Rema,[18] adopting the custom of R. Weil, opened the door while reciting *Shefokh Hamatkha.* This is based, he explained, on the *Or Zaru'a*[19] who, on Seder night, did not lock his doors because this night is called *leyl shimurim* in the Torah (Exodus 12:42), a night of watching (taken to mean a night when we are protected). By leaving the door unlocked, we demonstrate our belief in the Almighty and his promise of redemption. As the *Ḥok Ya'akov*,[20] quoting the *Manhig*, further noted, we are destined to be redeemed this night[21] and if Elijah happens to come, he will find the door open and we can go with him without undue delay. However, added the *Ḥok Ya'akov*, today we cannot leave the door open all night because we are afraid of thieves.

The custom of leaving the door open on Seder night is very old, going back to *gaonic* times,[22] but the association of this *minhag* with the final redemption was made much later, by the Maharil and the *Manhig*.[22]

The *Arukh ha-Shulḥan*[23] used to stand at the start of *Shefokh Hamatkha* and pronounce *Barukh Habah* (Blessed the one who is coming; Welcome) when the door was being opened. Both these actions show the wholehearted commitment to the idea that Elijah would come this night to herald the arrival of the Messiah. To emphasize the importance of this belief, stated the *Arukh ha-Shulḥan*, we break the general rule that the entire Seder should be conducted while seated, in the manner of free men and aristocrats.

Hodu and Ahna: Give Thanks and We Beseech Thee

The *Midrash Tehillim*[1] tells us that a minimum of three is needed to read the *Hallel* on Seder night so that one can recite the *Hodu* to the other two. The *Kol Bo*[2] explained that this is because one person acts as a leader and a minimum of two should respond. This same custom of one reciting to the other two, continued the *Kol Bo*, applies as well to the *Ahna* section of the *Hallel*. We would normally assume that the three have to be adult males. The Rosh,[3] however, stated that the Leader plus his wife and a child old enough to be educated, about five to six years of age,[4] are sufficient. The *Magen Avraham*,[5] on the other hand, felt that if possible one should try to have a minimum of three adult males for the *Hallel* since they can also serve as a *mezuman* for the Grace.[6]

The Maharil,[7] at the discretion of the Leader, permitted a child to lead in these prayers, for this keeps the child awake by involving him as a leader in the Seder, as well as giving him training in running a Seder. The *Magen Avraham*,[8] however, restricted the child to leading only the *Ahnas*. He believed that, as a minor, the child cannot exempt the adults from their duty of saying the verses of the *Hodu*, but as each verse in the *Ahnas* is repeated by the company, there is no harm in the child leading. The Maharil also allowed a woman to lead in the *Hodu* and the *Ahna*, as she is commanded equally with the men to say *Hallel*. However, the *Ḥok Ya'akov*[9] prohibited this, fearing that the voice of a woman might be too distracting.

It is not clear what exactly the *Midrash Tehillim* and the *rishonim* meant by "the Leader should say *Hodu* to the other two and that they should respond." It appears that the Leader has to read each sentence in full, but what do the other two answer? Some say that they answer just the second half of each passage, the *key leolam ḥasdaw*. The *Mishnah Berurah*[10] explained that the guests answer the Leader by reciting the next sentence. R. Emden[11] wrote that the guests repeat the first sentence as a refrain to the Leader's reading of each of the other sentences. This last *minhag* is in accordance with the way this prayer should be said in synagogue, with the *Ḥazan* or Cantor reading each of the verses and the congregants repeating the first verse as a refrain.[12] It is also evident from the *Magen Avraham*, cited above, and the *Arukh ha-Shulḥan*[13] that they too followed this custom. In the *Ahna* section, the Leader reads each verse and the company repeats it after him.[14]

The Fourth Cup

The Mishnah[1] states that we must drink the fourth wine cup after *Birkat ha-Shir*. There is a dispute in the Talmud[2] concerning which prayer the Mishnah refers to. Rabbi Judah said it was *Yehaleluha Hashem Elohaynu*, while Rabbi Johanan said it was *Nishmat Kol Ḥai*. Our Sages could not decide the issue,[3] and today there is a difference between the Ashkenazim and Sephardim. This *Haggadah* follows the Ashkenazic rite and places the fourth cup after *Nishmat*.

The *Baḥ*[4] cited old *Maḥzorim* and *Haggadahs* that delay the blessing over the fourth cup until after the liturgical songs which were later additions to the *Haggadah*. Nevertheless, he claimed that this practice was wrong, for the Mishnah states very clearly that the fourth cup must be drunk after *Birkat ha-Shir*. On the other hand, the *Magen Avraham*[5] observed that according to the old *Maḥzorim*, the Maharam of Rothenburg introduced this custom with the explanation that singing creates thirst, and the final cup of wine at the end will slake the thirst before retiring. The *Ḥayyei Adam* and the *Mishnah Berurah* apparently agreed that the Maharam's *minhag* was acceptable.[6] However, R. Emden did not cite it, while the *Arukh ha-Shulḥan*[7] strongly objected to it. The majority of *Haggadahs* today follow the *Arukh ha-Shulḥan* and place the blessing for the fourth cup after *Birkhat ha-Shir*.

It is most important to drink at least a *revi'it*[8] of wine for the fourth cup, as the special Grace over wine about to be said is only recited when at least a *revi'it* is drunk. This concluding blessing also applies to the third cup of wine.

After the fourth cup, one may not eat or drink anything except water, tea, and the like.[9] However, there is a long-standing dispute going back to *gaonic* and *rishonic* times, and continuing today, as to whether one must or may have a fifth cup of wine. The basis of the dispute is a variant reading of the *baraita* in *Pesaḥim*:[10] "On the fourth cup (variant reading fifth cup) we finish the *Hallel*." Although the rule is that one must have just four cups, many Sages permitted a fifth cup.[11] The *Mishnah Berurah*[12] allowed a fifth cup under certain circumstances, while R. Kasher[13] found great merit in drinking a fifth cup. However, the *Arukh ha-Shulḥan*[14] and R. Zevin[15] stated that our *minhag* is to drink only four cups, and today must people drink only the four required wine cups and use the Cup of Elijah[16] as a remembrance of a fifth cup.

The rest of the *Haggadah* is usually led by the children who sing the tunes written for the liturgical poems they have learned in yeshiva or Hebrew school. The Talmud encourages everyone to relate everything he knows about the Exodus in particular, and anything of merit concerning the Seder and Judaism in general. The Seder may continue as long as one wishes, provided it is finished before the time for morning prayers.

ABBREVIATIONS

The following abbreviations have been used in the notes.

Pes.	Babylonian Talmud Tractate *Pesaḥim*
TOH	*Tur Oraḥ Ḥayyim*
SAOH	*Shulḥan Arukh Oraḥ Ḥayyim*
Emden	*Siddur Beit Ya'akov* by Jacob Emden
MB	*Mishnah Berurah* by Israel Meir ha-Kohan
AH	*Arukh ha-Shulḥan* by Jehiel Epstein
Zevin	*Hamoadim be-Halakhah* by Solomon Zevin

NOTES

TABLE PREPARATION

1. Rashbam, Pes. 109a; TOH 472; SAOH 472:1. *Tosafoth*, Pes. 100b quoting the *She'iltot* relates that the table should be set before the onset of every Sabbath and Festival meal.

2. *Shabbath* 113a; SAOH 302:3; *Shabbath* 118a; SAOH 323:6.

3. *Betzah* 17a; SAOH 503:1; Emden, p. 227b; *Me'am Lo'ez*, p. 229.

4. Emden, p. 227a.

5. TOH 472. The SAOH 472:2 and all later Sages agreed.

6. *Sefer Maharil, Hilḥot Haggadah.*

7. Pes. 108b. The Talmud in *Berakoth* 51a lists ten requirements that a wine cup used in connection with a *mitzvah* must have.

8. *Midot u-Sherei Torah be'Siddur Minḥat Yerushalaym*, p. 414-426 (1977 edition). Throughout this work we have adopted the modern equivalent of *halakhic* measurements and sizes as estimated by this recently published prayer book for Jerusalem. Other estimates, usually more stringent, are given by the *Ḥazon Ish* and Rabbi Feinstein. For the *revi'it*, the *Ḥazon Ish* estimated 5.3 fluid ounces (150 grams) (*Ibid.*), while Rabbi Feinstein estimated it as 3.3–4.2 fluid ounces (see S.O.Y, *The Passover Haggadah*, p. 143).

9. Emden, p. 227a. Fine glass crystal is also suitable.

10. One Talmudic passage in Pes. 99b seems to indicate that only the Leader need drink the four cups. However, from another passage in Pes. 108b, one can draw the inference that the law of drinking four cups applies also to every child. The *Mordecai* (end of Pes.) and the Rosh (Pes. #21) ruled in favor of the Talmud in Pes. 108b, that everyone is commanded to drink the four cups. However, the Rosh in a responsa (*Teshuvot ha-Rosh* 14.5) explained the law to mean that only children who have reached the age of being able to be taught need drink the four wine cups. This latter rule was followed by the TOH 472, the SAOH 472:15, and all later authorities.

11. *Hok Ya'akov*, SAOH 472:27. The age is based on the Talmud *Eruvin* 82a-b.

12. *Hok Ya'akov*, SAOH 472:28.

13. MB 472:47; AH 472:15.

14. Pes. 109a. See also TOH 472 and SAOH 472:16.

15. Pes. 99b, 108a.

16. *Sefer Ravon, Pesaḥim* 108a.

17. *Sefer Ravyah, Pesaḥim, Seder Leyl Pesaḥ* #525.

18. Rambam, *Ḥametz u-Matzah* 7:6–7 and *Haggahot Maimuniyyot* #2.

19. AH 472:3.

20. SAOH 472:2; AH 472:3; MB 472:7–10 and virtually every later decisor required *heseba* at the specified times.

21. For the right-handed person, it was usual to lean on the left side as the right hand was necessary for eating. However, since it was considered biologically harmful to eat leaning on the right, one might catch food in the windpipe, even left-handed people were required to lean on the left. See TOH 472 and Rema, SAOH 472:3.

22. Pes. 108a.

23. *Talmudic Encyclopedia,* "Heseba."

24. Rema, SAOH 427:4; AH 472:6 and all later decisors. It is interesting to note that Rabbenu Jeruḥam, the Mordecai, and the Maharil, *Hilḥot Haggadah,* stated that since all women today are considered important, a statement attributed by the *Mordecai* (*Pesaḥim* 108a) and Rabbenu Jeruḥam (Nesiv 5:4) to *Tosafoth,* they must recline like the men.

25. *Sefer ha-Roke'aḥ,* end of *Hilḥot Aveiluth.*

26. *Haggahot Maimuniyyot,* Rambam, *Hilḥot Shabbath* 30:2.

27. *Shabbath* 113a. The Maharam applied the same reasoning to *Yom Tov* (see note 26).

28. *Tashbatz* 160.

29. Rema, SAOH 610:4.

30. *Magen Avraham,* SAOH 610:5.

31. AH 610:2; MB 610:16.

32. *Teshuvoth Maharam Mintz* 86.

33. Emden, p. 124b; *Kitzur Shulḥan Arukh* 147:4.

34. *Taz,* SAOH 472:1; *Magen Avraham,* SAOH 472:5; *Hok Ya'akov,* SAOH 472:5.

35. Menachem M. Kasher, *Israel Passover Haggadah,* p. 26.

36. At a later date, possibly as late as the 19th century, the *minhag* began for the *sheleah tzibur,* the Cantor, to wear a *kittel* on Rosh Hashannah, for *Tefilat Tal* on Passover, *Tefilat Geshem* on *Shemini Atzereth* and on *Hoshannah Rabbah,* as these were all solemn occasions and in some way analogous to Yom Kippur.

37. *Sefer Abudarham, Seder Haggadah.*

38. *Mishbetzot Zahav* 486.

39. TOH 473, following earlier *rishonim* such as the Rosh and *Tosafoth,* SAOH 473:4, AH 473:9.

40. *Ma'aseh Rav* 191.

41. Zevin, p. 273.

42. *Tosafoth,* Pes. 101b, *Shibbolei ha-Leket* 218, *Seder Pesaḥ.*

43. TOH 473, SAOH 473:4.

44. Kasher, *op. cit.,* p. 30. See also *Me'am Lo'ez,* p. 229, where Rabbi Culi recommended that the glass of vinegar also be included in the Seder plate in addition to the three matzot and all the other foods.

45. Hayyim Vital, *Etz Hayyim,* as quoted by the *Ba'er Heitev,* SAOH 473:8 and Ganzfried, *Siddur Avodath Yisrael,* Vol. II, p. 235b.

46. Emden, p. 227b; *Ba'er Heitev, ibid.*

47. We have examples of tiered Seder plates from the 19th century.

48. Pes. 114a.

49. Pes. 114b. The *Hok Ya'akov,* SAOH 473:15 quoted the *Roke'aḥ, Seder ha-*

Pesah 283, that the two cooked foods also represent Moses and Aaron, a thought echoed earlier by Rav Sherira Gaon.

50. Rashbam, Pes. 114b; Rosh, *Pesahim* #25.

51. Rambam, *Hametz u-Matzah* 8:1. Tosafoth, Pes. 114b; Haggahot Maimuniyyot, Rambam, *Hametz u-Matzah* 8:2. See *Bah*, TOH 473 for a complete listing of early opinions.

52. AH 473:9.

53. The *Kol Bo* #50, the *Aguddah, Arvei Pesahim*, and the Abudarham, *Seder Haggadah*, based on a passage in the Jerusalem Talmud which is not found in our edition. The TOH 473, the SAOH 473:4, and all later decisors followed this custom. The Kaufmann *Haggadah*, an early illustrated manuscript *Haggadah*, recommended a *ziroa* and an egg while the Prague *Haggadah*, the first printed illustrated *Haggadah*, recommended meat and an egg.

54. *Kol Bo* #50; TOH 473.

55. *Kol Bo* #50; Abudarham, *Seder Haggadah;* TOH 473; SAOH 473:4.

56. *Tosafoth*, Pes. 114b; Rashal #88; *Bah*, TOH 473; *Magen Avraham*, SAOH 473:8; AH 473:9; Zevin, *op. cit.*, p. 263.

57. TOH 476; *Magen Avraham*, SAOH 476:1; MB 476:1.

58. Emden, p. 227a; the Gra, SAOH 476:1; MB 476:1. The Rashal (#88) objected to the custom of leaving the *ziroa* until the second day of *Yom Tov* and therefore recommended cooking it and eating it at the Seder.

59. *Kol Bo* #50; Abudarham, *Seder Haggadah; Aguddah, Arvei Pesahim.*

60. *Kol Bo* #50; *Taz*, SAOH 473:4; MB 473:23.

61. *Ma'aseh Rav* 191.

62. *Darkei Moshe*, TOH 473:10; Rema, SAOH 476:2; AH 476:4. See section on *Shulhan Arukh*, p. 43 *this volume.*

63. See section on *Shulhan Arukh*, p. 97 Note 4.

64. *Magen Avraham*, SAOH 473:8; *Hok Ya'akov*, SAOH 473:17. This is based on the Rashal's (#88) interpretation of the *Mordecai* (*Pesahim* #608). However, as the *Taz* (SAOH 476:3) pointed out, a careful reading of our edition of the *Mordecai* rather leads one to the conclusion that the *Mordecai* permitted the eating of roasted eggs on Seder night.

65. Rema, SAOH 473:4; *Ba'er Heitev*, SAOH 473:10. See section on *Shulhan Arukh*, p. 44 and p. 98, note 11, *this volume.*

66. SAOH 473:4; Rashal #88; AH 473:9; Zevin, p. 263.

67. *Sheeloth u-Teshuvoth Rabbi Jacob Weil* 193, *Dinei Pesah; Darkei Moshe*, TOH 473:10.

68. Rashal #88.

69. *Hok Ya'akov*, SAOH 473:17. See also the Gra, SAOH 476:2.

70. See above, note 58.

71. AH 473:9.

72. Zevin, p. 263.

LIGHTING THE CANDLES

1. *Shabbath* 31b.

2. Rambam, *Hilḥot Shabbath* 5:3.

3. In the absence of a woman, it is incumbent upon the male to light candles for the Sabbath and *Yom Tov.*

4. The Midrash as quoted by TOH 263.

5. *Haggahot Maimuniyyot,* Rambam, *Hilḥot Shabbath* 5:1.

6. *Or Zaru'a, Hilḥot Erev Shabbath* #11. The Jerusalem Talmud cited is not extant in our edition.

7. The *Midrash Tanḥuma, Noah; Tosafoth, Shabbath* 25b, and the Rambam, *Hilḥot Shabbath* 5:1 all stated that the reason for the kindling of lights on the Sabbath is that it adds to the enjoyment of the occasion. Sitting and eating in darkness was considered by our Sages as a negation of the spirit of the day. Even today, candlelight is a mark of special festivity.

8. *Ḥayyei Adam, Hilḥot Shabbath* 5:1 and 5:9.

9. Only on the first day of the Festival, not for the second day observed in the Diaspora. She felt that the Festival deserved this honor just as the Sabbath did, even though one may kindle lights on *Yom Tov.* See Joseph son of Joshua Falk, *Introduction to the Derishah and Perishah, Tur Yoreh De'ah,* where *halakhic* reasons are cited and a short biography of this remarkable woman is given. See also Zevin, *op. cit.,* pp. 14–15.

10. *Kol Bo, Hilḥot Shabbath*; TOH 263.

11. Rema, SAOH 263:1.

12. Rabbi Weil, *op. cit., Dinim ve-Halakhot* #29; *Darkei Moshe,* TOH 263:2; Rema, SAOH 263:5. It should be noted that the Rambam and others stated that there is no exception made in candle lighting and the woman merely makes a condition saying that she does not assume the holiness of the Sabbath until after she lights the candles.

13. *Magen Avraham,* SAOH 263:12.

14. Joseph son of Joshua Falk, *ibid.*

15. The *Magen Avraham,* SAOH 263:12 and the *Ḥayyei Adam, Hilḥot Shabbath* 5:11 ruled that on *Yom Tov* one also lights the candles before the blessing, while the AH 263:13, the MB 263:27, and others agreed with the wife of the *Derishah.* See Zevin, pp. 14–15, who cited al the sources.

16. Rashi, *Sabbath* 25b; *Or Zaru'a, ibid.; Darkei Moshe,* TOH 263: 4; Rema, SAOH 263:10; *Magen Avraham,* SAOH 263:21; MB 263:45.

17. Rashi, *Shabbath* 25b.

THE SEDER PROGRAM

1. *Otzar ha-Tefillot,* Vol. II, p. 964; E. D. Goldschmidt, *The Passover Haggadah* (Hebrew), p. 72, based on a manuscript seen by the Shadal (Samuel David Luzzatto).

2. Menachem M. Kasher, *Haggadah Shelemah*, pp. 77–82. Rabbi Kasher listed 14 different Programs which he found in various manuscript *Haggadahs*. The earliest was the one by Rabbi Joseph Tov Elam (Joseph ben Samuel Bonfils), of the 11th century, found in *ha-Pardes, Hilḥot Pesaḥ*, p. 55.

3. The Venice *Haggadah* of 1629 was the first to use the terms of the Program as titles of various sections, though they were inserted on the side, not in the body of the *Haggadah*.

KADDESH: Recite the Kiddush

1. *Tosefta Pesaḥim*, Ch. II; *Tosafoth*, Pes. 99b; Rosh, Pes. #10.

2. *Terumat ha-Deshen* 137; SAOH 472:1; Zevin, *op. cit.*, p. 264, and all later decisors. See also the Maharil, *Hilḥot Haggadah* who argued that only that part of the *Haggadah* from Karpas onward must be performed after nightfall.

3. Pes. 100a,; SAOH 271:9 and all later decisors.

4. TOH 271 quoting the Jerusalem Talmud. See the *Haggahot Maimuniyyot*, Rambam, *Shabbath* 29:100 where it appears that he is the source of this idea.

5. *Haggahot Maimuniyyot, ibid.* See also TOH 271.

6. *Ḥayyei Adam, Hilḥot Shabbath* 6:13; AH 271:22; MB 271:41.

7. *Berakoth* 51a; SAOH 271:10 and all the decisors.

8. *Shekalim* 3:2.

9. *Magen Avraham*, SAOH 472:13; *Taz*, SAOH 472:9.

10. *Roke'aḥ* 283, *Seder ha-Pesaḥ*; TOH 472. See also the *Beth Yosef*, TOH 272 who quoted a Sage who found a basis for this ruling in the *Jerusalem Targum* on the Song of Songs.

11. *Taz*, SAOH 472:9; *Hok Ya'akov*, SAOH 472:24.

12. Pes. 114a.

13. TOH 473; Rema, SAOH 473:1; *Hok Ya'akov;* SAOH 473:8.

14. AH 473:6.

15. Emden, p. 231b. Emden recommended announcing each of the mnemonic devices as they occur.

16. Emden, p. 231b; *Ḥayyei Adam, Ha-Seder b'Ktzarah* 130:2; MB introduction to 473; Ganzfried, *Siddur Avodath Yisrael*, Vol. II, . 236b. M. Kasher, *Israel Passover Haggadah*, p. 32, put the *hinne memuḥan* only before the blessings over the four wine cups, following, he said, the Maharal of Prague. Rabbi Emden's *Haggadah* was the first to recommend the reciting of all the *hinne memuḥans*. Rabbi Ganzfried, *Siddur*, p. 235b, implied that R. Emden originated this custom.

17. Pes. 99b.

18. Jerusalem Talmud, *Pesaḥim* 10:1.

19. Kasher, *op. cit.*, pp. 165–166.

20. *Midrash ha-Gadol* I, pp. 675–677; Ginzberg, *Legend of The Laws*, Vol. II, pp. 61–62.

21. *Taz*, SAOH 183:2.

22. *Shibbolei ha-Leket* #156, *Berakoth*; SAOH 183:5.

23. *Magen Avraham,* SAOH 183:9.

24. SAOH 183:5; *Mahazit ha-Shekel,* SAOH 183:9, AH 183:5. The MB 183:20 also agreed.

25. *Berakoth* 51a. See also Rashi, *Berakoth* 51a, and SAOH 183:1–5.

26. AH 271:24.

27. Emden, p. 231a.

28. Pes. 108a. See also section on *heseba,* p. 2.

29. SAOH 472:7. See also Rema, SAOH 472:7, and AH 472:9.

30. Pes. 108b and all the decisors.

31. Student Organization of Yeshiva, *The Passover Haggadah,* p. 143.

32. See note 8, p. 84.

33. *Tosafoth,* Pes. 108b and all the decisors.

34. Pes. 108b.

35. *Roke'aḥ* 283; Rema, SAOH 472:9.

36. The *halakhic* time stated for *aḥilat p'ras* (piece of bread) is subject to the various opinions of the Sages cited. The time ranges from 2–9 minutes. See note 8, p. 84.

37. The *Kol Bo* #50 ruled that most of a *revi'it* is sufficient, while the Ramban and the *Mordecai* felt that one must drink most of the wine in the cup, no matter how large the cup is. See *Beth Yosef* and *Darkei Moshe,* TOH 472 who cited all the early sources.

38. SAOH 472:9 quoted both opinions, while the *Magen Avraham,* SAOH 472:10 tended toward the view of the Ramban.

39. AH 472:13.

40. MB 472:33.

41. See p. [12].

Kiddush for Saturday Night

1. Rambam, *Shabbath* 29:1.

2. *Berakoth* 33a.

3. Mishnah, *Berakoth* 8:1; Talmud *Berakoth* 52a.

4. *Tosafoth, Betzah* 33b. See also Rambam, *Shabbath* 29:29, and the *Baḥ,* TOH 297 who added an additional reason.

5. *Betzah* 16a.

6. Pes. 54a.

7. *Genesis Rabbah* XI.

8. *Otzar ha-Tefillot,* Vol. II, p. 868.

9. *Pirkei de-Rabbi Eliezer,* Chap. 20.

10. *Shibbolei ha-Leket* #130, *Din Havdalah*; TOH 298; *Beth Yosef,* TOH 298; *Siddur* Rashi #525; *Pirkei de-Rabbi Eliezer, ibid.*; Levi, *Yesodei ha-Tefillah,* p. 205.

11. *Berakoth* 53b.

12. Rav Hai Goan, as quoted by the *Baḥ,* TOH 298.

13. *Ibid.* See also Rabbi Yona as quoted by *Baḥ,* TOH 298.
14. *Baḥ,* TOH 298.
15. Emden, p. 204b.
16. TOH 298.
17. Rema, SAOH 298:3.
18. *Magen Avraham,* SAOH 298:5.
19. Rema, SAOH 298:3.
20. Following the ideas of the *geonim.* See note 10.
21. Rema, SAOH 298:3; *Zohar,* Vol. I, *Berashith,* pp. 87–88, and *Veyakhel,* Vol. IV, pp. 205–208. The *Zohar* goes into a much fuller mystical explanation.
22. AH 298:8. See Rema, SAOH 298:3 and *Magen Avraham,* 298:5. However, both the *Pirkei de-Rabbi Eliezer* and the *Shibbolei ha-Leket* said both hands are used. See *Pirkei de-Rabbi Eliezer,* English translation by Gerald Friedlander, chap. 20, p. 145, note #4.

U'REḤATZ: Lave the Hands

1. TOH 158, and 473 and SAOH 158, and all their commentaries.
2. Pes. 115a.
3. SAOH 158:4.
4. The Gra, SAOH 158:4.
5. AH 158:4.
6. *Hok Ya'akov,* SAOH 473:2.
7. Rabbi Naphtali Berlin, *Imrey Sefer,* pp. 5–6.
8. *Leket Yosher,* p. 88.
9. Kasher, *op. cit.,* p. 22.
10. SAOH 158–62.
11. MB 162:49, mentioned as an alternative.
12. AH 162:19.
13. MB 162:49.

KARPAS: Eat the Karpas

1. M. Jastrow, *Dictionary of the Talmud Bavli,* explained that *karpas* is either celery or a type of parsley. H. Danby, *The Mishnah,* Shebiith 9:1, translates *karpas* as celery.
2. Pes. 114a–115a.
3. TOH 473; SAOH 473:4. The MB 473:20 preferred the use of a vegetable that requrires the blessing of *boreh pri ha-adamah;* then one will not have to make this blessing when eating the *maror.*
4. *Seder Rav Amram Gaon, Haggadah.*
5. *Shibbolei ha-Leket* #218, *Seder Pesaḥ.*
6. p.10.

7. *Sefer Abudarham, Seder Haggadah.*

8. Rashi, Pes. 144a.

9. *Sefer Maharil, Hilḥot Haggadah.*

10. SAOH 473:6 and all decisors. See *Beth Yosef,* TOH 473 for other opinions.

11. MB 473:56 following most later authorities. See *Ba'er Heitev,* SAOH 473:18.

12. See TOH 473 and the *Beth Yosef* who discuss the problem in detail and cite all the authorities.

13. *Beth Yosef,* TOH 473; SAOH 473:6; MB 473:54.

14. Zevin, p. 258.

15. Emden, p. 232a.

16. AH 473:18; MB 473:5.

17. *Magen Avraham,* SAOH 473:5; Emden, p. 232a.

18. See p.6.

YAḤATZ: Divide the Middle Matzah

1. *Berakoth* 39b. See also p.34.

2. TOH 475 and the *Beth Yosef* there discussed this question in detail, as did Zevin, p. 268.

3. SAOH 473:4 and all later decisors. However, the Gra, SAOH 473:4 insisted on only two matzot for the *motzi* and for the Seder plate.

4. Rosh, *Pesaḥim* #30.

5. TOH 473.

6. See *Baḥ,* TOH 473 for a fuller explanation of all these positions.

7. SAOH 473:6 and all the later decisors.

8. *Kol Bo* #50.

9. Pes. 115b–116a.

10. Ran, *Pesaḥim,* chap. 10.

11. Rambam, *Ḥametz u-Matzah* 8:6.

12. *Sefer Maharil, Hilḥot Haggadah.* Emden, p. 232a; *Magen Avraham,* SAOH 473:21 and the MB 473:58 agree with the Maharil.

13. *Baḥ,* TOH 473.

14. See section on *afikoman,* p.65.

15. *Roke'aḥ* 283, *Seder ha-Pesaḥ;* TOH 473; SAOH 473:6.

16. Emden, p. 232a.

17. *Piskei ha-Rosh, Hilḥot Pesaḥim.*

18. Rashal #88.

19. Emden, p. 232a; AH 473:20. However, the *Arukh ha-Shulḥan* recommended placing it under someone else's pillow so that he may watch it.

20. Ganzfried, *Siddur,* p. 237a.

21. *Hok Ya'akov,* SAOH 472:2.

22. Pes. 109a.

23. Rambam, *Ḥametz u-Matzah* 7:2.

MAGGID: Recite the Haggadah

Ha Laḥma Anya: This Is the Bread of Affliction

1. Pes. 115b.

2. *Tosafoth,* Pes. 115b. It seems that during the Rambam's time small tables were used, similar to the ones in the time of the Talmud, as he also recommended removing the table, *Ḥametz u-Matzah* 8:2.

3. Rashbam, Pes. 115b.

4. In a responsa quoted by the *Beth Yosef,* TOH 473 and in the Rosh, *Hilḥot Pesaḥim B'Kitzarah.*

5. TOH 473.

6. SAOH 473:6.

7. MB 473:60.

8. AH 473:20. The *Me'am Lo'ez,* p. 233, recommended lifting the Seder plate with the right hand and holding the matzah with the left.

9. *Mahzor Vitry,* see Eisenstein, *Otzar Perushim,* p. 138. However, in many editions of the *Mahzor Vitry* this *minhag* is not cited.

10. *Shibbolei ha-Leket* #218, *Seder Pesaḥ.*

11. Emden, p. 232b.

12. Abrabanel, *Zevaḥ Pesaḥ,* Eisenstein, *op. cit.,* p. 74.

13. Emden, p. 232b.

14. Rashal #88.

15. Emden, p. 232b; MB 473:61.

16. Maharal mi-Prag, Eisenstein, *op. cit.,* p. 199, explained that this passage introduces the matzah, the food over which the entire *Haggadah* is recited.

17. Rambam, *Ḥametz u-Matzah* 7:1, based on Pes. 116a–116b.

18. See Zevin, pp. 279–280, for a comprehensive analysis of this question and a citing of all the sources.

19. Rema, SAOH 473:6. See also the *Kol Bo* #50 who had the same tradition.

20. AH 473:20.

Mah Nishtannah: The Four Questions

1. Pes. 115b. See also proceding section.

2. Rosh, *Hilḥot Pesaḥim* and his commentary on *Pesaḥim* #29. See also Maharal, Eisenstein, *op. cit.,* p. 202.

3. It seems that the Rashbam and *Tosafoth,* Pes. 115b, just left the Seder plate at the end of the table where it was placed for the *Ha Laḥma Anya.*

4. TOH 473; also the *Hok Ya'akov,* SAOH 473:33.

5. Emden, p. 233a.

6. SAOH 473:6.

7. MB 473:65.

8. *Magen Avraham*, SAOH 473:25.
9. AH 473:21.
10. Pes. 116a.
11. Rashbam, Pes. 116a.
12. Pes. 116a.
13. Pes. 115b.
14. Goldschmidt, *The Passover Haggadah*, pp. 10–11, cited all the authorities. Goldschmidt believed that the Ravya's *minhag* was based on an incorrect reading of a Mishnah and Baraitha. It is also interesting to note that the Rambam had two separate opinions on this matter. *Ḥametz u-Matzah* 7:3 seems to indicate that the son asks these four questions, while in *Ḥametz u-Matzah* 8:2 he stated that the Leader recites these questions.
15. Emden, p. 233a.See also the Bertinoro, Mishnah *Pesaḥim* 10:4.
16. Ganzfried, *Siddur*, p. 237b.
17. MB 43:69–70.
18. AH 473:21.

Avadim Hahyenu: We Were Slaves

1. TOH 473.
2. Pes. 108b.
3. *Baḥ*, TOH 473.
4. It should be noted that the Rambam did not require the return of the Seder plate until needed for *Matzah Zu* and *Maror Zeh*. See Rambam, *Ḥametz u-Matzah* 8:4.
5. SAOH 473:7.
6. MB 473:71.
7. AH 473:22.

Vehe Sheamdah: This Covenant Has Sustained

1. *Shenei Luḥot ha-Berit, Pesaḥim* 2b; Emden, p. 237a; see also *Shulḥan Arukh ha-Rav*, 473:44.
2. Amsterdam *Haggadah* 1712.
3. *Magen Avraham*, SAOH 473:27; MB 473:73; AH 473:23.
4. AH 473:23
5. See p.11.
6. Ganzfried, *Siddur*, p. 239b.

Dam, Ve-Esh . . . B'aḥav: The Ten Plagues

1. *Sefer Maharil, Hilhot Haggadah*. The Maharil cited the *Roke'aḥ* as his source, a fact lacking in our editions of the *Roke'aḥ*.

2. Rema, SAOH 473:7.

3. The Prague *Haggadah*; *Magen Avraham*, SAOH 473:28; Emden, p. 242a; MB 473:74 note #81; AH 473:24. The Sephardim have a custom of pouring out drops with the left hand from a glass of wine vinegar into a wash basin; see *Me'am Lo'ez*, p. 254.

4. *Magen Avraham*, SAOH 473:28; *Hok Ya'akov*, SAOH 473:37.

5. Ganzfried, *Siddur*, p. 241b; MB 473:71 and his note #81.

6. AH 473:24.

7. The *Sefer Amrakhal* is printed in *Alexander Marx Jubilee Volume* (Hebrew Volume), p. 162 ff.

8. The Ari, *Etz Ḥayyim* as quoted by Kasher, *Haggadah Shelemah*, p. 126–127; Emden, p. 227a. See also *Me'am Lo'ez*, cited in note 3.

9. Emden, p. 242a; Ganzfried, *Siddur*, p. 242b.

10. As quoted by Goldschmidt, *Seder Haggadah Shel Pesaḥ*, p. 22.

11. *Darkei Moshe*, TOH 473:18.

12. MB 473:75.

13. Emden, p. 242a; Ganzfried, *Siddur*, p. 241b in the name of the Ari.

Matzah Zu and Maror Zeh: This Matzah and This Maror

1. Pes. 116b.

2. Rashbam, Pes. 116b.

3. Rambam, *Ḥametz u-Matzah* 8:4; TOH 473; SAOH 473:7; Emden, p. 246b; AH 473:23.

4. *Rabbi Weil* #193, *Dinei Pesaḥ*.

5. *Brother to the Rylands Spanish Haggadah* as seen in Narkis, B., *Hebrew Illuminated Manuscripts*, p. 68.

6. Kasher, *op. cit.*, pp. 142–152.

7. Rema, SAOH 473:7.

8. *Sefer Maharil*, *Ḥilhot Haggadah*.

9. Rema, SAOH 473:7. Also agreeing with the Rema are: the Prague *Haggadah*, Ganzfried, *Siddur*, p. 243b and AH 473:23.

10. Ganzfried, *Siddur*, p. 243b.

Lefeḥaḥ . . . Go'al Yisrael: Therefore . . . Who Redeemed Israel

1. *Midrash Shoḥer Tov* as quoted by TOH 473 and the *Sefer Abudarham*. This quote is not found in our editions. Kasher, *Haggadah Shelemah*, p. 133, cited 12th century *rishonim* who had this custom. The *Haggahot Maimuniyyot*, Rambam, *Haggadah* #3, and the TOH 473 in the name of other Ashkenazic Sages

stated that everyone at the Seder should lift their wine cups. All later decisors agreed.

2. *Sefer Abudarham, Seder Haggadah.*

3. See also the Gra on SAOH 473:7 who cited sources for the statement that *Hallel* is considered a song.

4. *Haggahot Maimuniyyot,* Rambam, *Ḥametz u-Matzah, Nusaḥ Haggadah* #3.

5. TOH 473.

6. SAOH 473:7.

7. Abudarham, *ibid.*

8. Emden, p. 249b.

9. AH 473:23. Ganzfried, *Siddur,* p. 243b and p. 244a also follows this *minhag.*

10. *Beth Yosef,* TOH 473; *Agur, Hilḥot Leyl Pesaḥ* #798.

11. Rema, SAOH 473:7.

12. AH 473:23.

13. See p. 11. The *Me'am Lo'ez,* p. 269, wrote that it was his custom to raise the wine cup in his right, cover the matzot, and put the Seder plate on the heads of the children from *Lefeḥaḥ* until *Go'al Yisrael.*

The Second Cup

1. For a complete discussion of this topic, see TOH 474, SAOH 474, and Zevin, *op. cit.,* p. 269 the notes.

2. Rema, SAOH 474.

3. Emden, pp. 249b–250a.

4. MB 474:4–5.

5. Zevin, p. 269.

6. AH 474:3.

RAḤTZAH: Lave the Hands

1. *Minhag Ḥatam Sofer* 10:17; *Moadim u-Z'manim,* p. 104.

2. Pes. 115b.

3. *Magen Avraham,* SAOH 475:1; MB 475: *Be'ur Halakhah;* AH 475:1.

4. See p. [9].

5. SAOH 158:11; AH 158:17.

6. See p. 12.

7. TOH 475 and all later Sages. The *Beth Yosef,* TOH 475 wrote that the *Agur* quoted the same *minhag* in the name of the *Ba'al ha-Ma'or.*

MOTZI—MATZAH: Blessings over the Matzah

1. See the Seder plate, p. 7.
2. Pes. 40a.
3. Some *rishonim* required the eating of *shemurah* matzah during all of Passover. For a discussion of this question, see Zevin, pp. 242–245; MB 453:4, *Be'ur Halakhah*.
4. TOH 453 and the commentaries; SAOH 453:4; MB 453:4, *Be'ur Halakhah;* AH 453:23.
5. See S.O.Y., *Haggadah,* pp. 152–153, and Zevin, pp. 242–245, for a fuller discussions of this problem.
6. Emden, p. 227b. Emden stated that no expense should be spared in order to obtain *shemurah* matzah.
7. *Berakoth* 39b.
8. *Tosafoth, Berakoth* 39b; Rosh, *Pesaḥim,* chap. 10; TOH 475.
9. *Shibbolei ha-Leket* 218, *Seder Pesaḥ;* TOH 475.
10. Rabbi Menoaḥ from Vienna, *Tosafoth, Berakoth* 39b; *Ha-Manhig, Hilḥot Pesaḥ* 82.
11. *Tosafoth, Berakoth* 39b.
12. TOH 475; SAOH 475:10; *Taz,* SAOH 475:1; Emden, p. 250a; AH 475:3.
13. Rashal #88; *Baḥ,* TOH 475.
14. *Sefer Maharil, Hilḥot Haggadah.*
15. *Ba'er Heitev,* SAOH 475:1; *Ḥok Ya'akov,* SAOH 475:2; MB 475:2; Zevin, p. 270.
16. *Siddur Minhat Yerushalaym,* pp. 416–426. The estimates for the size of a *kezayit* range from 1–1.5 ounces. See S.O.Y., *Haggadah,* p. 154 and see also p. 81, note 8.
17. TOH 475.
18. SAOH 475:1.
19. MB 475:1, *Be'ur Halakhah.*
20. See directions to *Raḥtzah,* p. [30].
21. *Minhagei Hatam Sofer* 10:17; Moshe Sternbuch, *Moadim u-Z'manim,* p. 104.
22. Rambam, *Ḥametz u-Matzah* 8:8; Toh 475.
23. TOH 475.
24. SAOH 475:1; Ari as quoted by Ganzfried, *Siddur,* p. 244b.
25. Rema, SAOH 475:1.
26. *Berakoth* 40a.
27. *Sefer Maharil, Hilḥot Haggadah.*
28. *Levush* 475:1; *Hok Ya'akov,* SAOH 475:4.
29. Emden, p. 250a.
30. AH 475:5.
31. Kasher, *op. cit.,* p. 168.
32. *Ḥayyei Adam* 130, *Ha-Seder B'Ktzarah* #9; MB 475:4.
33. Pes. 114b and all the decisors.

34. *Siddur Minhat Yerushalaym*, p. 418; S.O.Y., *op cit.*, p. 153; Gersion Appel, *The Concise Code of Jewish Law*, p. 188; Adin Steinsaltz, *The Passover Haggadah*, p. 2.

35. *Darkei Moshe*, TOH 475:1.

36. TOH 475.

37. SAOH 475:1.

38. *Sefer Maharil, Hilḥot Haggadah*. The *Magen Avraham*, SAOH 475:4 deemed this ruling of the Maharil to apply only if one could not fulfill the requirement of eating it all together and swallowing it at one time.

39. MB 475:9.

40. AH 475:4.

41. Pes. 108a.

MAROR: Bitter Herb

1. Pes. 39a.

2. *Ibid.*

3. AH 473:16.

4. *Me'am Lo'ez*, p. 269.

5. See Rabbi A. Steinsaltz, *Pesaḥim* 39a and Appendix; also Dr. Felix, *Mareath Ha-Mishnah, Zeraim*, pp. 44, 58, 88, 98, as quoted by S.O.Y., *op cit.*, p. 147.

6. The *Aguddah* as quoted by the *Sefer Maharil, Hilḥot Haggadah*, and *Rabbi Weil #193, Dinei Pesaḥ*. The *Aguddah, Arvei Pesaḥim*, recommends that lettuce be used for the *maror*, while the citation of the Maharil and R. Weil does not seem to be in our editions of the *Sefer ha-Aguddah*.

7. *Baḥ*, TOH 473; *Tosafoth Yom Tov, Pesaḥim* 2:6; *Magen Avraham*, SAOH 473:11.

8. The *Haggahot Maimuniyyot*, Rambam, *Ḥametz u-Matzah* 7:20 defines *tamḥa* as *mirtaḥ*. This word had a similar sound to *reitaḥ*, the Yiddish word for radish. In fact, the *Magen Avraham*, SAOH 473:11 wrote that *mirtaḥ* and horseradish are one and the same. However, a careful reading of the *Haggahot Maimuniyyot* shows that by *mirtaḥ* he meant the same vegetable identified by Rashi, marrubium,a type of mint. It is questionable whether our Mishnaic and Talmudic Sages were at all familiar with horseradish.

9. AH 473:13.

10. See also the *Ḥayyei Adam* 130:3. Although in Israel in his day (18th century) they used lettuce for the *maror*, in his own country (Eastern Europe), Passover falls at the beginning of spring, and there is no lettuce; the only vegetable he felt could be used for *maror* was horseradish.

11. For a short review of the extensive Rabbinic literature on these questions, see MB 475:33–40 and Zevin, p. 271.

12. *Ḥatam Sofer*, SAOH 473:5. Although, said the *Ḥatam Sofer*, lettuce was the preferred *maror* of our Sages, he was so fearful of the worms in the lettuce of his day

that he recommended the use of horseradish. He, too, was under the impression that *tamḥa* meant horseradish. Today, scholarly opinion views *tamḥa* as something other than horseradish, and, as our lettuce is not wormy or unduly difficult to wash, there is no question that we should revert to the *minhag* of our forefathers and use lettuce as the *maror*.

13. Pes. 116a.
14. Jerusalem Talmud *Pesaḥim* 9:5.
15. Pes. 116a.
16. For a recipe see p. 47.
17. Pes. 39a, the Mishnah, and all the decisors. See also Zevin, p. 271 for a fuller discussion of this point.
18. See p. 81, note 8.
19. Pes. 116a and all the decisors.
20. Rashi, Pes. 115b.
21. *Tosafoth*, Pes. 115b.
22. Rashi and Rashbam, Pes. 116a quoting the Talmud *Sotah* 11b.
23. TOH 475. Also the *Sefer ha-Roke'aḥ* #283 and all the later Sages.
24. Pes. 115b and all the decisors.
25. TOH 475.
26. Emden, p. 250a.
27. *Sefer ha-Roke'aḥ* # 283; TOH 475; SAOH 475:1; AH 475:6.
28. Pes. 115b.
29. *Peri Ḥadosh*, SAOH 475:1. The *Peri Ḥadosh* probably felt that the Talmud in *Pesaḥim* is not definitive. See *Beth Yosef*, TOH 475.
30. MB 475:13.
31. *Sefer Maharil, Hilḥot Haggadah; Magen Avraham*, SAOH 473:19.
32. TOH 475; SAOH 475:1; *Ḥok Ya'akov*, SAOH 475:8.
33. Pes. 108a and all the decisors.
34. Rashi, Pes. 108a.

KOREKH: Combine Matzah and Bitter Herb

1. TOH 475.
2. *Baḥ*, TOH 475.
3. All this does not apply to those like the Gra who recommended the use of only two matzot on the Seder plate.
4. See section on *Maror*, pp. 38–39.
5. *Ḥayyei Adam* 130, The Seder #11; see also Emden, p. 227b.
6. *Halakhically*, one may use a combination of any of the permitted vegetables to make up the *kezayit* necessary for the *maror* and the *korekh*. As noted previously, only lettuce is known with certainty as one of the acceptable vegetables mentioned by the Mishnah; therefore, it alone should be used for the *maror*. But for the *korekh*, since the requirement of *maror* has been fulfilled, some of the other vegetables believed to have been mentioned in the Mishnah, especially in combina-

tion with lettuce, may be used.

7. *Shibbolei ha-Leket* #218, *Seder Pesaḥ.*

8. The Rosh stated, as a general rule, that only when a blessing is said need there be a *kezayit.* Therefore, reasoned the *Sha'agat Aryeh* #100, for the *korekh* where no blessing is made, the Rosh would rule that no *kezayit* is necessary.

9. *Sha'agat Aryeh* #100; Emden, p. 250a; *Ḥayyei Adam* 130, The Seder #11; *Ma'amar Mordecai,* Vol III, 475:7.

10. MB 475:16.

11. For a discussion on this point and a reference to the sources, see Rambam, *Ḥametz u-Matzah* 8:8, and the *Haggahot Maimuniyyot;* Tur 475: *Baḥ* and *Darkei Moshe,* TOH 475; SAOH 475:1 and commentaries; Zevin, p. 275.

12. TOH 475.

13. *Taz,* SAOH 475:6.

14. *Magen Avraham,* SAOH 475:7.

15. MB 475:19.

16. Emden, p. 250a.

17. *Ḥayyei Adam* 130, The Seder #11.

18. AH 475:8.

19. Zevin, p. 273.

20. *Beth Yosef,* TOH 475. In our editions of the *Maharil* no dipping for the *korekh* is required at all.

21. *Ma'amar Mordecai,* Vol. III, 475:7.

22. MB 475:17.

23. *Shibbolei ha-Leket* #218; *Sefer ha-Roke'aḥ, Seder ha-Pesaḥ* #283; *Ha-Manhig, Hilḥot Pesaḥ* #83; *Or Zaru'a* 2:256. See Zevin, *ibid.*

24. SAOH 475:1.

25. MB 475:23.

26. AH 475:7.

27. *Beth Yosef,* TOH 475.

28. *Ibid.*

29. See section on *Motzi,* p. 36, for a discussion of the modern equivalent of this measurement.

SHUḤAN ARUKH: The Meal

1. Rema, SAOH 476:2.

2. Lentils are often served instead of eggs, as is seen in the story of Jacob and Esau and the selling of the birthright. The round lentil symbolizes death: as the lentil rolls, so death, sorrow, and mourning constantly roll about among men, from one to another. See Louis Ginzberg, *Legends of the Jews,* Vol I., p. 319; Vol. V, p. 277.

3. *Mishbetzet Zahav,* SAOH 476:3.

4. *Ḥatam Sofer* as quoted by Kasher, *op. cit.,* p. 94. See also Kasher's, *Ha-Rambam ve-Hamehilta d'Rabbi Shimeon ben Joḥai,* p. 154–155 for six reasons why an egg is eaten on Seder night.

5. Gra, SAOH 476:2.

6. See p. 5.

7. MB 476:11; *Ḥayyei Adam* 130, The Seder #12.

8. See p. 42 and p. 44.

9. See section on Recipes, p. 51. *this volume.*

10. *Pes. 53a. The Jerusalem Talmud Pesaḥim* 4:4 states that the prohibition against eating roasted meat on Seder night applies to anything that requires ritual slaughtering.

11. *Magen Avraham,* SAOH 476:1; *Ḥayyei Adam* 130, The Seder #12; MB 476:1; AH 476:1. Roasted eggs and roasted fish are permitted.

12. AH 476:1–2.

13. *Magen Avraham,* SAOH 476:1; *Ḥayyei Adam, ibid.;* MB 476:1.

14. *Sefer Maharil, Hilḥot Haggadah;* Rema, SAOH 476:2.

15. See section on Menu and Recipes for Seder nights, p. 45 ff. *this volume.*

16. AH 476:4. See also Ganzfried, *Siddur,* p. 254a.

17. *Sefer Maharil, ibid.*

18. *Sefer ha-Roke'aḥ* #283, *Hilḥot Pesaḥ.* The *Roke'aḥ* based his *halakhah* on the *Gemara* in *Nazir* 23a.

19. See the *Mordecai,* end of Pes., *Seder shel Pesaḥ,* where it appears that he disagreed with the *Roke'aḥ.* Of the later Sages, the Rema, SAOH 476:1; the *Magen Avraham,* SAOH 476:2; the *Hok Ya'akov,* SAOH 476:4; the AH 476:4; the MB 476:6 and Zevin, p. 273, all agreed with the *Roke'aḥ* and the Maharil.

20. See section on *Afikoman,* pp. 66, *this volume.*

TZAFUN: The Hidden Matzah

1. See p. 10.

2. Kasher, *op. cit.,* p. 26. Kasher further explained that the word also denotes a custom prevalent in ancient times. After a party where the wine flowed freely and everyone was merry, the guests, often accompanied by music, made the rounds of friends, joined in turn by others and finally finished in a final bout of drinking and merrymaking. See also Steinsaltz, *Haggadah shel Pesaḥ* , "Yaḥatz".

3. Pes. 119b.

4. *Ibid.* See also Rashbam, Pes. 119b and Pes. 115a.

5. Pes. 119b.

6. See *Beth Yosef,* TOH 477 who cites all the early sources.

7. Rambam, *Ḥametz u-Matzah* 8:9; Rashbam, Pes. 119b; Rosh, *Pesaḥim* #35, *Haggadah.*

8. *Or Zaru'a* 2:256; *Shibbolei ha-Leket* #218, *Seder Pesaḥ; Ha-Manhig, Hilḥot Pesaḥ* # 86; *Haggahot Maimuniyyot,* Rambam, *Ḥametz u-Matzah* 7:5; *Sefer ha-Roke'aḥ* #283, *Hilḥot Pesaḥ.*

9. Pes. 119b.

10. Rosh, Pes. 119b #34; *Baḥ,* TOH 477.

11. *Sefer Maharil, Hilḥot Haggadah; Baḥ,* TOH 477; *Magen Avraham,* SAOH

477:1; *Taz,* SAOH 477:1; MB 477:1; AH 477:3; Zevin, p. 274.

12. See MB 477:4, subnote 4, where he explained that Rashi and the Rashbam definitely required *heseba* because according to them the *mitzvah* of eating matzah on Passover is fulfilled through the eating of the *afikoman.*

13. Rosh, Pes. 108a, #20; *Haggahot Maimuniyyot,* Rambam, *Ḥametz u-Matzah* 7:5; TOH 477; SAOH 477:1.

14. Rambam, *Ḥametz u-Matzah* 7:8.

15. *Ḥayyei Adam* 130, The Seder #13; MB 477:4; Ah 477:4.

16. Pes. 120b.

17. Rambam, *Ḥametz u-Matzah* 6:1.

18. *Baḥ,* TOH 477 deduced the Rif's position on this *Halakhah.*

19. Rosh, Pes. 120b, #38, who also quoted the Rabbenu Tam.

20. All quoted by the *Baḥ,* TOH 477.

21. TOH 477; SAOH 477:1.

22. Emden, p. 250b; *Ḥayyei Adam* 130, The Seder #13.

23. MB 477:6; AH 477:5; see also Zevin, p. 274.

24. *Tosafoth,* Pes. 117b.

25. See the extensive literature on this subject in TOH 481 and the commentaries; SAOH 481:1 and commentaries; Zevin, p. 274.

26. *Ḥayyei Adam* 130, The Seder #13. However, in section 130:14 he allowed some liquids if one is very thirsty.

27. MB 481:1; AH 478:3 and 481:3.

28. AH 477:4; Zevin, p. 275.

29. See p. 21 for a full explanation of this *minhag* and its origin.

BAREKH: Grace

1. TOH 182 and SAOH 182 and their commentaries; AH 182: 1–5. All agreed that if possible, whenever three, and of course ten, say Grace together it should be said over wine. Today, when ten eat together, especially at any special occasion, Grace is always said over wine.

2. Pes. 117b.

3. *Midrash Tehillim,* Psalm 113.

4. *Baḥ,* TOH 479.

5. Emden, p. 250a.

6. Rabbi Naphtali Berlin, *Imrey Sefer, Barekh,* pp. 46–47.

7. *Ḥayyei Adam* 130:11; AH 479:1.

8. MB 479:9, subnote 12.

9. *Darkei Moshe,* TOH 479:2; Rema, SAOH 479:1.

10. *Sefer ha-Aguddah, Arvei Pesaḥim; Ḥok Ya'akov,* SAOH 479:7.

11. MB 479:13; AH 479:2.

12. *Berakoth* 51b and 52b.

13. Ganzfried, *Kitzur Shulḥan Arukh* 45:4 based on the *Kav Hayashor* #64.

14. *Hullin* 105b.

15. *Sanhedrin* 92a.

16. See AH 180:2.

17. AH 180:3.

18. See *Otzar ha-Tefillot, Berhat ha-Mazon.* It is the *Shenei Luḥot ha-Berit* who probably originated the idea of reciting a Psalm before Grace.

19. R. Steinsaltz, *Haggadah shel Pesaḥ, Barekh.*

20. *Ethics of Our Fathers* 3:4.

21. *Hullin* 105a.

22. See SAOH 181; MB 181; AH 181.

23. *Berakoth* 45a.

24. Rashi, *Berakoth* 45a.

25. See p. [36].

26. Most of the passages of the *Zimun* are taken from the Mishnah in *Berakoth* 45a, while the introductory phrase, *Rabbotei mir veel benchen,* was set by the *Magen Avraham* who based it on the Talmud and *Zohar.* See SAOH 192:1; *Magen Avraham,* Introduction to SAOH 192.

27. AH 192:5.

28. *Magen Avraham, ibid.,* cited the *Tur,* Abudarham, *Roke'aḥ,* Maharal mi-Prag, and *Levush* as a source for this passage.

29. Emden, p. 121a; *Sha'arei Teshuvah,* SAOH 192:3; MB 192:4; Ganzfried, *Kitzur Shulḥan Arukh* 45:6. See also the *Otzar ha-Tefillot, Grace,* who cited a Rabbi who recommended that the company wait for the Leader to say the first three words of the Grace, then answer *Barukh who u-barukh Shemo* and proceed with the Grace. This is too complicated to follow and none of our decisors or later Sages recommended it.

30. SAOH 183:7.

31. *Ḥayyei Adam* 48:1; see also MB 183: 27–28; Appel, *op, cit.,* p. 172:8, note 6.

32. *Otzar ha-Tefillot, Berḥat ha-Mazon.*

HALLEL: Praise
Shefokh Hamatkha: Pour Out Thy Wrath

1. Pes. 117b.

2. Goldschmidt, *Haggadah shel Pesaḥ,* p. 58, placed the introduction of this paragraph during the Middle Ages, possibly around the time of the Crusades. See also his *Passover Haggadah,* p. 143.

3. Maharal, *Gevurot ha-Shem;* see Eisenstein end of chapter 17.

4 *Sefer Abudarham, Seder Haggadah.* See also p. 12.

5. *Sefer Abudarham, ibid.*

6. TOH 480; SAOH 480:1; Emden, p. 251a; *Ḥayyei Adam* 130, The Seder #15; AH 480:2.

7. *Sefer Abudarham, ibid.;* Maharal, *ibid.*

8. The reasons will be discussed in the next few paragraphs.

9. *Shetei ha-Leḥem,* end of the book. This responsa is quoted verbatim in the *Berkhat Eliyahu,* also at the end of the book.

10. *Ḥok Ya'akov,* SAOH 480:6.

11. Emden, p. 227a and 231a. Many Sages felt that once wine in a cup was tasted, the remaining wine was rendered unfit for further use in connection with a *mitzvah.*

12. Prof. Goldschmidt, *Seder Haggadah shel Pesaḥ,* p. 22, probably did not see the original responsa of R. Hagiz.

13. R. Hagiz, *ibid.*

14. *Divrei Eliyahu, Ve-Ayra.*

15. See p. 12 for the other four phrases of redemption which are represented by the four wine cups.

16. See p. 68 on the prohibition against destroying food.

17. *Sefer Minhage Baal Ḥatam Sofer* 10:12.

18. *Darkei Moshe,* TOH 480; Rema, SAOH 480:1.

19. *Or Zaru'a* 2:254, in the name of R. Nissim Gaon.

20. *Ḥok Ya'akov,* SAOH 480:6.

21. The Talmud, *Rosh Hashannah* 11b, states that we were redeemed the first time on Passover and the final redemption will also take place on Passover.

22. Goldschmidt, *op. cit.,* p. 22.

23. AH 480:1.

Hodu and Ahna: Give Thanks and We Beseech Thee

1. *Midrash Tehillim,* Psalm 113; TOH 479.
2. *Kol Bo* #50; Rema, SAOH 479:1.
3. Rosh, *Pesaḥim* #32.
4. See p. 1.
5. *Magen Avraham,* SAOH 479:2, and all later decisors.
6. See p. 67.
7. *Sefer Maharil, Hilḥot Haggadah;* Rema, SAOH 479:1.
8. *Magen Avraham,* SAOH 479:2. See also *Rabbi Weil* #193 who also felt the same.
9. *Hok Ya'akov,* SAOH 479:6.
10. MB 479:9.
11. Emden, p. 251a.
12. *Otzar ha-Tefillot,* Vol. II, p. 905.
13. AH 479:3.
14. *Magen Avraham,* SAOH 479:2 says it explicitly.

The Fourth Cup

1. Pes. 117b.
2. Pes. 118a.
3. See the *rishonim* on Pes. 118a; TOH 480 and commentaries; SAOH 480

and commentaries; AH 480:3; MB 480:4–5.

4. *Baḥ*, TOH 480.

5. *Magen Avraham*, SAOH 480:2.

6. *Ḥayyei Adam* 130, The Seder #15; MB 479:6.

7. AH 480:3.

8. See p. 1 for a complete discussion concerning the proper size of the wine cup.

9. See Section on *Afikoman*, p. 66, this volume.

10. Pes. 118a.

11. Our tradition that only four cups of wine are required follows the *Haggahot Maimuniyyot*, Rambam, *Ḥametz u-Matzah* 8:30. For a complete discussion of this entire problem, see TOH 481 and commentaries; SAOH 481:1 and commentaries; AH 481:1–2; Kasher, *op. cit.*, p. 332.

12. MB 481:3.

13. Kasher, *op. cit.*, pp. 204, 212, 332.

14. AH 481:2.

15. Zevin, p. 276.

16. See p. 73.

BIBLIOGRAPHY

Abrabanel, Isaac ben Judah (1437–1508). *Zevaḥ Pesaḥ*. Reprinted in Eisenstein, *Ozar Perushim ve-Ziyurim el Haggadah shel Pesah*, New York, 1920.

Abraham ben Nathan ha-Yarḥi of Lunel (c. 1155–1215). *Sefer ha-Manhig*, Jerusalem, 1978.

Abudarham, David ben Joseph (14th century). *Sefer Abudarham ha-Shalem*, Jerusalem, 1962.

Adani, David ben Amrah (13th century). *Midrash ha-Gadol*, Vol. I, Jerusalem, 1947.

Aguddah. *See* Alexander Suslin ha-Kohen.

Agur. *See* Landau, Jacob.

Aḥai Gaon (680–752). *She'iltot*, Jerusalem, 1967.

Alexander Marx Jubilee Volume (Hebrew Volume), New York, 1950.

Alexander Suslin ha-Kohen (d. 1349). *Sefer ha-Aguddah*, New York, 1958.

Alfasi, Isaac ben Jacob (1013–1103). *Sefer ha-Halakhot*. Printed in most editions of the Talmud.

Amram Gaon (9th century). *Seder Rav Amram Gaon*, Jerusalem, 1971.

Anav, Zedekiah ben Abraham (13th century). *Shibbolei ha-Leket ha-Shalem*, New York, 1959.

Appel, Gersion. *The Concise Code of Jewish Law*, New York, 1977.

Ari. *See* Luria, Isaac.

Arukh ha-Shulḥan. *See* Epstein, Jehiel.

Asher ben Jehiel (1250–1327). *Sefer ha-Asheri*. Printed in most editions of the Talmud.

———. *She'elot u-Teshuvot ha-Rosh*, New York, 1954.

Ashkenazi, Judah ben Simeon (c. 1730–1791). *Ba'er Heitev*. Printed in most editions of the *Shulḥan Arukh*.

Ashkenazi, Tzevi Hirsch ben Jacob (1660–1718). *Sefer She'elot u-Teshuvot Hakham Tzevi*, Jerusalem, 1970.

Avi ha-Ezri. *See* Eliezer ben Joel.

Ba'er Heitev. *See* Ashkenazi, Judah.

Baḥ. *See* Sirkes, Joel.

Berkhat Eliyahu. *See* Elijah ben Jacob.

Berlin, Naphtali Zevi Judah (1817–1893). *Imrey Sefer*, Tel Aviv, 1960.

Bertinoro, Obadiah ben Abraham Yare (c. 1450–1516). Printed in most editions of the Mishnah.

Beth Yosef. *See* Caro, Joseph.

Be'ur ha-Gra. *See* Zalman, Elijah.

Caro, Joseph ben Ephraim (1488–1575). *Beth Yosef.* Printed in most editions of the *Tur.*

———. *Shulḥan Arukh,* New York, 1951.

Cremieux, Mordecai ben Abraham (1749–1865). *Ma'amar Mordecai,* Vol. III, Jerusalem, 1970.

Culi, Jacob (c. 1685–1732). *Yalkut Me'am Lo'ez,* Exodus, Vol. I. Hebrew translation by A. Yerushalmi, Jerusalem, 1967.

Danby, Herbert (1889–1953). *The Mishnah,* London, 1933.

Danzig, Abraham ben Jehiel Michal (1748–1820). *Ḥayyei Adam,* Jerusalem, 1975.

Darkei Moshe. See Isserles, Moses.

De Silva, Hezekiah ben David (1659–1695). *Peri Ḥadash.* Printed in most editions of the *Shulḥan Arukh.*

David ben Samuel ha-Levi (1586–1667). *Turei Zahav.* Printed in most editions of the *Shulḥan Arukh.*

Derishah u-Perishah. See Falk, Joshua.

Divrei Eliyahu. See Zalman, Elijah.

Duran, Simeon ben Zemaḥ (1361–1444). *Teshuvot Simeon ben Zemaḥ, Sefer ha-Tashbatz,* Tel Aviv, 1964.

Eisenstein, Judah David (1854–1956). *Ozar Perushim ve-Ziyurim el Haggadah shel Pesah,* New York, 1920.

Eleazar ben Judah of Worms (c. 1165–1230). *Sefer ha-Roke'aḥ ha-Gadol,* Jerusalem, 1966.

Eliezer ben Joel ha-Levi (1140–1225). *Sefer Ravyah,* Jerusalem, 1964.

Eliezer ben Nathan (c. 1090–1170). *Sefer ha-Ravon* or *Even ha-Ezer,* Israel, 1975.

Elijah ben Jacob (18th century). *Berkhat Eliyahu,* Wandsbeck, 1728.

Emden, Jacob (1697–1776). *Siddur Beit Ya'akov,* New York, 1950.

Encyclopedia Talmudit, Vol. 9, Jerusalem, 1951.

Epstein, Jehiel Michal ben Aaron Isaac Halevi (1829–1908). *Arukh ha-Shulḥan,* New York, 1941.

Etz ha-Hayyim. See Vital, Hayyim.

Falk, Joshua ben Alexander ha-Kohen (c. 1555–1614). *Derishah u-Perishah.* Printed in most editions of the *Tur.*

Ganzfried, Solomon ben Joseph (1804–1886). *Kitzur Shulḥan Arukh,* New York, 1945.

———. *Siddur Avodath Yisrael,* New York, 1971.

Genesis Rabbah (5th–6th century exegetical Midrash). Soncino English translation, London, 1951.

Ginzberg, Louis (1873–1953). *The Legends of the Jews,* Philadelphia, 1938.

Goldschmidt, Ernst Daniel (1895–1974). *Seder Haggadah shel Pesaḥ,* Jerusalem, 1947.

———. *The Passover Haggadah, Its Sources and History*, Jerusalem, 1969.

Gombiner, Abraham Abele ben Hayyim ha-Levi (1637–1683). *Magen Avraham*. Printed in most editions of the *Shulḥan Arukh*.

Gra. *See* Zalman, Elijah.

Gunzberg, Aryeh Leib ben Asher (1695–1785). *Sha'agat Aryeh*, Jerusalem, 1974.

Ḥafetz Ḥayyim. *See* Israel Meir.

Haggahot Maimuniyyot. *See* Meir ha-Kohen.

Hagiz, Moses (1672–1751). *Sefer Shetei ha-Leḥem*, Jerusalem, 1970.

Hakham Tzevi. *See* Ashkenazi, Tzevi.

Hamoadim be-Halakha. *See* Zevin, Solomon.

Ha-Pardes. (School of Rashi). Budapest, 1923.

Ḥatam Sofer. *See* Sofer, Moses.

Ḥayyei Adam. *See* Danzig, Abraham.

Heller, Yom Tov Lipmann ben Nathan ha-Levi (1579–1654). *Tosefoth Yom Tov*. Printed in most editions of the Mishnah.

Ḥok Ya'akov. *See* Reischer, Jacob.

Horowitz, Isaiah ben Abraham ha-Levi (c. 1565–1630). *Sefer Shenei Luḥot ha-Berit*, Jerusalem, 1969.

Isaac ben Moses of Vienna (c. 1180–1250). *Or Zaru'a*, Israel, 1958.

Israel Meir ha-Kohen (Kagan) (1838–1933). *Mishnah Berurah*, New York, 1952.

Issachar Ber of Vilna (19th century). *Ma'aseh Rav*. Collection of writings of the Gra reprinted at the end of *Otzar ha-Tefillot*, Vol. II.

Isserlein, Israel ben Pethaḥiah (1390–1460). *Terumat ha-Deshen*, Tel Aviv, 1957.

Isserles, Moses (c. 1525–1572). *Darkei Moshe*. Printed in most editions of the *Tur*.

———. *Ha-Mappah*. Printed in most editions of the *Shulḥan Arukh*.

Jacob ben Asher (c. 1270–1340). *Arba'ah Turim*, New York, 1964.

Jaffe, Mordecai ben Abraham (c. 1535–1612). *Levushim*, Jerusalem, 1967,

Jastrow, Marcus Mordecai (1829–1903). *Dictionary of the Targumin, the Talmud Bavli and Yerushalmi and the Midrashic Literature*, New York, 1950.

Jeroḥam ben Meshullam (c. 1290–1350). *Sefer Meshorim and Toledot Adam ve-Havvah*, Israel, 1974.

Joseph ben Moses (1423–c. 1490). *Leket Yosher*, New York, 1959.

Joseph son of Joshua Falk (17th century). *Introduction to the Derishah and Perishah*. Printed in most editions of the *Tur Yoreh De'ah*, New York, 1964.

Judah Loew ben Bezalel (c. 1525–1609). *Gevurot ha-Shem*. Reprinted in Eisenstein, *Ozar Perushim ve-Ziyurim el Haggadah shel Pesah*, New

York, 1920.
Kasher, Menachem (1895–). *Haggadah Shelemah,* Jerusalem, 1960.
———. *The Passover Haggadah,* New York, 1955.
———. *Ha-Rambam ve-Hameḥilta d'Rabbi Shimeon ben Joḥai,* New York, 1943.
Kitzur Shulḥan Arukh. See Ganzfried, Solomon.
Kol Bo (end of 13th century or beginning of 14th century, anonymous work). *Sefer Kol Bo,* New York, 1946.
Kolin, Samuel ben Nathan ha-Levi (1720–1806). *Maḥazit ha-Shekel.* Printed in most editions of the *Shulḥan Arukh.*
Landau, Jacob (15th century). *Sefer Ha-Agur ha-Shalem,* Jerusalem, 1959.
Leket Yosher. See Joseph ben Moses.
Levi, Eliezer (20th century). *Yesodot ha-Tefillah,* Tel Aviv, 1958.
Levush. See Jaffe, Mordecai.
Luria, Isaac ben Solomon (1534–1572). Most original of the kabbalistic thinkers.
Luria, Solomon (Shlomo) ben Jehiel (c. 1510–1574). *She'eloth u-Teshuvot ha-Rashal,* Jerusalem, 1969.
Luzzatto, Samuel David (1800–1865). Italian scholar, philosopher, Biblical commentator, and translator.
Ma'amar Mordecai. See Cremieux, Mordecai.
Ma'aseh Rav. See Issachar Ber.
Magen Avraham. See Gombiner, Abraham.
Maharal. *See* Judah Loew ben Bezalel.
Maharam of Rothenburg. *See* Meir ben Baruch of Rothenburg.
Maharil. *See* Moellin, Jacob.
Maḥzit ha-Shekel. See Kolin, Samuel.
Maḥzor Vitry. See Simḥah ben Samuel.
Maimonides, Moses (1135–1204). *Mishneh Torah,* New York, 1967.
Manhig. See Abraham ben Nathan ha-Yarḥi.
Margolis, Hayyim (d. 1818). *Sha'arei Teshuvah.* Printed in most editions of the *Shulḥan Arukh.*
Me'am Loez. See Culi, Jacob.
Meir ben Baruch of Rothenburg (c. 1215–1293). Outstanding scholar of the period.
Meir ha-Kohen of Rothenburg (13th century). *Haggahot Maimuniyyot.* Printed in most editions of Maimonides, *Mishneh Torah.*
Midrash ha-Gadol. See Adani, David.
Midrash Shoḥer Tov. See Midrash Tehillim.
Midrash Tanḥuma (homiletical Midrash of unknown date, probably 9th century), Jerusalem, 1964.
Midrash Tehillim (group of Midrashim compiled from the 3rd–13th cen-

turies), Jerusalem, 1966.
Minhage Ḥatam Sofer. See Shil, Yosh'a.
Mintz, Moses ben Isaac (15th century). *Teshuvot Maharam Mintz,* Tel Aviv, 1968.
Mishbetzot Zahav. See Teomim, Joseph.
Mishnah. Pardes edition, New York, 1953.
Mishnah Berurah. See Israel Meir.
Moadim u-Z'manim. See Sternbuch, Moshe.
Moellin, Jacob ben Moses (c. 1360–1427). *Sefer Maharil,* Jerusalem, 1949.
Mordecai. See Mordecai ben Hillel.
Mordecai ben Hillel ha-Kohen (c. 1240–1298). *Sefer Mordecai.* Printed in many editions of the Talmud.
Moses ben Jacob Coucy (13th century). *Sefer Mitzvot Gadol* Jerusalem, 1963.
Moses ben Naḥman (1194–1270). Famous Biblical commentator and Talmudic scholar.
Narkis, Bezalel (1926–). *Hebrew Illuminated Manuscripts,* Jerusalem, 1969.
Netziv. *See* Berlin, Naphtali.
Nissim ben Reuben Gerondi (c. 1310–1375). Commentary on the Rif and printed with most editions of the Rif.
Or Zaru'a. See Isaac ben Moses.
Otzar ha-Tefillot (first published in 1915). The most complete anthology of commentaries on the prayerbook. New York, 1946.
Peri Ḥadash. See DaSilva, Hezekiah.
Peri Megadim. See Teomim, Joseph.
Pirkei de-Rabbi Eliezer (8th century *aggadic* work). Jerusalem, 1970. English translation by Gerald Friedlander, New York, 1965.
Rabbenu Jeroḥam. *See* Jeroḥam ben Meshullam.
Rambam. *See* Maimonides, Moses.
Ramban. *See* Moses ben Naḥman.
Ran. *See* Nissim ben Reuben.
Rashal. *See* Luria, Solomon.
Rashba. *See* Adret, Solomon.
Rashbam. *See* Samuel ben Meir.
Rashi, *See* Solomon ben Isaac.
Ravon. *See* Eliezer ben Nathan.
Ravyah. *See* Eliezer ben Joel.
Reischer, Jacob ben Joseph (c. 1670–1733). *Hok le-Ya'akov.* Printed in most editions of the *Shulḥan Arukh.*
Rema. *See* Isserles, Moses.
Rif. *See* Alfasi, Isaac.
Roke'ah. See Eleazar ben Judah.
Rosh. *See* Asher ben Jehiel.

Saadiah (ben Joseph) Gaon (882–942). *Siddur Rav Saadiah Gaon*, Jerusalem, 1970.

Samuel ben Meir (c. 1080–1174). Printed in most editions of the tractate *Pesaḥim*.

Sefer Amrakhal (13th or 14th century anonymous work). See *Alexander Marx Jubilee Volume*.

Semag. *See* Moses ben Jacob Coucy.

Sha'agat Aryeh. *See* Gunzberg, Aryeh.

Sha'arei Teshuvah. *See* Margolis, Hayyim.

Shadal. *See* Luzzatto, Samuel.

She'iltot. *See* Aḥai Gaon.

Shenei Luḥot ha-Berit. See Horowitz, Isaiah.

Shetei ha-Leḥem. *See* Hagiz, Moses.

Shibbolei ha-Leket. *See* Anav, Zedekiah.

Shil, Yosh'a Leib (19th century). *Minage Ḥatam Sofer*, Jerusalem, 1965.

Shulḥan Arukh. *See* Caro, Joseph.

Shulḥan Arukh ha-Rav. *See* Shneur Zalman of Lyady.

Shneur Zalman of Lyady (1745–1813). *Shulḥan Arukh ha-Rav*, Brooklyn, 1965.

Siddur Minḥat Yerushalaym (20th century comprehensive Siddur compiled by I. Adi and Y.A. Dvorkes), Jerusalem, 1977.

Siddur Rav Amram Gaon. *See* Amram Gaon.

Siddur Rav Saadiah Gaon. *See* Saadiah Gaon.

Simḥah ben Samuel of Vitry (11th–12th century). *Maḥzor Vitry*, Jerusalem, 1963.

Sirkes, Joel ben Samuel (1561–1640). *Bayit Ḥadash*. Printed in most editions of the *Tur*.

Sofer, Moses (1762–1839). *Haggahot on Shulḥan Arukh Oraḥ Ḥayyim*. Printed in most editions of the *Shulḥan Arukh*.

Solomon ben Isaac (1040–1105). Wrote the classic commentary on the Talmud. Printed in most editions of the Talmud.

S.O.Y. (Student Organization of Yeshiva University). *The Passover Haggadah*, New York, 1974.

Steinsaltz, Adin (20th century). *The Passover Haggadah*, Jerusalem, 1977.

Sternbuch, Moshe (19th century). *Haggadah shel Pesaḥ Moadim u-Z'manim*, Jerusalem, 1963.

Talmud. Shulsinger Brothers edition, New York, 1950.

Tashbatz. *See* Duran, Simeon.

Taz. See David ben Samuel.

Teomim, Joseph ben Meir (c. 1727–1792). *Mishbetzot Zahav* and *Peri Megadim*. Printed in most editions of the *Shulḥan Arukh*.

Terumat ha-Deshen. *See* Isserlein, Israel.

Teshuvot Maharam Mintz. See Moses ben Isaac.
Tosafoth (12th–14th centuries). Printed in most editions of the Talmud.
Tosefoth Yom Tov. See Heller, Yom Tov Lipmann.
Tosefta (4th century). Printed in most editions of the Talmud.
Tur. See Jacob ben Asher.
Vilna Gaon. *See* Zalman, Elijah.
Vital, Ḥayyim ben Joseph (1542–1620). *Etz ha-Ḥayyim,* Tel-Aviv, 1960.
Weil, Jacob ben Judah (d. 1456). *Sheeloth u-Teshuvot Rabbi Jacob Weil,* Jerusalem, 1958.
Zalman, Elijah ben Solomon (1720–1797). *Be'ur ha-Gra.* Printed in most editions of the *Shulḥan Arukh.*
———. *Divrei Eliyahu,* edited by Y.L. Papel and A.D. Bloch, Jerusalem, 1966.
Zevaḥ Pesaḥ. See Abrabanel, Isaac.
Zevin, Solomon Joseph (1890–1975). *Hamoadim be-Halakhah,* Tel Aviv, 1953.
Zohar. English translation by Soncino Press. London, 1949.

INDEX

הגדה של פסח

PASSOVER HAGGADAH: THE COMPLETE SEDER

By

Arthur M. Silver

Menorah Publishing Company, Inc.
New York, N.Y.

First edition
Library of Congress Catalog Card Number: 79-92726
ISBN 0-932232-06-x
Manufactured in the United States of America

Table Preparation

The table should be set before evening and the Seder should begin immediately after nightfall upon returning from the *Ma'ariv* (evening prayer) service in the synagogue. However, if Passover eve falls on Saturday night, then the table may not be set until after nightfall. Similarly, for the second Seder (in the Diaspora), one must wait until after nightfall before setting the table. Cover the table with a beautiful white cloth and set it with the finest silverware and table appointments. Every place setting should have an unblemished wine cup or goblet, preferably silver, holding at least 3.1 fluid ounces, and each chair at the table to be occupied by a male over thirteen should have a pillow for reclining. A *kittel* should be prepared at the chair of the Leader, the person who is to conduct the Seder. The Seder plate or basket containing the various traditional Passover items should be set before the Leader's place at the table. This plate should contain: three unbroken matzoth (preferably hand *shemurah*), *ziroa* (a boiled or roasted lamb or other animal shankbone with some meat on it), *betzah* (a hard-boiled egg), *karpas* (celery), *ḥaroset* (a paste prepared from pounded fruits and nuts and mixed with cinnamon and wine (see p. 47 for recipe), *maror* (romaine or any other type of lettuce), and *ḥazeret* (preferably lettuce, but endive or chicory or any combination of these may be chosen). Either diagram A or B of the Seder plate (p. 7) is acceptable (see recipes, p. 45 for exact quantities). A bowl containing salt water is placed near the Seder plate next to the *karpas*. Several broken vessels should be placed near the table within easy reach of all. A beautiful silver wine goblet, to be used as the Cup of Elijah, is placed in the center of the table. The candles that will be lighted by the mistress of the house to usher in the Festival may be placed either on the table or on a sideboard in the room where the Seder is to be held. Extra portions of *karpas, shemurah* matzah, *maror,* and *ḥazeret* are prepared and left in the kitchen, to be brought in when needed. It is customary to arrange for at least three adult males to be present at the Seder.

Lighting the Candles הַדְלָקַת נֵר שֶׁל יוֹם טוֹב

Approximately one hour before nightfall (check a Jewish calendar for the exact time), the mistress of the house must light the candles. She should be dressed in Sabbath holiday clothes and must wear some type

of head covering. The minimum number of candles is two, although many women light more. The mistress lights the candles, puts her hands over and above them, hiding them from her sight, and pronounces the blessings below. She then takes her hands away so that she can see and enjoy the candlelight. On Friday night include the words in parentheses.

Blessed art Thou, Lord our God, King of the universe, who hast sanctified us by His commandments and commanded us to light (the Sabbath and) the festival lights.

בָּרוּךְ אַתָּה יְיָ אֱלֹהֵינוּ מֶלֶךְ הָעוֹלָם, אֲשֶׁר קִדְּשָׁנוּ בְּמִצְוֹתָיו וְצִוָּנוּ לְהַדְלִיק נֵר שֶׁל (שַׁבָּת וְשֶׁל) יוֹם טוֹב.

Blessed art Thou, Lord our God, King of the universe, who hast kept us alive, and hast sustained us and enabled us to reach this season.

בָּרוּךְ אַתָּה יְיָ אֱלֹהֵינוּ מֶלֶךְ הָעוֹלָם, שֶׁהֶחֱיָנוּ וְקִיְּמָנוּ וְהִגִּיעָנוּ לַזְּמַן הַזֶּה.

The Seder Program

סֵדֶר לֵיל פֶּסַח

Recite the *Kiddush*
Lave the hands
Eat the *karpas*
Divide the middle matzah
Recite the *Haggadah*
Lave the hands
Blessing over bread
Blessing over the matzah
Bitter herb
Combine matzah with bitter herb
The meal
The hidden matzah
Grace
Praise
Acceptance prayer

קַדֵּשׁ וּרְחַץ
כַּרְפַּס יַחַץ
מַגִּיד רָחְצָה
מוֹצִיא מַצָּה
מָרוֹר כּוֹרֵךְ
שֻׁלְחָן עוֹרֵךְ
צָפוּן בָּרֵךְ
הַלֵּל נִרְצָה

Kaddesh: *Recite the Kiddush* קַדֵּשׁ

As soon as the stars appear, the Leader dons his *kittel.* The matzoth on the Seder plate are covered, the wine goblets are filled to the brim with a fine red wine, and the Leader commences the Seder by announcing *Kaddesh* and giving a short explanation of this rite. The Leader may also recite the *hinnene memuḥan.* All present stand, the *Kiddush* cup is lifted with both hands at least 3½ inches above the table and just before the start of the *Kiddush* is held with the right hand alone (throughout the Seder a right-handed person raises the wine cup with the right hand and a left-handed participant uses the left hand). The leader intones the *Kiddush* and the company repeats it quietly after him, word by word.

הִנְנִי מוּכָן וּמְזֻמָּן לְקַיֵּם מִצְוַת כּוֹס רִאשׁוֹן מֵאַרְבַּע כּוֹסוֹת לְשֵׁם יִחוּד קוּדְשָׁא בְּרִיךְ הוּא וּשְׁכִינְתֵּיהּ עַל יְדֵי הַהוּא טָמִיר וְנֶעְלָם בְּשֵׁם כָּל יִשְׂרָאֵל.

I am ready and prepared to perform the commandment of the first of the four cups, to honor the Holy One, blessed be He and His Divine Presence, through the hidden and secret Guardian, on behalf of all Israel.

When Seder night falls Sunday through Thursday, say the following:

סַבְרִי מָרָנָן וְרַבָּנָן וְרַבּוֹתַי.

בָּרוּךְ אַתָּה יְיָ אֱלֹהֵינוּ מֶלֶךְ הָעוֹלָם, בּוֹרֵא פְּרִי הַגָּפֶן.

בָּרוּךְ אַתָּה יְיָ אֱלֹהֵינוּ מֶלֶךְ הָעוֹלָם, אֲשֶׁר בָּחַר בָּנוּ מִכָּל עָם, וְרוֹמְמָנוּ מִכָּל לָשׁוֹן וְקִדְּשָׁנוּ בְּמִצְוֹתָיו. וַתִּתֶּן לָנוּ יְיָ אֱלֹהֵינוּ בְּאַהֲבָה מוֹעֲדִים לְשִׂמְחָה, חַגִּים וּזְמַנִּים לְשָׂשׂוֹן, אֶת יוֹם חַג הַמַּצּוֹת הַזֶּה, זְמַן חֵרוּתֵנוּ מִקְרָא קֹדֶשׁ זֵכֶר לִיצִיאַת מִצְרָיִם. כִּי בָנוּ

With your permission, gentlemen:

Blessed art Thou, Lord our God, King of the universe, creator of the fruit of the vine.

Blessed art Thou, Lord our God, King of the universe, who hast chosen us from all peoples, and hast exalted us among the nations, and hast sanctified us by His commandments. And Thou hast given us with love, Lord our God, Sabbaths for rest and Holydays for rejoicing, festivals and seasons for gladness, this festival of Passover, the season of our freedom, a holy convocation in remem-

brance of our departure from Egypt. For Thou hast chosen and sanctified us from among the nations; and Thou hast given us a heritage, Thy Holydays in joy and in gladness. Blessed art Thou, O Lord, who sanctifiest Israel and the Festivals.

בָחַרְתָּ וְאוֹתָנוּ קִדַּשְׁתָּ מִכָּל הָעַמִּים, וּמוֹעֲדֵי קָדְשְׁךָ בְּשִׂמְחָה וּבְשָׂשׂוֹן הִנְחַלְתָּנוּ. בָּרוּךְ אַתָּה יְיָ מְקַדֵּשׁ יִשְׂרָאֵל וְהַזְּמַנִּים.

Blessed art Thou, Lord our God, King of the universe, who hast kept us alive, and sustained us and enabled us to reach this season.

בָּרוּךְ אַתָּה יְיָ אֱלֹהֵינוּ מֶלֶךְ הָעוֹלָם, שֶׁהֶחֱיָנוּ וְקִיְּמָנוּ וְהִגִּיעָנוּ לַזְּמַן הַזֶּה.

(*continue on page [9]*)

When Seder falls on Friday night, say the following:

And there was evening and there was morning
the sixth day.

And the heaven and the earth were finished, and all the host of them. And on the seventh day God finished His work which He had made; and He rested on the seventh day from all His work which He had made. And God blessed the seventh day, and hallowed it; because on it He rested from all His work which God in creating had made (Gen. 1:31–2:3).

וַיְהִי עֶרֶב וַיְהִי בֹקֶר

יוֹם הַשִּׁשִּׁי. וַיְכֻלּוּ הַשָּׁמַיִם וְהָאָרֶץ וְכָל צְבָאָם. וַיְכַל אֱלֹהִים בַּיּוֹם הַשְּׁבִיעִי מְלַאכְתּוֹ אֲשֶׁר עָשָׂה, וַיִּשְׁבֹּת בַּיּוֹם הַשְּׁבִיעִי מִכָּל מְלַאכְתּוֹ אֲשֶׁר עָשָׂה. וַיְבָרֶךְ אֱלֹהִים אֶת יוֹם הַשְּׁבִיעִי וַיְקַדֵּשׁ אֹתוֹ, כִּי בוֹ שָׁבַת מִכָּל מְלַאכְתּוֹ אֲשֶׁר בָּרָא אֱלֹהִים לַעֲשׂוֹת.

With your permission, gentlemen:

סַבְרִי מָרָנָן וְרַבָּנָן וְרַבּוֹתַי.

Blessed art Thou, Lord our God, King of the universe, creator of the fruit of the vine.

בָּרוּךְ אַתָּה יְיָ אֱלֹהֵינוּ מֶלֶךְ הָעוֹלָם, בּוֹרֵא פְּרִי הַגָּפֶן.

Blessed art Thou, Lord our God, King of the universe, who hast

בָּרוּךְ אַתָּה יְיָ אֱלֹהֵינוּ מֶלֶךְ הָעוֹלָם, אֲשֶׁר בָּחַר בָּנוּ מִכָּל עָם

וְרוֹמְמָנוּ מִכָּל לָשׁוֹן וְקִדְּשָׁנוּ בְּמִצְוֹתָיו. וַתִּתֶּן לָנוּ יְיָ אֱלֹהֵינוּ בְּאַהֲבָה שַׁבָּתוֹת לִמְנוּחָה וּמוֹעֲדִים לְשִׂמְחָה, חַגִּים וּזְמַנִּים לְשָׂשׂוֹן, אֶת יוֹם הַשַּׁבָּת הַזֶּה וְאֶת יוֹם חַג הַמַּצּוֹת הַזֶּה, זְמַן חֵרוּתֵנוּ בְּאַהֲבָה מִקְרָא קֹדֶשׁ זֵכֶר לִיצִיאַת מִצְרָיִם. כִּי בָנוּ בָחַרְתָּ וְאוֹתָנוּ קִדַּשְׁתָּ מִכָּל הָעַמִּים, וְשַׁבָּת וּמוֹעֲדֵי קָדְשְׁךָ בְּאַהֲבָה וּבְרָצוֹן בְּשִׂמְחָה וּבְשָׂשׂוֹן הִנְחַלְתָּנוּ. בָּרוּךְ אַתָּה יְיָ מְקַדֵּשׁ הַשַּׁבָּת וְיִשְׂרָאֵל וְהַזְּמַנִּים.

chosen us from all peoples, and hast exalted us among the nations, and hast sanctified us by His commandments. And Thou hast given us with love, Lord our God, Sabbaths for rest and Holydays for rejoicing, festivals and seasons for gladness, this Sabbath day and this festival of Passover, the season of our freedom, with love a holy convocation in remembrance of our departure from Egypt. For Thou hast chosen and sanctified us from among the nations; and Thou hast given us a heritage, Thy Sabbath and Holydays with love and favor, in joy and in gladness. Blessed art Thou, O Lord, who sanctfiest the Sabbath and Israel and the Festivals.

בָּרוּךְ אַתָּה יְיָ אֱלֹהֵינוּ מֶלֶךְ הָעוֹלָם, שֶׁהֶחֱיָנוּ וְקִיְּמָנוּ וְהִגִּיעָנוּ לַזְּמַן הַזֶּה.

Blessed art Thou, Lord our God, King of the universe, who hast kept us alive, and sustained us and enabled us to reach this season.

(*continue on p. [9]*)

When Seder falls on Saturday night, say the following:

סַבְרִי מָרָנָן וְרַבָּנָן וְרַבּוֹתַי.

בָּרוּךְ אַתָּה יְיָ אֱלֹהֵינוּ מֶלֶךְ הָעוֹלָם, בּוֹרֵא פְּרִי הַגָּפֶן.

בָּרוּךְ אַתָּה יְיָ אֱלֹהֵינוּ מֶלֶךְ הָעוֹלָם, אֲשֶׁר בָּחַר בָּנוּ מִכָּל עָם,

With your permission, gentlemen:

Blessed art Thou, Lord our God, King of the universe, creator of the fruit of the vine.

Blessed art Thou, Lord our God, King of the universe, who hast chosen us from all peoples, and has exalted

וְרוֹמְמָנוּ מִכָּל לָשׁוֹן וְקִדְּשָׁנוּ
בְּמִצְוֹתָיו. וַתִּתֶּן לָנוּ יְיָ אֱלֹהֵינוּ
בְּאַהֲבָה מוֹעֲדִים לְשִׂמְחָה, חַגִּים
וּזְמַנִּים לְשָׂשׂוֹן, אֶת יוֹם חַג
הַמַּצּוֹת הַזֶּה, זְמַן חֵרוּתֵנוּ מִקְרָא
קֹדֶשׁ זֵכֶר לִיצִיאַת מִצְרָיִם. כִּי בָנוּ
בָחַרְתָּ וְאוֹתָנוּ קִדַּשְׁתָּ מִכָּל
הָעַמִּים, וּמוֹעֲדֵי קָדְשְׁךָ בְּשִׂמְחָה
וּבְשָׂשׂוֹן הִנְחַלְתָּנוּ. בָּרוּךְ אַתָּה יְיָ
מְקַדֵּשׁ יִשְׂרָאֵל וְהַזְּמַנִּים.

us among the nations, and hast sanctified us by His commandments. And Thou hast given us with love, Lord our God, Sabbaths for rest and Holydays for rejoicing, festivals and seasons for gladness, this festival of Passover, the season of our freedom, a holy convocation in remembrance of our departure from Egypt. For Thou hast chosen and sanctified us from among the nations; and Thou hast given us a heritage, Thy Holydays in joy and in gladness. Blessed art Thou, O Lord, who sanctifiest Israel and the Festivals.

Place the wine cup in the left hand or place it on the table. Bend all four fingers of the right hand (not both hands) over the thumb and look at both the fingernails and the palm at the same time, making sure that the light of the candles is reflected by the fingernails. Open the fingers slightly so that light now reaches the palm. Recite the blessing below.

בָּרוּךְ אַתָּה יְיָ אֱלֹהֵינוּ מֶלֶךְ
הָעוֹלָם, בּוֹרֵא מְאוֹרֵי הָאֵשׁ.

Blessed art Thou, Lord our God, King of the universe, Creator of light of the fire.

Stretch out the fingers and turn the palm to face the candlelight and look at the nails from the back side of the hand. Take the wine cup in the right hand and continue.

בָּרוּךְ אַתָּה יְיָ אֱלֹהֵינוּ מֶלֶךְ
הָעוֹלָם, הַמַּבְדִּיל בֵּין קֹדֶשׁ לְחוֹל,
בֵּין אוֹר לְחֹשֶׁךְ, בֵּין יִשְׂרָאֵל

Blessed art Thou, Lord our God, King of the universe, who hast made a distinction between holy and profane, between light and darkness, between Israel

לָעַמִּים, בֵּין יוֹם הַשְּׁבִיעִי לְשֵׁשֶׁת יְמֵי הַמַּעֲשֶׂה. בֵּין קְדֻשַּׁת שַׁבָּת לִקְדֻשַּׁת יוֹם טוֹב הִבְדַּלְתָּ, וְאֶת יוֹם הַשְּׁבִיעִי מִשֵּׁשֶׁת יְמֵי הַמַּעֲשֶׂה קִדַּשְׁתָּ; הִבְדַּלְתָּ וְקִדַּשְׁתָּ אֶת עַמְּךָ יִשְׂרָאֵל בִּקְדֻשָּׁתֶךָ. בָּרוּךְ אַתָּה יְיָ הַמַּבְדִּיל בֵּין קֹדֶשׁ לְקֹדֶשׁ.

and the nations, between the seventh day and the six days of work. Thou hast made a distinction between the sanctity of the Sabbath and the sanctity of the Festivals, and hast sanctified the seventh day above the six days of work; Thou hast distinguished and sanctified Thy people Israel with Thy holiness. Blessed art Thou, O Lord, who makest distinction between holy and holy.

בָּרוּךְ אַתָּה יְיָ אֱלֹהֵינוּ מֶלֶךְ הָעוֹלָם, שֶׁהֶחֱיָנוּ וְקִיְּמָנוּ וְהִגִּיעָנוּ לַזְּמַן הַזֶּה.

Blessed art Thou, Lord our God, King of the universe, who hast kept us alive, and sustained us and enabled us to reach this season.

At the conclusion of the *Kiddush,* before the wine is drunk, all are seated; the males must recline on the left side. Everyone should try to drink all the wine in his goblet or at least most of it as quickly as possible, the maximum allowable time being four minutes. Before continuing, anyone present may present a *d'var Torah,* an insight or review of halakhic, aggadic, or historical material concerning this section of the Seder. Hereafter, at the conclusion of any section or paragraph, a *d'var Torah,* or any appropriate comment, may be offered concerning the section just concluded.

U'reḥatz: *Lave the Hands* וּרְחַץ

The Leader announces *U'reḥatz* and gives a short explanation of this rite. Proceed with the ritual washing of the hands but without the usual blessing. According to some, only the Leader washes; according to others, all perform this rite. A bowl, a pitcher with water, and a proper laver are brought to the table, or the usual ritual washing procedure may be used (see *Raḥtzah*, p. [30]). Before the hands may be washed ritually, they must be clean and all rings removed. The laver should hold at least

a half pint of water, the larger the better, and should be free of holes, cracks, or protruding parts. Its mouth should be wide and level. The vessel is taken in the right hand, placed in the left hand, filled with water, and a half pint is poured over the right hand covering it entirely up to the wrist. In order to leave no part of the hand unwashed, the fingers should be slighty separated and raised upward so that the water will run down the length of the fingers. The entire hand must be thus washed by the one act of pouring out the water. This process is repeated. The laver is then taken in the right hand and the same procedure repeated for the left hand. After washing, both hands are rubbed together and raised upward. The hands are then dried.

Karpas: *Eat the Karpas* כַּרְפַּס

The Leader announces *Karpas* and provides a short introduction. He then breaks off small pieces of the celery on the Seder plate. Each piece should be less than a *kezayit* (about one ounce). He dips them in the salt water and gives everyone a piece. If more is necessary, it is brought in from the kitchen. The Leader then explains to all present that when they pronounce the blessing of *boreh pri ha-adamah* below, it also applies to the *maror* and *korekh* that will follow later in the *Haggadah* service. He recites the blessing below aloud and everyone follows along word by word.

Blessed art Thou, Lord our God, King of the universe, Creator of the fruit of the earth.

בָּרוּךְ אַתָּה יְיָ אֱלֹהֵינוּ מֶלֶךְ
הָעוֹלָם, בּוֹרֵא פְּרִי הָאֲדָמָה.

The small pieces of *karpas* are eaten. The salt water and remaining *karpas* may be removed from the table.

Yaḥatz: *Divide the Middle Matzah* יַחַץ

The Leader announces *Yaḥatz* and explains the significance of what is to follow. He takes the middle matzah on the Seder plate and breaks it into two uneven parts. The smaller part he returns to its original position, and the larger part he wraps in a napkin which he puts between the pillows of his chair. This will be used as the *afikoman* which, according to custom, the children ''steal'' and hold for ransom.

Maggid: *Recite the Haggadah* מַגִּיד

The Leader announces *Maggid*, commenting that everyone present will now begin the recital of the main body of the *Haggadah*, the story of the Exodus. He uncovers the matzoth, raises the Seder plate, and reads aloud the *Ha Laḥma Anya.* From this point on, all present at the Seder recite the *Haggadah* with the Leader, unless otherwise instructed. It is a positive Biblical commandment that each person must recite the *Maggid* section. If one does not understand Hebrew, one should follow along in the English translation.

הִנְנִי מוּכָן וּמְזֻמָּן לְקַיֵּם הַמִּצְוָה לְסַפֵּר בִּיצִיאַת מִצְרַיִם, לְשֵׁם יִחוּד קוּדְשָׁא בְּרִיךְ הוּא וּשְׁכִינְתֵּיהּ עַל יְדֵי הַהוּא טָמִיר וְנֶעְלָם בְּשֵׁם כָּל יִשְׂרָאֵל.

I am ready and prepared to perform the commandment of relating the story of the Exodus out of Egypt, to honor the Holy One, blessed be He and His Divine Presence, through the hidden and secret Guardian, on behalf of all Israel.

הָא לַחְמָא עַנְיָא דִּי אֲכַלוּ אַבְהָתָנָא בְּאַרְעָא דְמִצְרָיִם. כָּל דִּכְפִין יֵיתֵי וְיֵיכֻל, כָּל דִּצְרִיךְ יֵיתֵי וְיִפְסַח. הָשַׁתָּא הָכָא, לַשָּׁנָה הַבָּאָה בְּאַרְעָא דְיִשְׂרָאֵל; הָשַׁתָּא עַבְדֵי, לַשָּׁנָה הַבָּאָה בְּנֵי חוֹרִין.

This is the bread of affliction that our ancestors ate in the land of Egypt. All who are hungry, let them come in and eat; all who are in need come in and celebrate the Passover. Now we are here, but next year may we be in the land of Israel. Now we are subjects, but next year may we be free men.

Put the Seder plate down, cover the matzoth (others remove the Seder plate from the table or move it to the end of the table). The wine goblets are filled. The Leader calls on the youngest present to ask or sing the *Mah Nishtannah*, the four questions.

מַה נִּשְׁתַּנָּה הַלַּיְלָה הַזֶּה מִכָּל הַלֵּילוֹת?
שֶׁבְּכָל הַלֵּילוֹת אָנוּ אוֹכְלִין חָמֵץ וּמַצָּה, הַלַּיְלָה הַזֶּה — כֻּלּוֹ מַצָּה.

Why is this night different from all other nights? On all other nights we may eat leavened bread and matzah, but on this night only matzah; on all

שֶׁבְּכָל הַלֵּילוֹת אָנוּ אוֹכְלִין שְׁאָר יְרָקוֹת, הַלַּיְלָה הַזֶּה — מָרוֹר. שֶׁבְּכָל הַלֵּילוֹת אֵין אָנוּ מַטְבִּילִין אֲפִילוּ פַּעַם אֶחָת, הַלַּיְלָה הַזֶּה — שְׁתֵּי פְעָמִים. שֶׁבְּכָל הַלֵּילוֹת אָנוּ אוֹכְלִין בֵּין יוֹשְׁבִין וּבֵין מְסֻבִּין, הַלַּיְלָה הַזֶּה — כֻּלָּנוּ מְסֻבִּין.

other nights we may eat all kinds of herbs, but on this night we must eat bitter herbs; on all other nights we need not dip even once, but on this night we must do so twice; on all other nights we eat either sitting upright or reclining, but on this night we all recline.

If the Seder plate had been removed, it is now returned, the matzoth are uncovered, and the Leader and company reply:

עֲבָדִים הָיִינוּ לְפַרְעֹה בְּמִצְרָיִם וַיּוֹצִיאֵנוּ יְיָ אֱלֹהֵינוּ מִשָּׁם בְּיָד חֲזָקָה וּבִזְרוֹעַ נְטוּיָה. וְאִלּוּ לֹא הוֹצִיא הַקָּדוֹשׁ בָּרוּךְ הוּא אֶת אֲבוֹתֵינוּ מִמִּצְרַיִם, הֲרֵי אָנוּ וּבָנֵינוּ וּבְנֵי בָנֵינוּ מְשֻׁעְבָּדִים הָיִינוּ לְפַרְעֹה בְּמִצְרָיִם. וַאֲפִילוּ כֻּלָּנוּ חֲכָמִים, כֻּלָּנוּ נְבוֹנִים, כֻּלָּנוּ זְקֵנִים, כֻּלָּנוּ יוֹדְעִים אֶת הַתּוֹרָה, מִצְוָה עָלֵינוּ לְסַפֵּר בִּיצִיאַת מִצְרָיִם. וְכָל הַמַּרְבֶּה לְסַפֵּר בִּיצִיאַת מִצְרַיִם הֲרֵי זֶה מְשֻׁבָּח.

We were slaves unto Pharaoh in Egypt, and the Lord our God brought us out from there with a mighty hand and an outstretched arm. If the Holy One, blessed be He, had not brought our ancestors out of Egypt, then we and our children, and our children's children, would still be in bondage to Pharaoh in Egypt. Even if we were all wise, all understanding, all intelligent, and all endowed with knowledge of the Torah, it would nevertheless be our duty to tell the story of the Exodus from Egypt, and whoever discusses more about the Exodus from Egypt, that one merits more praise.

מַעֲשֶׂה בְּרַבִּי אֱלִיעֶזֶר וְרַבִּי יְהוֹשֻׁעַ,

It is told of Rabbi

וְרַבִּי אֶלְעָזָר בֶּן עֲזַרְיָה וְרַבִּי עֲקִיבָא וְרַבִּי טַרְפוֹן, שֶׁהָיוּ מְסֻבִּין בִּבְנֵי בְרַק, וְהָיוּ מְסַפְּרִים בִּיצִיאַת מִצְרַיִם כָּל אוֹתוֹ הַלַּיְלָה, עַד שֶׁבָּאוּ תַלְמִידֵיהֶם וְאָמְרוּ לָהֶם: רַבּוֹתֵינוּ, הִגִּיעַ זְמַן קְרִיאַת שְׁמַע שֶׁל שַׁחֲרִית.

Eliezer, Rabbi Joshua, Rabbi Elazar ben Azariah, Rabbi Akiba and Rabbi Tarphon, that they were once reclining at the Seder together at Bene Brak and were recounting the story of the Exodus from Egypt the entire night until their pupils came and said to them: "Our Masters, it is time to recite the morning *Shema.*"

אָמַר רַבִּי אֶלְעָזָר בֶּן עֲזַרְיָה: הֲרֵי אֲנִי כְּבֶן שִׁבְעִים שָׁנָה, וְלֹא זָכִיתִי שֶׁתֵּאָמֵר יְצִיאַת מִצְרַיִם בַּלֵּילוֹת, עַד שֶׁדְּרָשָׁהּ בֶּן זוֹמָא. שֶׁנֶּאֱמַר: „לְמַעַן תִּזְכֹּר אֶת יוֹם צֵאתְךָ מֵאֶרֶץ מִצְרַיִם כֹּל יְמֵי חַיֶּיךָ”. „יְמֵי חַיֶּיךָ” — הַיָּמִים, „כֹּל יְמֵי חַיֶּיךָ” — הַלֵּילוֹת. וַחֲכָמִים אוֹמְרִים: „יְמֵי חַיֶּיךָ” — הָעוֹלָם הַזֶּה, „כֹּל יְמֵי חַיֶּיךָ” — לְהָבִיא לִימוֹת הַמָּשִׁיחַ.

Rabbi Elazar ben Azariah said: I am like one who is seventy years old and I have never been able to prove that the story of the Exodus from Egypt ought to be related at night, during the evening service, until Ben Zoma explained it: It is said, "That thou mayest remember the day when thou camest forth out of the land of Egypt all the days of thy life" (Deut. 16:3). "The days of thy life" would imply the days only; "all the days of thy life" indicates that the nights are included. The other Sages, however, expound it thus: "The days of thy life" refers to this world; "all the days of thy life" indicates that the days of the Messiah are included.

בָּרוּךְ הַמָּקוֹם, בָּרוּךְ הוּא. בָּרוּךְ שֶׁנָּתַן תּוֹרָה לְעַמּוֹ יִשְׂרָאֵל, בָּרוּךְ הוּא.

Blessed be the All-Present, blessed be He. Blessed be He who gave the Torah to His people Israel, blessed be He.

כְּנֶגֶד אַרְבָּעָה בָנִים דִּבְּרָה תוֹרָה: אֶחָד חָכָם, וְאֶחָד רָשָׁע, וְאֶחָד תָּם, וְאֶחָד שֶׁאֵינוֹ יוֹדֵעַ לִשְׁאוֹל.

The Torah speaks concerning four sons: one wise, one wicked, one simple, and one who

חָכָם מַה הוּא אוֹמֵר: „מָה הָעֵדֹת וְהַחֻקִּים וְהַמִּשְׁפָּטִים אֲשֶׁר צִוָּה יְיָ אֱלֹהֵינוּ אֶתְכֶם". וְאַף אַתָּה אֱמָר לוֹ כְּהִלְכוֹת הַפֶּסַח: אֵין מַפְטִירִין אַחַר הַפֶּסַח אֲפִיקוֹמָן.

רָשָׁע מַה הוּא אוֹמֵר: „מָה הָעֲבֹדָה הַזֹּאת לָכֶם". „לָכֶם" — וְלֹא לוֹ. וּלְפִי שֶׁהוֹצִיא אֶת עַצְמוֹ מִן הַכְּלָל כָּפַר בָּעִקָּר. וְאַף אַתָּה הַקְהֵה אֶת שִׁנָּיו וֶאֱמָר לוֹ: „בַּעֲבוּר זֶה עָשָׂה יְיָ לִי בְּצֵאתִי מִמִּצְרָיִם". „לִי" — וְלֹא לוֹ, אִלּוּ הָיָה שָׁם לֹא הָיָה נִגְאָל.

תָּם מַה הוּא אוֹמֵר: „מַה זֹּאת". וְאָמַרְתָּ אֵלָיו: „בְּחֹזֶק יָד הוֹצִיאָנוּ יְיָ מִמִּצְרַיִם מִבֵּית עֲבָדִים".

וְשֶׁאֵינוֹ יוֹדֵעַ לִשְׁאוֹל — אַתְּ פְּתַח לוֹ, שֶׁנֶּאֱמַר: „וְהִגַּדְתָּ לְבִנְךָ בַּיּוֹם הַהוּא לֵאמֹר, בַּעֲבוּר זֶה עָשָׂה יְיָ לִי בְּצֵאתִי מִמִּצְרָיִם".

does not know how to ask.

The Wise Son, what does he say? "What mean the testimonies, and the statutes, and the ordinances, which the Lord our God hath commanded you?" (Deut. 6:20). You must explain to him that the laws of Passover state: no dessert may be eaten after partaking of the paschal lamb.

The Wicked Son, what does he say? "What mean ye by this service?" (Ex. 12:26). "Ye," he insinuates, not himself. Since he has excluded himself from the community, he has denied a cardinal principle. Therefore you should counter abruptly, "It is because of that which the Lord did for me when I came forth out of Egypt" (Ex. 13:8): for *me*, not for *him*, for if he had been there he would not have been redeemed.

The Simple Son, what does he say? "What is this?" (Ex. 13:14). And you shall say to him, "By strength of hand the Lord brought us out from Egypt, from the house of bondage" (*Ibid.*).

As for him who does not know how to ask, you must begin for him, as it is said: "And thou shalt tell thy son in that day, saying: It is because of that which the Lord did for me when I came

יָכוֹל מֵרֹאשׁ חֹדֶשׁ? — תַּלְמוּד לוֹמַר: „בַּיּוֹם הַהוּא". אִי בַּיּוֹם הַהוּא, יָכוֹל מִבְּעוֹד יוֹם? — תַּלְמוּד לוֹמַר: „בַּעֲבוּר זֶה". „בַּעֲבוּר זֶה", לֹא אָמַרְתִּי אֶלָּא בְּשָׁעָה שֶׁיֵּשׁ מַצָּה וּמָרוֹר מֻנָּחִים לְפָנֶיךָ.

מִתְּחִלָּה עוֹבְדֵי עֲבוֹדָה זָרָה הָיוּ אֲבוֹתֵינוּ, וְעַכְשָׁו קֵרְבָנוּ הַמָּקוֹם לַעֲבוֹדָתוֹ, שֶׁנֶּאֱמַר: „וַיֹּאמֶר יְהוֹשֻׁעַ אֶל כָּל הָעָם, כֹּה אָמַר יְיָ אֱלֹהֵי יִשְׂרָאֵל: בְּעֵבֶר הַנָּהָר יָשְׁבוּ אֲבוֹתֵיכֶם מֵעוֹלָם, תֶּרַח אֲבִי אַבְרָהָם וַאֲבִי נָחוֹר, וַיַּעַבְדוּ אֱלֹהִים אֲחֵרִים. וָאֶקַּח אֶת אֲבִיכֶם אֶת אַבְרָהָם מֵעֵבֶר הַנָּהָר וָאוֹלֵךְ אוֹתוֹ בְּכָל אֶרֶץ כְּנָעַן, וָאַרְבֶּה אֶת זַרְעוֹ וָאֶתֵּן לוֹ אֶת יִצְחָק. וָאֶתֵּן לְיִצְחָק אֶת יַעֲקֹב וְאֶת עֵשָׂו, וָאֶתֵּן לְעֵשָׂו אֶת הַר שֵׂעִיר לָרֶשֶׁת אוֹתוֹ, וְיַעֲקֹב וּבָנָיו יָרְדוּ מִצְרָיִם."

בָּרוּךְ שׁוֹמֵר הַבְטָחָתוֹ לְיִשְׂרָאֵל, בָּרוּךְ הוּא. שֶׁהַקָּדוֹשׁ בָּרוּךְ הוּא

forth out of Egypt" (Ex. 13:8).

It might be thought that the *Haggadah* should be recited on the first day of Nison. The text says, however, "in that day." It might be thought that the *Haggadah* should begin in the daytime, but the text says, "because of that," which applies only to the time when the matzah and bitter herb are set before you.

In the beginning our ancestors were idol worshippers but now the All-Present has brought us to His service, as it is said: "And Joshua said unto all the people: Thus saith the Lord, the God of Israel: Your father dwelt of old time beyond the River, even Terah, the father of Abraham, and the father of Nahor; and they served other gods. And I took your father Abraham from beyond the River, and led him throughout the land of Canaan, and multiplied his seed, and gave him Isaac. And I gave unto Isaac, Jacob and Esau; and I gave unto Esau mount Seir, to possess it; and Jacob and his children went down into Egypt" (Joshua 24:2–4).

Blessed be He who keeps his promise to Israel; blessed be He. For the Holy One, blessed be He, determined the end of the bondage in order to fulfill that which He

חִשַּׁב אֶת הַקֵּץ, לַעֲשׂוֹת כְּמָה שֶּׁאָמַר לְאַבְרָהָם אָבִינוּ בִּבְרִית בֵּין הַבְּתָרִים, שֶׁנֶּאֱמַר: „וַיֹּאמֶר לְאַבְרָם יָדֹעַ תֵּדַע כִּי גֵר יִהְיֶה זַרְעֲךָ בְּאֶרֶץ לֹא לָהֶם וַעֲבָדוּם וְעִנּוּ אֹתָם אַרְבַּע מֵאוֹת שָׁנָה. וְגַם אֶת הַגּוֹי אֲשֶׁר יַעֲבֹדוּ דָּן אָנֹכִי, וְאַחֲרֵי כֵן יֵצְאוּ בִּרְכֻשׁ גָּדוֹל״.

had said to Abraham our father in the Pact between the Portions, as it is said: "And He said unto Abram: Know of a surety that thy seed shall be a stranger in a land that is not theirs, and shall serve them; and they shall afflict them four hundred years; and also that nation, whom they shall serve, will I judge; and afterward shall they come out with great substance" (Gen. 15:13–14).

The Leader first covers the matzoth, then he and the company raise the wine cups and sing the following passage:

וְהִיא שֶׁעָמְדָה לַאֲבוֹתֵינוּ וְלָנוּ; שֶׁלֹּא אֶחָד בִּלְבָד עָמַד עָלֵינוּ לְכַלּוֹתֵנוּ, אֶלָּא שֶׁבְּכָל דּוֹר וָדוֹר עוֹמְדִים עָלֵינוּ לְכַלּוֹתֵנוּ, וְהַקָּדוֹשׁ בָּרוּךְ הוּא מַצִּילֵנוּ מִיָּדָם.

This covenant has sustained our fathers and us. For not only one man has risen up against us to destroy us, but in every generation men rise up against us to destroy us; but the Holy One, blessed be He, delivers us from their hands.

The wine goblets are put down and the Leader uncovers the matzoth.

צֵא וּלְמַד מַה בִּקֵּשׁ לָבָן הָאֲרַמִּי לַעֲשׂוֹת לְיַעֲקֹב אָבִינוּ. שֶׁפַּרְעֹה לֹא גָזַר אֶלָּא עַל הַזְּכָרִים, וְלָבָן בִּקֵּשׁ לַעֲקֹר אֶת הַכֹּל, שֶׁנֶּאֱמַר: „אֲרַמִּי אֹבֵד אָבִי, וַיֵּרֶד מִצְרַיְמָה וַיָּגָר שָׁם בִּמְתֵי מְעָט, וַיְהִי שָׁם לְגוֹי גָּדוֹל, עָצוּם וָרָב״.

Go forth and learn what Laban the Aramite sought to do to Jacob our father. For Pharaoh issued his edict only against the males, but Laban sought to uproot all, as it is said: "The Aramite would have destroyed my father, and he went down into Egypt and sojourned there, few in number; and he became there a

„וַיֵּרֶד מִצְרַיְמָה" — אָנוּס עַל פִּי הַדִּבּוּר. „וַיָּגָר שָׁם" — מְלַמֵּד שֶׁלֹּא יָרַד יַעֲקֹב אָבִינוּ לְהִשְׁתַּקֵּעַ בְּמִצְרַיִם אֶלָּא לָגוּר שָׁם, שֶׁנֶּאֱמַר: „וַיֹּאמְרוּ אֶל פַּרְעֹה לָגוּר בָּאָרֶץ בָּאנוּ, כִּי אֵין מִרְעֶה לַצֹּאן אֲשֶׁר לַעֲבָדֶיךָ כִּי כָבֵד הָרָעָב בְּאֶרֶץ כְּנָעַן, וְעַתָּה יֵשְׁבוּ נָא עֲבָדֶיךָ בְּאֶרֶץ גֹּשֶׁן".

„בִּמְתֵי מְעָט" — כְּמָה שֶׁנֶּאֱמַר: „בְּשִׁבְעִים נֶפֶשׁ יָרְדוּ אֲבֹתֶיךָ מִצְרָיְמָה וְעַתָּה שָׂמְךָ יְיָ אֱלֹהֶיךָ כְּכוֹכְבֵי הַשָּׁמַיִם לָרֹב". „וַיְהִי שָׁם לְגוֹי" — מְלַמֵּד שֶׁהָיוּ יִשְׂרָאֵל מְצֻיָּנִים שָׁם. „גָּדוֹל עָצוּם" —כְּמָה שֶׁנֶּאֱמַר: „וּבְנֵי יִשְׂרָאֵל פָּרוּ וַיִּשְׁרְצוּ וַיִּרְבּוּ וַיַּעַצְמוּ בִּמְאֹד מְאֹד וַתִּמָּלֵא הָאָרֶץ אֹתָם". „וָרָב" — כְּמָה שֶׁנֶּאֱמַר: „רְבָבָה כְּצֶמַח הַשָּׂדֶה נְתַתִּיךְ, וַתִּרְבִּי וַתִּגְדְּלִי וַתָּבֹאִי בַּעֲדִי עֲדָיִים, שָׁדַיִם נָכֹנוּ וּשְׂעָרֵךְ צִמֵּחַ וְאַתְּ עֵרֹם וְעֶרְיָה".

„וַיָּרֵעוּ אֹתָנוּ הַמִּצְרִים וַיְעַנּוּנוּ

nation, great, mighty, and populous" (Deut. 26:5). "And he went down into Egypt," compelled by the Divine Decree. "And sojourned there," teaching us that he did not go to settle but only to reside there temporarily, as it is said: "And they said unto Pharaoh: To sojourn in the land are we come; for there is no pasture for thy servants' flocks; for the famine is sore in the land of Canaan. Now therefore, we pray thee, let thy servants dwell in the land of Goshen" (Gen. 47:4).

"Few in number," as it is said: "Thy fathers went down into Egypt with threescore and ten persons; and now the Lord thy God hath made thee as the stars of heaven for multitude" (Deut. 10:22). "And he became there a nation:" teaching us that Israel was a distinctive nation there. "Great, mighty," as it is said: "And the children of Israel were fruitful, and increased abundantly, and multiplied, and waxed exceedingly mighty; and the land was filled with them" (Ex. 1:7). "And populous," as it is said: "I caused thee to increase, even as the growth of the field. And thou didst increase and grow up, and thou camest to excellent beauty: thy breasts were fashioned, and thy hair

וַיִּתְּנוּ עָלֵינוּ עֲבֹדָה קָשָׁה". „וַיָּרֵעוּ אֹתָנוּ הַמִּצְרִים" — כְּמָה שֶׁנֶּאֱמַר: „הָבָה נִתְחַכְּמָה לוֹ פֶּן יִרְבֶּה וְהָיָה כִּי תִקְרֶאנָה מִלְחָמָה וְנוֹסַף גַּם הוּא עַל שֹׂנְאֵינוּ וְנִלְחַם בָּנוּ וְעָלָה מִן הָאָרֶץ". „וַיְעַנּוּנוּ" — כְּמָה שֶׁנֶּאֱמַר: „וַיָּשִׂימוּ עָלָיו שָׂרֵי מִסִּים לְמַעַן עַנֹּתוֹ בְּסִבְלֹתָם וַיִּבֶן עָרֵי מִסְכְּנוֹת לְפַרְעֹה אֶת פִּתֹם וְאֶת רַעַמְסֵס". „וַיִּתְּנוּ עָלֵינוּ עֲבֹדָה קָשָׁה" — כְּמָה שֶׁנֶּאֱמַר: „וַיַּעֲבִדוּ מִצְרַיִם אֶת בְּנֵי יִשְׂרָאֵל בְּפָרֶךְ".

„וַנִּצְעַק אֶל יְיָ אֱלֹהֵי אֲבֹתֵינוּ, וַיִּשְׁמַע יְיָ אֶת קֹלֵנוּ, וַיַּרְא אֶת עָנְיֵנוּ וְאֶת עֲמָלֵנוּ וְאֶת לַחֲצֵנוּ". „וַנִּצְעַק אֶל יְיָ אֱלֹהֵי אֲבוֹתֵינוּ" — כְּמָה שֶׁנֶּאֱמַר: „וַיְהִי בַיָּמִים הָרַבִּים הָהֵם וַיָּמָת מֶלֶךְ מִצְרַיִם וַיֵּאָנְחוּ בְנֵי יִשְׂרָאֵל מִן הָעֲבֹדָה וַיִּזְעָקוּ, וַתַּעַל שַׁוְעָתָם אֶל הָאֱלֹהִים מִן הָעֲבֹדָה". „וַיִּשְׁמַע יְיָ אֶת קוֹלֵנוּ" — כְּמָה שֶׁנֶּאֱמַר: „וַיִּשְׁמַע אֱלֹהִים אֶת נַאֲקָתָם, וַיִּזְכֹּר אֱלֹהִים אֶת בְּרִיתוֹ אֶת אַבְרָהָם אֶת יִצְחָק וְאֶת

was grown; yet thou wast naked and bare" (Ezek. 16:7).

"And the Egyptians dealt ill with us, and afflicted us, and laid upon us hard bondage" (Deut. 26:6). "And the Egyptians dealt ill with us," as it is said: "Come, let us deal wisely with them, lest they multiply, and it came to pass, that, when there befalleth us any war, they also join themselves unto our enemies, and fight against us, and get them up out of the land" (Ex. 1:10). "And afflicted us," as it is said: "Therefore they did set over them taskmasters to afflict them with their burdens. And they built for Pharaoh storecities, Pithom and Raamses" (Ex. 1:11). "And laid upon us hard bondage," as it is said: "And the Egyptians made the children of Israel to serve with rigor" (Ex. 1:13).

"And we cried unto the Lord, the God of our fathers, and the Lord heard our voice, and saw our affliction, and our toil, and our oppression" (Deut. 26:7). "And we cried unto the Lord, the God of our fathers," as it is said: "And it came to pass in the course of those many days that the king of Egypt died; and the children of Israel sighed by reason of the bondage, and they cried, and

יַעֲקֹב". „וַיַּרְא אֶת עָנְיֵנוּ" — זוֹ פְּרִישׁוּת דֶּרֶךְ אֶרֶץ, כְּמָה שֶׁנֶּאֱמַר: „וַיַּרְא אֱלֹהִים אֶת בְּנֵי יִשְׂרָאֵל וַיֵּדַע אֱלֹהִים". „וְאֶת עֲמָלֵנוּ" — אֵלּוּ הַבָּנִים, כְּמָה שֶׁנֶּאֱמַר: „כָּל הַבֵּן הַיִּלּוֹד הַיְאֹרָה תַּשְׁלִיכֻהוּ וְכָל־הַבַּת תְּחַיּוּן". „וְאֶת לַחֲצֵנוּ" — זֶה הַדְּחַק, כְּמָה שֶׁנֶּאֱמַר: „וְגַם רָאִיתִי אֶת הַלַּחַץ אֲשֶׁר מִצְרַיִם לֹחֲצִים אֹתָם".

„וַיּוֹצִאֵנוּ יְיָ מִמִּצְרַיִם בְּיָד חֲזָקָה וּבִזְרֹעַ נְטוּיָה וּבְמֹרָא גָּדֹל וּבְאֹתוֹת וּבְמֹפְתִים". „וַיּוֹצִאֵנוּ יְיָ מִמִּצְרַיִם" —לֹא עַל יְדֵי מַלְאָךְ, וְלֹא עַל יְדֵי שָׂרָף, וְלֹא עַל יְדֵי שָׁלִיחַ, אֶלָּא הַקָּדוֹשׁ בָּרוּךְ הוּא בִּכְבוֹדוֹ וּבְעַצְמוֹ, שֶׁנֶּאֱמַר: „וְעָבַרְתִּי בְאֶרֶץ מִצְרַיִם בַּלַּיְלָה הַזֶּה וְהִכֵּיתִי כָל בְּכוֹר בְּאֶרֶץ מִצְרַיִם מֵאָדָם וְעַד בְּהֵמָה, וּבְכָל אֱלֹהֵי מִצְרַיִם אֶעֱשֶׂה שְׁפָטִים אֲנִי יְיָ". „וְעָבַרְתִּי בְאֶרֶץ מִצְרַיִם בַּלַּיְלָה הַזֶּה" אֲנִי וְלֹא מַלְאָךְ, „וְהִכֵּיתִי כָל בְּכוֹר בְּאֶרֶץ מִצְרַיִם" —אֲנִי וְלֹא שָׂרָף. „וּבְכָל

their cry came up unto God by reason of the bondage'' (Ex. 2:23). ''And the Lord heard our voice,'' as it is said: ''And God heard their groaning, and God remembered His covenant with Abraham, with Isaac, and with Jacob'' (Ex. 2:24). ''And saw our affliction,'' this refers to the separation of husband and wife, as it is said: ''And God saw the children of Israel, and God took cognizance of them'' (Ex. 2:25). ''And our toil,'' this refers to the sons, as it is said: ''Every son that is born ye shall cast into the river, and every daughter ye shall save alive'' (Ex. 1:22). ''And our oppression,'' this refers to the severity, as it is said: ''Moreover, I have seen the oppression wherewith the Egyptians oppress them'' (Ex. 3:9).

''And the Lord brought us forth out of Egypt with a mighty hand, and with an outstretched arm, and with great terribleness, and with signs, and with wonders'' (Deut. 26:8). ''And the Lord brought us forth out of Egypt,'' not by the hand of an angel, and not by the hand of a seraph, and not by the hand of a messenger, but the Holy One, blessed be He, in His glory and in His Self, as it is said: ''For I will go through the land

of Egypt in that night, and will smite all the first-born in the land of Egypt, both man and beast; and against all the gods of Egypt I will execute judgments: I am the Lord" (Ex. 12:12). "For I will go through the land of Egypt in that night," I, not an angel: "And will smite all the first-born in the land of Egypt," I, not a seraph: "And against all the gods of Egypt I will execute judgments," I, not a messenger. "I am the Lord," I am He, and no other. "With a mighty hand," this refers to the murrain, as it is said: "Behold, the hand of the Lord is upon thy cattle which are in the field, upon the horses, upon the asses, upon the camels, upon the herds, and upon the flocks; there shall be a very grievous murrain" (Ex. 9:3). "And with an outstretched arm," this refers to the sword, as it is said: "Having a drawn sword in his hand stretched out over Jerusalem" (I Chron. 21:16). "And with great terribleness," this refers to the manifestation of the Divine Presence, as it is said: "Or hath God assayed to go and take Him a nation from the midst of another nation, by trials, by signs, and by wonders, and by war, and by a mighty hand, and by an outstretched arm, and by great ter-

אֱלֹהֵי מִצְרַיִם אֶעֱשֶׂה שְׁפָטִים" — אֲנִי וְלֹא הַשָּׁלִיחַ. „אֲנִי יְיָ" — אֲנִי הוּא וְלֹא אַחֵר. „בְּיָד חֲזָקָה" — זוֹ הַדֶּבֶר, כְּמָה שֶׁנֶּאֱמַר: „הִנֵּה יַד יְיָ הוֹיָה בְּמִקְנְךָ אֲשֶׁר בַּשָּׂדֶה, בַּסּוּסִים, בַּחֲמֹרִים, בַּגְּמַלִּים, בַּבָּקָר וּבַצֹּאן דֶּבֶר כָּבֵד מְאֹד". „וּבִזְרֹעַ נְטוּיָה" — זוֹ הַחֶרֶב, כְּמָה שֶׁנֶּאֱמַר: „וְחַרְבּוֹ שְׁלוּפָה בְּיָדוֹ נְטוּיָה עַל יְרוּשָׁלָםִ".

„וּבְמֹרָא גָּדֹל" — זֶה גִּלּוּי שְׁכִינָה, כְּמָה שֶׁנֶּאֱמַר: „אוֹ הֲנִסָּה אֱלֹהִים לָבוֹא לָקַחַת לוֹ גוֹי מִקֶּרֶב גּוֹי, בְּמַסֹּת בְּאֹתֹת וּבְמוֹפְתִים וּבְמִלְחָמָה וּבְיָד חֲזָקָה וּבִזְרוֹעַ נְטוּיָה וּבְמוֹרָאִים גְּדֹלִים; כְּכֹל אֲשֶׁר עָשָׂה לָכֶם יְיָ אֱלֹהֵיכֶם בְּמִצְרַיִם לְעֵינֶיךָ".

„וּבְאֹתוֹת" — זֶה הַמַּטֶּה, כְּמָה שֶׁנֶּאֱמַר: „וְאֶת הַמַּטֶּה הַזֶּה תִּקַּח

בְּיָדֶךָ אֲשֶׁר תַּעֲשֶׂה בּוֹ אֶת הָאֹתֹת".

rors, according to all that the Lord your God did for you in Egypt before thine eyes?" (Deut. 4:4). "And with signs," this refers to the rod, as it is said: "And thou shalt take in thy hand this rod, wherewith thou shalt do the signs" (Ex. 4:17). "And with wonders," this refers to the blood, as it is said: "And I will show wonders in the heavens and in the earth" (Joel 3:3).

„וּבְמֹפְתִים" — זֶה הַדָּם, כְּמָה שֶׁנֶּאֱמַר: „וְנָתַתִּי מוֹפְתִים בַּשָּׁמַיִם וּבָאָרֶץ":

When pronouncing each of the three words below, *Dam, Ve-Ash, Ve-Simrat Oshen,* each person dips the index finger into the wine cup and removes a drop of wine (some use the fourth finger, some the pinky, while others tip the cup), one drop for each of the words, onto a broken plate or vessel.

„דָּם, וָאֵשׁ, וְתִימְרוֹת עָשָׁן".

"Blood, and fire, and pillars of smoke" (*Ibid.*).

דָּבָר אַחֵר: „בְּיָד חֲזָקָה" — שְׁתַּיִם, „וּבִזְרֹעַ נְטוּיָה" — שְׁתַּיִם, „וּבְמֹרָא גָּדֹל" — שְׁתַּיִם, „וּבְאֹתוֹת" — שְׁתַּיִם, „וּבְמֹפְתִים" — שְׁתַּיִם, אֵלּוּ עֶשֶׂר מַכּוֹת שֶׁהֵבִיא הַקָּדוֹשׁ בָּרוּךְ הוּא עַל הַמִּצְרִים בְּמִצְרַיִם. וְאֵלּוּ הֵן:

Another explanation is as follows: "with a mighty hand," indicates two; "and with an outstretched arm," two; "and with great terribleness," two; "and with signs," two; "and with wonders," two. These indicate the ten plagues which the Holy One, blessed be He, brought upon the Egyptians in Egypt, to wit:

At the mention of each of the ten plagues, a drop of wine is removed from the wine cups as described previously.

דָּם · צְפַרְדֵּעַ · כִּנִּים · עָרוֹב · דֶּבֶר · שְׁחִין · בָּרָד · אַרְבֶּה · חֹשֶׁךְ · מַכַּת בְּכוֹרוֹת.

BLOOD, FROGS, VERMIN, WILD BEASTS, MURRAIN, BOILS, HAIL, LOCUSTS, DARKNESS, SLAYING OF THE FIRST-BORN.

Rabbi Judah used to refer to them by abbreviation, thus:

רַבִּי יְהוּדָה הָיָה נוֹתֵן בָּהֶם סִמָּנִים:

At the mention of each of the mnemonics below, remove a drop of wine and place it on the broken plate as described previously. After the final drop of wine is spilled, the broken plates are removed from the table and the wine cups are refilled.

D'tzaḥ, Adash, B'aḥav.

דְּצַ״ךְ, עֲדַ״שׁ, בְּאַחַ״ב.

Rabbi Jose the Galilean says: From where can one deduce that if the Egyptians received ten plagues in Egypt, they received fifty plagues on the sea? With regard to Egypt, what does the text say? "Then the magicians said unto Pharaoh: This is the finger of God" (Ex. 8:15); and at the sea, what does the text say? "And Israel saw the great hand which the Lord laid upon the Egyptians, and the people feared the Lord; and they believed in the Lord, and in His servant Moses" (Ex. 14:31). How many plagues did they receive by one finger? Ten plagues. Hence you can deduce, that in Egypt they received ten plagues, while at the sea they received fifty plagues.

רַבִּי יוֹסֵי הַגְּלִילִי אוֹמֵר: מִנַּיִן אַתָּה אוֹמֵר שֶׁלָּקוּ הַמִּצְרִים בְּמִצְרַיִם עֶשֶׂר מַכּוֹת, וְעַל הַיָּם לָקוּ חֲמִשִּׁים מַכּוֹת? בְּמִצְרַיִם מַה הוּא אוֹמֵר: „וַיֹּאמְרוּ הַחַרְטֻמִּם אֶל פַּרְעֹה אֶצְבַּע אֱלֹהִים הִוא״. וְעַל הַיָּם מַה הוּא אוֹמֵר — „וַיַּרְא יִשְׂרָאֵל אֶת הַיָּד הַגְּדֹלָה אֲשֶׁר עָשָׂה יְיָ בְּמִצְרַיִם, וַיִּירְאוּ הָעָם אֶת יְיָ וַיַּאֲמִינוּ בַּייָ וּבְמשֶׁה עַבְדּוֹ״. כַּמָּה לָקוּ בְּאֶצְבַּע — עֶשֶׂר מַכּוֹת, אֱמוֹר מֵעַתָּה: בְּמִצְרַיִם לָקוּ עֶשֶׂר מַכּוֹת, וְעַל הַיָּם לָקוּ חֲמִשִּׁים מַכּוֹת.

Rabbi Eliezar says: From where can one deduce that every plague which the Holy One, blessed be He, brought upon the Egyptians in Egypt was equivalent to four plagues? It is said: "He sent forth upon them the fierceness of

רַבִּי אֱלִיעֶזֶר אוֹמֵר: מִנַּיִן שֶׁכָּל מַכָּה וּמַכָּה שֶׁהֵבִיא הַקָּדוֹשׁ בָּרוּךְ הוּא עַל הַמִּצְרִים בְּמִצְרַיִם הָיְתָה שֶׁל אַרְבַּע מַכּוֹת, שֶׁנֶּאֱמַר: „יְשַׁלַּח בָּם חֲרוֹן אַפּוֹ עֶבְרָה וָזַעַם וְצָרָה

מִשְׁלַחַת מַלְאֲכֵי רָעִים". „עֶבְרָה" — אַחַת, „וָזַעַם" — שְׁתַּיִם, „וְצָרָה" — שָׁלֹשׁ, „מִשְׁלַחַת מַלְאֲכֵי רָעִים" — אַרְבַּע. אֱמוֹר מֵעַתָּה: בְּמִצְרַיִם לָקוּ אַרְבָּעִים מַכּוֹת, וְעַל הַיָּם, לָקוּ מָאתַיִם מַכּוֹת.

His anger, wrath, and indignation, and trouble, a sending of messengers of evil" (Ps. 78:49). "Wrath" indicates one; "indignation," two; "trouble," three; "a sending of messengers of evil," four. Hence you can deduce that in Egypt they received forty plagues, while at the sea they received two hundred plagues.

רַבִּי עֲקִיבָא אוֹמֵר: מִנַּיִן שֶׁכָּל מַכָּה וּמַכָּה שֶׁהֵבִיא הַקָּדוֹשׁ בָּרוּךְ הוּא עַל הַמִּצְרִים בְּמִצְרַיִם הָיְתָה שֶׁל חָמֵשׁ מַכּוֹת — שֶׁנֶּאֱמַר: „יְשַׁלַּח בָּם חֲרוֹן אַפּוֹ עֶבְרָה וָזַעַם וְצָרָה מִשְׁלַחַת מַלְאֲכֵי רָעִים". „חֲרוֹן אַפּוֹ" — אַחַת, „עֶבְרָה" — שְׁתַּיִם, „וָזַעַם" — שָׁלֹשׁ, „וְצָרָה" — אַרְבַּע, „מִשְׁלַחַת מַלְאֲכֵי רָעִים" — חָמֵשׁ. אֱמוֹר מֵעַתָּה: בְּמִצְרַיִם לָקוּ חֲמִשִּׁים מַכּוֹת, וְעַל הַיָּם לָקוּ חֲמִשִּׁים וּמָאתַיִם מַכּוֹת.

Rabbi Akiba says: From where can one deduce that every plague which the Holy One, blessed be He, brought upon the Egyptians in Egypt was equivalent to five plagues? It is said: "He sent forth upon them the fierceness of His anger, wrath, and indignation, and trouble, a sending of messengers of evil" (*Ibid.*). "The fierceness of His anger" indicates one; "wrath," two; "indignation," three; "trouble," four; "a sending of messengers of evil," five. Hence you can deduce that in Egypt they received fifty plagues, while at the sea they received two hundred and fifty plagues.

כַּמָּה מַעֲלוֹת טוֹבוֹת לַמָּקוֹם עָלֵינוּ!

How many are the favors that the Almighty has bestowed upon us.

אִלּוּ הוֹצִיאָנוּ מִמִּצְרַיִם וְלֹא עָשָׂה בָהֶם שְׁפָטִים — דַּיֵּנוּ,

Had He brought us out of Egypt and not executed judgment upon the Egyptians, IT WOULD HAVE BEEN SUFFICIENT.

Had He executed judgment on them and not wrought justice on their gods, IT WOULD HAVE BEEN SUFFICIENT.

Had He wrought justice on their gods and not slain their first-born, IT WOULD HAVE BEEN SUFFICIENT.

Had He slain their first-born and not given us their wealth, IT WOULD HAVE BEEN SUFFICIENT.

Had He given us their wealth and not split the sea for us, IT WOULD HAVE BEEN SUFFICIENT.

Had He split the sea for us and not led us through it on dry land, IT WOULD HAVE BEEN SUFFICIENT.

Had He led us through it on dry land and not sunk our oppressors in its depths, IT WOULD HAVE BEEN SUFFICIENT.

Had He sunk our oppressors in its depths and not satisfied our wants in the wilderness for forty years, IT WOULD HAVE BEEN SUFFICIENT.

Had He satisfied our wants in the wilderness for forty years and not fed us the manna, IT WOULD HAVE BEEN SUFFICIENT.

Had He fed us with the manna and not given us the Sabbath, IT WOULD HAVE BEEN SUFFICIENT.

Had He given us the Sabbath and not brought us to Mount

אִלּוּ עָשָׂה בָהֶם שְׁפָטִים וְלֹא עָשָׂה בֵאלֹהֵיהֶם — דַּיֵּנוּ,

אִלּוּ עָשָׂה בֵאלֹהֵיהֶם וְלֹא הָרַג אֶת בְּכוֹרֵיהֶם — דַּיֵּנוּ,

אִלּוּ הָרַג אֶת בְּכוֹרֵיהֶם וְלֹא נָתַן לָנוּ אֶת מָמוֹנָם — דַּיֵּנוּ,

אִלּוּ נָתַן לָנוּ אֶת מָמוֹנָם וְלֹא קָרַע לָנוּ אֶת הַיָּם — דַּיֵּנוּ,

אִלּוּ קָרַע לָנוּ אֶת הַיָּם וְלֹא הֶעֱבִירָנוּ בְתוֹכוֹ בֶּחָרָבָה — דַּיֵּנוּ,

אִלּוּ הֶעֱבִירָנוּ בְתוֹכוֹ בֶּחָרָבָה וְלֹא שִׁקַּע צָרֵינוּ בְּתוֹכוֹ — דַּיֵּנוּ,

אִלּוּ שִׁקַּע צָרֵינוּ בְּתוֹכוֹ וְלֹא סִפֵּק צָרְכֵּנוּ בַּמִּדְבָּר אַרְבָּעִים שָׁנָה — דַּיֵּנוּ,

אִלּוּ סִפֵּק צָרְכֵּנוּ בַּמִּדְבָּר אַרְבָּעִים שָׁנָה וְלֹא הֶאֱכִילָנוּ אֶת הַמָּן — דַּיֵּנוּ,

אִלּוּ הֶאֱכִילָנוּ אֶת הַמָּן וְלֹא נָתַן לָנוּ אֶת הַשַּׁבָּת — דַּיֵּנוּ,

אִלּוּ נָתַן לָנוּ אֶת הַשַּׁבָּת וְלֹא קֵרְבָנוּ לִפְנֵי הַר סִינַי — דַּיֵּנוּ,

אִלּוּ קֵרְבָנוּ לִפְנֵי הַר סִינַי וְלֹא נָתַן לָנוּ אֶת הַתּוֹרָה — דַּיֵּנוּ,

Sinai, IT WOULD HAVE BEEN SUFFICIENT.

Had He brought us to Mount Sinai and not given us the Torah, IT WOULD HAVE BEEN SUFFICIENT.

Had He given us the Torah and not brought us into the Land of Israel, IT WOULD HAVE BEEN SUFFICIENT.

Had He brought us into the Land of Israel and not built us the Temple, IT WOULD HAVE BEEN SUFFICIENT.

How much more so, then, hath the Almighty a double, and redoubled, call upon our thankfulness. For He brought us out of Egypt, and executed judgment upon the Egyptians, and wrought justice on their gods, and slew their first-born, and gave us their wealth, and split the sea for us, and led us through it on dry land, and sank our oppressors in its depths, and satisfied our wants in the wilderness for forty years, and fed us with the manna, and gave us the Sabbath, and brought us to Mount Sinai, and gave us the Torah, and brought us into the Land of Israel, and built us the Temple to atone for all our sins.

Rabban Gamaliel said: Any person who does not mention the following three things on Passover has not fulfilled his obligation; and these are: The Passover

אִלּוּ נָתַן לָנוּ אֶת הַתּוֹרָה וְלֹא הִכְנִיסָנוּ לְאֶרֶץ יִשְׂרָאֵל — דַּיֵּנוּ,

אִלּוּ הִכְנִיסָנוּ לְאֶרֶץ יִשְׂרָאֵל וְלֹא בָנָה לָנוּ אֶת בֵּית הַבְּחִירָה — דַּיֵּנוּ,

עַל אַחַת כַּמָּה וְכַמָּה, טוֹבָה כְפוּלָה וּמְכֻפֶּלֶת לַמָּקוֹם עָלֵינוּ: שֶׁהוֹצִיאָנוּ מִמִּצְרַיִם, וְעָשָׂה בָהֶם שְׁפָטִים, וְעָשָׂה בֵאלֹהֵיהֶם, וְהָרַג אֶת בְּכוֹרֵיהֶם, וְנָתַן לָנוּ אֶת מָמוֹנָם, וְקָרַע לָנוּ אֶת הַיָּם, וְהֶעֱבִירָנוּ בְתוֹכוֹ בֶּחָרָבָה, וְשִׁקַּע צָרֵינוּ בְּתוֹכוֹ, וְסִפֵּק צָרְכֵּנוּ בַּמִּדְבָּר אַרְבָּעִים שָׁנָה, וְהֶאֱכִילָנוּ אֶת הַמָּן, וְנָתַן לָנוּ אֶת הַשַּׁבָּת, וְקֵרְבָנוּ לִפְנֵי הַר סִינַי, וְנָתַן לָנוּ אֶת הַתּוֹרָה, וְהִכְנִיסָנוּ לְאֶרֶץ יִשְׂרָאֵל, וּבָנָה לָנוּ אֶת בֵּית הַבְּחִירָה, לְכַפֵּר עַל כָּל עֲוֹנוֹתֵינוּ.

רַבָּן גַּמְלִיאֵל הָיָה אוֹמֵר: כָּל שֶׁלֹּא אָמַר שְׁלֹשָׁה דְבָרִים אֵלּוּ בַּפֶּסַח לֹא יָצָא יְדֵי חוֹבָתוֹ, וְאֵלּוּ הֵן:

פֶּסַח, מַצָּה, וּמָרוֹר.

פֶּסַח שֶׁהָיוּ אֲבוֹתֵינוּ אוֹכְלִים בִּזְמַן שֶׁבֵּית הַמִּקְדָּשׁ קַיָּם, עַל שׁוּם מָה —עַל שׁוּם שֶׁפָּסַח הַקָּדוֹשׁ בָּרוּךְ הוּא עַל בָּתֵּי אֲבוֹתֵינוּ בְּמִצְרַיִם, שֶׁנֶּאֱמַר: „וַאֲמַרְתֶּם זֶבַח פֶּסַח הוּא לַייָ, אֲשֶׁר פָּסַח עַל בָּתֵּי בְנֵי יִשְׂרָאֵל בְּמִצְרַיִם בְּנָגְפּוֹ אֶת מִצְרַיִם וְאֶת בָּתֵּינוּ הִצִּיל, וַיִּקֹּד הָעָם וַיִּשְׁתַּחֲווּ".

Sacrifice; the Matzah; the Bitter Herb.

The Passover Sacrifice which our fathers used to eat at the time when the Temple was standing, of what does it remind us? It reminds us that the Holy One, blessed be He, passed over the houses of our fathers in Egypt, as it is said: "That ye shall say: It is the sacrifice of the Lord's Passover, for that He passed over the houses of the children of Israel in Egypt, when He smote the Egyptians, and delivered our houses. And the people bowed the head and worshipped" (Ex. 12:27).

The Leader takes the broken middle matzah in his hand, shows it to all present, and intones the following:

מַצָּה זוֹ שֶׁאָנוּ אוֹכְלִים עַל שׁוּם מָה —עַל שׁוּם שֶׁלֹּא הִסְפִּיק בְּצֵקָם שֶׁל אֲבוֹתֵינוּ לְהַחֲמִיץ עַד שֶׁנִּגְלָה עֲלֵיהֶם מֶלֶךְ מַלְכֵי הַמְּלָכִים הַקָּדוֹשׁ בָּרוּךְ הוּא וּגְאָלָם, שֶׁנֶּאֱמַר: „וַיֹּאפוּ אֶת הַבָּצֵק אֲשֶׁר הוֹצִיאוּ מִמִּצְרַיִם, עֻגֹת מַצּוֹת כִּי לֹא חָמֵץ; כִּי גֹרְשׁוּ מִמִּצְרַיִם וְלֹא יָכְלוּ לְהִתְמַהְמֵהַּ, וְגַם צֵדָה לֹא עָשׂוּ לָהֶם".

This Matzah which we eat, of what does it remind us? It reminds us that there was no time for the dough of our fathers to become leavened before the supreme King of Kings, the Holy One, blessed be He, revealed himself to them and redeemed them, as it is said: "And they baked unleavened cakes of the dough which they brought forth out of Egypt, for it was not leavened: because they were thrust out of Egypt, and could not tarry, neither had they prepared for themselves any victual" (Ex. 12:39).

Return the matzah to its place between the two whole matzoth. The Leader takes the *maror* in his hand, displays it, and says the following:

מָרוֹר זֶה שֶׁאָנוּ אוֹכְלִים עַל שׁוּם מָה — עַל שׁוּם שֶׁמֵּרְרוּ הַמִּצְרִים אֶת חַיֵּי אֲבוֹתֵינוּ בְּמִצְרַיִם, שֶׁנֶּאֱמַר: „וַיְמָרְרוּ אֶת חַיֵּיהֶם בַּעֲבֹדָה קָשָׁה בְּחֹמֶר וּבִלְבֵנִים וּבְכָל עֲבֹדָה בַּשָּׂדֶה, אֵת כָּל עֲבֹדָתָם אֲשֶׁר עָבְדוּ בָהֶם בְּפָרֶךְ".

This Bitter Herb which we eat, of what does it remind us? It reminds us that the Egyptians embittered the lives of our fathers in Egypt, as it is said: "And they made their lives bitter with hard service, in mortar and in brick, and in all manner of service in the field; in all their service, wherein they made them serve with rigor" (Ex. 1:14).

Return the *maror* to its original position on the Seder plate.

בְּכָל דּוֹר וָדוֹר חַיָּב אָדָם לִרְאוֹת אֶת עַצְמוֹ כְּאִלּוּ הוּא יָצָא מִמִּצְרַיִם, שֶׁנֶּאֱמַר: „וְהִגַּדְתָּ לְבִנְךָ בַּיּוֹם הַהוּא לֵאמֹר, בַּעֲבוּר זֶה עָשָׂה יְיָ לִי בְּצֵאתִי מִמִּצְרָיִם". לֹא אֶת אֲבוֹתֵינוּ בִּלְבָד גָּאַל הַקָּדוֹשׁ בָּרוּךְ הוּא, אֶלָּא אַף אוֹתָנוּ גָּאַל עִמָּהֶם, שֶׁנֶּאֱמַר: „וְאוֹתָנוּ הוֹצִיא מִשָּׁם לְמַעַן הָבִיא אֹתָנוּ, לָתֶת לָנוּ אֶת הָאָרֶץ אֲשֶׁר נִשְׁבַּע לַאֲבֹתֵינוּ".

In every single generation it is a man's duty to regard himself as if he had come out of Egypt, as it is said: "And thou shalt tell thy son in that day, saying: It is because of that which the Lord did for me when I came forth out of Egypt" (Ex. 13:8). Not only our fathers did the Holy One, blessed be He, redeem, but us also He redeemed with them; as it is said: "And He brought us out from thence, that He might bring us in, to give us the land which He swore unto our fathers" (Deut. 6:23).

The Leader covers the matzah and everyone raises his wine cup. The Leader intones the following aloud:

לְפִיכָךְ אֲנַחְנוּ חַיָּבִים לְהוֹדוֹת, לְהַלֵּל, לְשַׁבֵּחַ, לְפָאֵר, לְרוֹמֵם, לְהַדֵּר, לְבָרֵךְ, לְעַלֵּה וּלְקַלֵּס לְמִי שֶׁעָשָׂה לַאֲבוֹתֵינוּ וְלָנוּ אֶת כָּל הַנִּסִּים הָאֵלּוּ; הוֹצִיאָנוּ מֵעַבְדוּת לְחֵרוּת, מִיָּגוֹן לְשִׂמְחָה, מֵאֵבֶל לְיוֹם טוֹב, וּמֵאֲפֵלָה לְאוֹר גָּדוֹל, וּמִשִּׁעְבּוּד לִגְאֻלָּה, וְנֹאמַר לְפָנָיו שִׁירָה חֲדָשָׁה; הַלְלוּיָהּ.

Therefore, it is our duty to thank, praise, laud, glorify, exalt, honor, bless, extol, and adore Him who performed for our fathers and for us all these wonders. He brought us forth from slavery to freedom, from anguish to joy, from mourning to festivity, from darkness to great light, and from bondage to redemption. Let us sing before Him a new song. Hallelujah!

The wine cups are put down. The following two Psalms are chanted in a joyful and melodious manner.

הַלְלוּיָהּ; הַלְלוּ עַבְדֵי יְיָ הַלְלוּ אֶת שֵׁם יְיָ. יְהִי שֵׁם יְיָ מְבֹרָךְ מֵעַתָּה וְעַד עוֹלָם. מִמִּזְרַח שֶׁמֶשׁ עַד מְבוֹאוֹ מְהֻלָּל שֵׁם יְיָ. רָם עַל כָּל גּוֹיִם יְיָ, עַל הַשָּׁמַיִם כְּבוֹדוֹ. מִי כַּייָ אֱלֹהֵינוּ הַמַּגְבִּיהִי לָשָׁבֶת. הַמַּשְׁפִּילִי לִרְאוֹת בַּשָּׁמַיִם וּבָאָרֶץ. מְקִימִי מֵעָפָר דָּל, מֵאַשְׁפֹּת יָרִים אֶבְיוֹן. לְהוֹשִׁיבִי עִם נְדִיבִים, עִם נְדִיבֵי עַמּוֹ. מוֹשִׁיבִי עֲקֶרֶת הַבַּיִת אֵם הַבָּנִים שְׂמֵחָה; הַלְלוּיָהּ.

Hallelujah. Praise, O ye servants of the Lord, praise the name of the Lord. Blessed be the name of the Lord from this time forth and for ever. From the rising of the sun unto the going down thereof the Lord's name be praised. The Lord is high above all nations, His glory is above the heavens. Who is like unto the Lord our God, that is enthroned on high; that looketh down low upon heaven and upon the earth? Who raiseth up the poor out of the dust, and lifteth up the needy out of the dunghill; that He may set him with princes, even with the princes of His people. Who maketh the barren

בְּצֵאת יִשְׂרָאֵל מִמִּצְרָיִם בֵּית יַעֲקֹב מֵעַם לֹעֵז. הָיְתָה יְהוּדָה לְקָדְשׁוֹ יִשְׂרָאֵל מַמְשְׁלוֹתָיו. הַיָּם רָאָה וַיָּנֹס, הַיַּרְדֵּן יִסֹּב לְאָחוֹר. הֶהָרִים רָקְדוּ כְאֵילִים גְּבָעוֹת כִּבְנֵי צֹאן. מַה לְּךָ הַיָּם כִּי תָנוּס, הַיַּרְדֵּן תִּסֹּב לְאָחוֹר. הֶהָרִים תִּרְקְדוּ כְאֵילִים, גְּבָעוֹת כִּבְנֵי צֹאן. מִלִּפְנֵי אָדוֹן חוּלִי אָרֶץ מִלִּפְנֵי אֱלוֹהַּ יַעֲקֹב. הַהֹפְכִי הַצּוּר אֲגַם מָיִם חַלָּמִישׁ לְמַעְיְנוֹ מָיִם.

woman to dwell in her house as a joyful mother of children. Hallelujah. (Ps. 113)

When Israel came forth out of Egypt, the house of Jacob from a people of strange language, Judah became His sanctuary, Israel his dominion. The sea saw it, and fled; the Jordan turned backward. The mountains skipped like rams, the hills like young sheep. What aileth thee, O thou sea, that thou fleest? Thou Jordan, that thou turnest backward? Ye mountains, that ye skip like rams; ye hills, like young sheep? Tremble, thou earth, at the presence of the Lord, at the presence of the God of Jacob; who turned the rock into a pool of water, the flint into a fountain of waters. (Ps. 114)

The wine cups are raised and the Leader and company recite the following.

בָּרוּךְ אַתָּה יְיָ אֱלֹהֵינוּ מֶלֶךְ הָעוֹלָם, אֲשֶׁר גְּאָלָנוּ וְגָאַל אֶת אֲבוֹתֵינוּ מִמִּצְרַיִם, וְהִגִּיעָנוּ הַלַּיְלָה הַזֶּה לֶאֱכָל בּוֹ מַצָּה וּמָרוֹר. כֵּן יְיָ אֱלֹהֵינוּ וֵאלֹהֵי אֲבוֹתֵינוּ הַגִּיעֵנוּ לְמוֹעֲדִים וְלִרְגָלִים אֲחֵרִים הַבָּאִים לִקְרָאתֵנוּ לְשָׁלוֹם, שְׂמֵחִים בְּבִנְיַן עִירֶךָ וְשָׂשִׂים בַּעֲבוֹדָתֶךָ, וְנֹאכַל

Blessed art Thou, Lord our God, King of the universe, who redeemed us and redeemed our fathers from Egypt, and enabled us to reach this night, to eat matzah and bitter herb. So may the Lord, our God, and the God of our fathers, enable us to reach other anniversaries and feasts which shall come to us in peace, happy in the building of Thy city and

exultant in Thy service. There we shall eat of the sacrifices and of the paschal lambs, the blood of which shall be sprinkled upon the wall of Thy altar for Thy acceptance. And there we shall chant unto Thee a new song for our redemption and for the salvation of our soul. Blessed art Thou, O Lord, who redeemed Israel.

שָׁם מִן הַזְּבָחִים וּמִן הַפְּסָחִים, אֲשֶׁר יַגִּיעַ דָּמָם עַל קִיר מִזְבַּחֲךָ לְרָצוֹן, וְנוֹדֶה לְךָ שִׁיר חָדָשׁ עַל גְּאֻלָּתֵנוּ וְעַל פְּדוּת נַפְשֵׁנוּ. בָּרוּךְ אַתָּה יְיָ גָּאַל יִשְׂרָאֵל.

At this point, the wine cups may be put down if somebody wishes to deliver a *d'var Torah* or offer some comment. The wine cups are raised for the blessing over the second of the four cups.

I am ready and prepared to perform the commandment of the second of the four cups, to honor the Holy One, blessed be He and His Divine Presence, through the hidden and secret Guardian, on behalf of all Israel.

הִנְנִי מוּכָן וּמְזֻמָּן לְקַיֵּם מִצְוַת כּוֹס שֵׁנִי מֵאַרְבַּע כּוֹסוֹת לְשֵׁם יִחוּד קוּדְשָׁא בְּרִיךְ הוּא וּשְׁכִינְתֵּיהּ עַל יְדֵי הַהוּא טָמִיר וְנֶעְלָם בְּשֵׁם כָּל יִשְׂרָאֵל.

Blessed art Thou, Lord our God, King of the universe, Creator of the fruit of the vine.

בָּרוּךְ אַתָּה יְיָ אֱלֹהֵינוּ מֶלֶךְ הָעוֹלָם, בּוֹרֵא פְּרִי הַגָּפֶן.

Drink most of the wine in the cup within four minutes. All males must recline on the left side while they drink the wine.

Raḥtzah: *Lave the Hands* רָחְצָה

Before the ritual washing of the hands, prepare the following for each person but do not bring it into the dining room: two large pieces of matzoth (preferably hand *shemurah* matzah), each piece approximately

4'' × 7'' (26 grams or about one ounce in weight). If possible, one section should be broken off from a whole matzah while the other should be broken off from a broken matzah. The Leader announces *Raḥtzah* and gives a short explanation of this and the following three rites. He then proceeds to the washroom. The Leader washes first and then everyone else follows in order of importance. The hands are ritually washed in the following manner: All rings must be removed from the fingers. The laver is taken with the right hand and placed in the left hand. Fill it with water and pour a half pint over the right hand covering the entire hand up to the wrist with water. In order to leave no part of the hand unwashed, the fingers should be slightly separated and raised upward so that the water can run down the entire length of the fingers and upon and around the fingertips. The entire hand must be washed by the one act of pouring out the water. Repeat this process. Then take the vessel in the right hand and repeat for the left hand. After both hands are washed, they are rubbed together and raised upward. The blessing below is recited while the hands are still wet, before being dried on a clean towel. This ritual may be performed either at the table, with a bowl, ewer, and laver brought to each person in turn, or in a washroom. If done in a washroom, care should be taken that the blessing is said in a clean and proper place (not in the toilet). There should be no talking between the ritual washing of the hands and eating the *korekh* except when necessary to the performance of the various ceremonies involved. Therefore, whoever wants to make some comment before the start of the meal on any of the following four sections must do so before *Raḥtzah*.

בָּרוּךְ אַתָּה יְיָ אֱלֹהֵינוּ מֶלֶךְ הָעוֹלָם, אֲשֶׁר קִדְּשָׁנוּ בְּמִצְוֹתָיו וְצִוָּנוּ עַל נְטִילַת יָדָיִם.

Blessed art Thou, Lord our God, King of the universe, who sanctified us with His commandments and commanded us concerning the washing of hands.

Motzi: *Blessing over Bread* מוֹצִיא

When everyone has returned to the table, the Leader picks up all three *shemurah* matzoth from the Seder plate, the two whole matzoth with the broken one in between. He pronounces the following blessing aloud while all the guests repeat the blessing silently with him:

הִנְנִי מוּכָן וּמְזֻמָּן לְקַיֵּם מִצְוַת אֲכִילַת מַצָּה, לְשֵׁם יִחוּד קוּדְשָׁא בְּרִיךְ הוּא וּשְׁכִינְתֵּיהּ עַל יְדֵי הַהוּא טָמִיר וְנֶעְלָם בְּשֵׁם כָּל יִשְׂרָאֵל.

I am ready and prepared to perform the commandment of eating matzah, to honor the Holy One, blessed be He and His Divine Presence, through the hidden and secret Guardian, on behalf of all Israel.

בָּרוּךְ אַתָּה יְיָ אֱלֹהֵינוּ מֶלֶךְ הָעוֹלָם, הַמּוֹצִיא לֶחֶם מִן הָאָרֶץ.

Blessed art Thou, Lord our God, King of the universe, who bringest forth bread from the earth.

Matzah: *Blessing over the Matzah* מַצָּה

The Leader puts down the bottom matzah and the prepared matzah portions are now distributed. Holding the two upper matzoth, the Leader pronounces the following blessing aloud while the guests, holding their portions, say the blessing quietly with him.

בָּרוּךְ אַתָּה יְיָ אֱלֹהֵינוּ מֶלֶךְ הָעוֹלָם, אֲשֶׁר קִדְּשָׁנוּ בְּמִצְוֹתָיו וְצִוָּנוּ עַל אֲכִילַת מַצָּה.

Blessed art Thou, Lord our God, King of the Universe, who sanctified us with His commandments and commanded us concerning the eating of matzah.

The Leader then breaks off a *kezayit* (the size of an olive, approximately 26 grams or one ounce in weight), a piece about 4″ × 7″, from each of the two matzoth in his hand for himself, and small pieces from the remainder of each of the same matzoth which he parcels out to the guests around the table. He then eats (some first dip the matzah in salt) both pieces of matzah together, in one mouthful. He must recline on the left and eat the matzah as quickly as possible. The first *kezayit* should be eaten within four minutes and both *kezaytim* within eight minutes. The guests also eat their matzah with the Leader within the allotted time, all the males reclining on the left.

Maror: *Bitter Herb* מָרוֹר

The Leader takes a *kezayit maror*, a lettuce leaf about 8″ × 10″, dips it completely in the *ḥaroset* (some dip only a part of the *maror* into the *ḥaroset*). After dipping it, he shakes all trace of the *ḥaroset* off the *maror*. He repeats this procedure until all participants are served. If

there is not enough *maror* on the Seder plate, more is brought in from the kitchen. The Leader then pronounces the following blessing aloud and everyone repeats it after him. When eating the *maror*, be sure to chew it thoroughly and to eat the entire portion within four minutes.

הִנְנִי מוּכָן וּמְזֻמָּן לְקַיֵּם מִצְוַת אֲכִילַת מָרוֹר, לְשֵׁם יִחוּד קוּדְשָׁא בְּרִיךְ הוּא וּשְׁכִינְתֵּיהּ עַל יְדֵי הַהוּא טָמִיר וְנֶעְלָם בְּשֵׁם כָּל יִשְׂרָאֵל.

I am ready and prepared to perform the commandment of eating the bitter herb, to honor the Holy One, blessed be He and His Divine Presence, through the hidden and secret Guardian, on behalf of all Israel.

בָּרוּךְ אַתָּה יְיָ אֱלֹהֵינוּ מֶלֶךְ הָעוֹלָם, אֲשֶׁר קִדְּשָׁנוּ בְּמִצְוֹתָיו וְצִוָּנוּ עַל אֲכִילַת מָרוֹר.

Blessed art Thou, Lord our God, King of the universe, who sanctified us with His commandments and commanded us concerning the eating of bitter herb.

Korekh: *Combine Matzah with Bitter Herb* כּוֹרֵךְ

The Leader takes a *kezayit* of the third (and as yet unbroken) matzah and a *kezayit* of the *ḥazeret* (lettuce, endive, or chicory). He dips the *ḥazeret* in the *ḥaroset* and shakes off any *ḥaroset* that might adhere (some Sages say there is no dipping for *korekh*). He then breaks the *kezayit* of matzah in half and puts the *ḥazeret* between, making a sandwich for himself. He gives each person similar portions, using additional *shemurah* matzah and *ḥazeret* which is brought in as needed. The Leader recites the following paragraph aloud and everyone joins in:

זֵכֶר לְמִקְדָּשׁ כְּהִלֵּל, כֵּן עָשָׂה הִלֵּל בִּזְמַן שֶׁבֵּית הַמִּקְדָּשׁ הָיָה קַיָּם. הָיָה כּוֹרֵךְ מַצָּה וּמָרוֹר וְאוֹכֵל בְּיַחַד, לְקַיֵּם מַה שֶּׁנֶּאֱמַר: „עַל מַצּוֹת וּמְרֹרִים יֹאכְלֻהוּ״.

In remembrance of the Temple, according to the custom of Hillel. Thus did Hillel do when the Temple was still extant: he used to combine matzah and bitter herb in a sandwich and eat them together, in observance of that which is said: "They shall eat it with unleavened bread and bitter herbs" (Num. 9:11).

The *korekh* should be eaten within eight minutes. The males recline on the left.

Shulḥan Arukh: *The Meal* שֻׁלְחָן עוֹרֵךְ

There are several customs pertaining to the Seder meal. It is customary to eat hard-boiled eggs and not to eat any broiled, roasted, or fried meats or fowl. Some do not eat any dipped foods; others do not eat any prepared food that contains matzah or matzah flour (*gebroks*). Although the meal is a festive occasion, one should nevertheless eat and drink with moderation. The meal should finish before midnight.

Tzafun: *The Hidden Matzah* צָפוּן

At the conclusion of the meal, the matzah that has been hidden, the *afikoman,* is ransomed from the children. The Leader breaks off one *kezayit,* a piece about 4″ × 7″, and takes another *kezayit* from other *shemurah* matzah. He then gives everyone seated at the table a small piece of whatever is left of the hidden matzah and makes each portion up to two *kezaytim* with other *shemurah* matzah. A minimum of one *kezayit* must be eaten but two *kezaytim* are recommended. Males must recline on the left. The afikoman should be eaten as quickly as possible; the first *kezayit* within four minutes and both *kezaytim* within eight minutes. It should be eaten before midnight. After the *afikoman,* no food or drink (water, seltzer, and tea excepted) may be taken except for the final two cups of wine.

הִנְנִי מוּכָן וּמְזֻמָּן לְקַיֵּם מִצְוַת אֲכִילַת אֲפִיקוֹמָן, לְשֵׁם יִחוּד קוּדְשָׁא בְּרִיךְ הוּא וּשְׁכִינְתֵּיהּ עַל יְדֵי הַהוּא טָמִיר וְנֶעְלָם בְּשֵׁם כָּל יִשְׂרָאֵל.

I am ready and prepared to perform the commandment of eating the *afikoman,* to honor the Holy One, blessed be He and His Divine Presence, through the hidden and secret Guardian, on behalf of all Israel.

Barekh: *Grace* בָּרֵךְ

The third wine cup is now filled for the Grace after the meal. The host should try to have a *mezuman,* three adult males over thirteen years of age, at his Seder so that the introductory lines of the Grace may be recited. It is customary that on Seder night the host should lead in the Grace. However, if he wishes, he may give this honor to a distinguished guest. The table should be cleared except for a small piece of matzah and the wine cups. The crumbs too should be removed. Before commencing Grace, the Leader and all present sing the following Psalm:

שִׁיר הַמַּעֲלוֹת, בְּשׁוּב יְיָ אֶת שִׁיבַת צִיּוֹן הָיִינוּ כְּחֹלְמִים. אָז יִמָּלֵא שְׂחוֹק פִּינוּ וּלְשׁוֹנֵנוּ רִנָּה, אָז יֹאמְרוּ בַגּוֹיִם הִגְדִּיל יְיָ לַעֲשׂוֹת עִם אֵלֶּה. הִגְדִּיל יְיָ לַעֲשׂוֹת עִמָּנוּ הָיִינוּ שְׂמֵחִים. שׁוּבָה יְיָ אֶת שְׁבִיתֵנוּ כַּאֲפִיקִים בַּנֶּגֶב. הַזֹּרְעִים בְּדִמְעָה בְּרִנָּה יִקְצֹרוּ. הָלוֹךְ יֵלֵךְ וּבָכֹה נֹשֵׂא מֶשֶׁךְ הַזָּרַע, בֹּא יָבֹא בְרִנָּה נֹשֵׂא אֲלֻמֹּתָיו.

A Song of Ascents. When the Lord brought back those that returned to Zion, we were like unto them that dream. Then was our mouth filled with laughter, and our tongue with singing; then said they among the nations: The Lord hath done great things with these. The Lord hath done great things with us; we are rejoiced. Turn our captivity, O Lord, as the streams in the dry land. They that sow in tears shall reap in joy. Though he goeth on his way weeping that beareth the measure of seed, he shall come home with joy, bearing his sheaves (Ps. 126).

Many customarily wash their hands before saying Grace. He who will lead in the Grace should wash his hands first. Only the first two joints of the fingers need be washed and the hands should be held downward before being dried. This washing is done at the table over a small bowl which must be removed from the table when everyone is done. The Leader lifts the wine cup with both hands at least 3½ inches off the table, and before starting, holds the wine cup with his right hand alone. If there are three adult males present, he says the following introductory lines to the Grace; when there are ten adult males present (a *minyan*), the words in parenthesis are included.

הִנְנִי מוּכָן וּמְזֻמָּן לְקַיֵּם מִצְוַת עֲשֵׂה שֶׁל בִּרְכַּת הַמָּזוֹן. שֶׁנֶּאֱמַר: וְאָכַלְתָּ וְשָׂבָעְתָּ, וּבֵרַכְתָּ אֶת יְיָ אֱלֹהֶיךָ, עַל הָאָרֶץ הַטֹּבָה אֲשֶׁר נָתַן לָךְ. לְשֵׁם יִחוּד קוּדְשָׁא בְּרִיךְ הוּא וּשְׁכִינְתֵּיהּ עַל יְדֵי הַהוּא טָמִיר וְנֶעְלָם בְּשֵׁם כָּל יִשְׂרָאֵל.

I am ready and prepared to perform the positive commandment of reciting Grace after the meal, as it is written: "When thou hast eaten, and art satisfied, then shalt thou bless the Lord thy God for the good land which he hath given thee;" to honor the Holy One, blessed be He and His Divine Presence, through the hidden and secret Guardian, on behalf of all Israel.

Leader:
Gentlemen, let us say Grace.

Leader:
רַבּוֹתַי נְבָרֵךְ.

Company:
May the name of the Lord be blessed from now unto eternity.

Company:
יְהִי שֵׁם יְיָ מְבֹרָךְ מֵעַתָּה וְעַד עוֹלָם.

Leader:
May the name of the Lord be blessed from now unto eternity. By permission of all assembled let us bless (our God) of whose bounty we have partaken.

Leader:
יְהִי שֵׁם יְיָ מְבֹרָךְ מֵעַתָּה וְעַד עוֹלָם בִּרְשׁוּת מָרָנָן וְרַבָּנָן וְרַבּוֹתַי, נְבָרֵךְ (אֱלֹהֵינוּ) שֶׁאָכַלְנוּ מִשֶּׁלּוֹ.

Company:
Blessed be He (our God) of whose bounty we have partaken and through whose goodness we live.

Company:
בָּרוּךְ (אֱלֹהֵינוּ) שֶׁאָכַלְנוּ מִשֶּׁלּוֹ וּבְטוּבוֹ חָיִינוּ.

Leader:
Blessed be He (our God) of whose bounty we have partaken and through whose goodness we live.
Blessed be He and blessed be His Name.

Leader:
בָּרוּךְ (אֱלֹהֵינוּ) שֶׁאָכַלְנוּ מִשֶּׁלּוֹ וּבְטוּבוֹ חָיִינוּ.
בָּרוּךְ הוּא וּבָרוּךְ שְׁמוֹ.

The Leader recites the entire Grace aloud. Everyone joins in, and recites *Amen* after the Leader completes each of the blessings of the Grace.

Blessed art Thou, Lord our God, King of the universe: who sustains the whole world in His goodness, in grace, loving kindness, and mercy. He giveth bread to all flesh, for his mercy endureth forever. And through His goodness, which is ever great, sustenance hath never failed us, nor will fail us, for ever and ever, for the

בָּרוּךְ אַתָּה יְיָ אֱלֹהֵינוּ מֶלֶךְ הָעוֹלָם הַזָּן אֶת הָעוֹלָם כֻּלּוֹ בְּטוּבוֹ בְּחֵן בְּחֶסֶד וּבְרַחֲמִים. הוּא נוֹתֵן לֶחֶם לְכָל בָּשָׂר, כִּי לְעוֹלָם חַסְדּוֹ. וּבְטוּבוֹ הַגָּדוֹל תָּמִיד לֹא חָסַר לָנוּ וְאַל יֶחְסַר לָנוּ מָזוֹן לְעוֹלָם וָעֶד. בַּעֲבוּר שְׁמוֹ הַגָּדוֹל, כִּי הוּא אֵל זָן

sake of His great Name. For He sustains and supports all, and does good to all, and prepares sustenance to all His creatures which He hath created. Blessed art Thou, O Lord, who sustainest all.

וּמְפַרְנֵס לַכֹּל וּמֵטִיב לַכֹּל, וּמֵכִין מָזוֹן לְכָל בְּרִיּוֹתָיו אֲשֶׁר בָּרָא. בָּרוּךְ אַתָּה יְיָ הַזָּן אֶת הַכֹּל.

We thank Thee, Lord our God, because Thou didst give our fathers as an inheritance a land which is pleasant, goodly, and spacious, and because Thou didst take us out, O Lord, our God, from the land of Egypt, and didst redeem us from the house of bondage, and for Thy covenant which Thou didst seal in our flesh, and for Thy law which Thou hast taught us, and for Thy statutes which Thou hast made known unto us, and for the life, grace, and loving kindness which Thou hast favored us, and for the partaking of this sustenance wherewith Thou dost sustain and support us continually, on every day and at every time, and in every hour.

נוֹדֶה לְּךָ יְיָ אֱלֹהֵינוּ עַל שֶׁהִנְחַלְתָּ לַאֲבוֹתֵינוּ אֶרֶץ חֶמְדָּה טוֹבָה וּרְחָבָה, וְעַל שֶׁהוֹצֵאתָנוּ יְיָ אֱלֹהֵינוּ מֵאֶרֶץ מִצְרַיִם וּפְדִיתָנוּ מִבֵּית עֲבָדִים, וְעַל בְּרִיתְךָ שֶׁחָתַמְתָּ בִּבְשָׂרֵנוּ, וְעַל תּוֹרָתְךָ שֶׁלִּמַּדְתָּנוּ וְעַל חֻקֶּיךָ שֶׁהוֹדַעְתָּנוּ, וְעַל חַיִּים חֵן וָחֶסֶד שֶׁחוֹנַנְתָּנוּ, וְעַל אֲכִילַת מָזוֹן שָׁאַתָּה זָן וּמְפַרְנֵס אוֹתָנוּ תָּמִיד בְּכָל יוֹם וּבְכָל עֵת וּבְכָל שָׁעָה.

And for all this, Lord our God, we render thanks to Thee and bless Thee. Blessed be Thy Name in the mouth of all that are alive, continually and for evermore: as it is written, "And thou shalt eat and be satisfied, and bless the Lord thy God for the good land which He hath given thee" (Deut. 8:10). Blessed art Thou, O

וְעַל הַכֹּל יְיָ אֱלֹהֵינוּ אֲנַחְנוּ מוֹדִים לָךְ וּמְבָרְכִים אוֹתָךְ יִתְבָּרַךְ שִׁמְךָ בְּפִי כָּל חַי תָּמִיד לְעוֹלָם וָעֶד. כַּכָּתוּב: „וְאָכַלְתָּ וְשָׂבָעְתָּ וּבֵרַכְתָּ אֶת יְיָ אֱלֹהֶיךָ עַל הָאָרֶץ הַטֹּבָה אֲשֶׁר נָתַן לָךְ". בָּרוּךְ אַתָּה יְיָ עַל הָאָרֶץ וְעַל הַמָּזוֹן.

Lord, for the land and the sustenance.

Have mercy, Lord our God, upon Israel, Thy people, and upon Jerusalem, Thy city, and upon Zion, the abiding place of Thy glory, and upon the kingdom of the house of David, Thine annointed, and upon the great and holy House which is called by Thy Name. Our God, our Father, do Thou pasture us, sustain us, support us, maintain us, and relieve us. Give us relief, Lord our God, speedily from all our troubles. And we beseech Thee, Lord our God, make us not dependent upon the gifts of flesh and blood, nor upon their loans, but only upon Thy full, open, holy, and ample hand, so that we may not be ashamed nor abashed for ever and ever.

רַחֵם נָא יְיָ אֱלֹהֵינוּ עַל יִשְׂרָאֵל עַמֶּךָ, וְעַל יְרוּשָׁלַיִם עִירֶךָ, וְעַל צִיּוֹן מִשְׁכַּן כְּבוֹדֶךָ, וְעַל מַלְכוּת בֵּית דָּוִד מְשִׁיחֶךָ, וְעַל הַבַּיִת הַגָּדוֹל וְהַקָּדוֹשׁ שֶׁנִּקְרָא שִׁמְךָ עָלָיו. אֱלֹהֵינוּ אָבִינוּ, רְעֵנוּ זוּנֵנוּ פַּרְנְסֵנוּ וְכַלְכְּלֵנוּ וְהַרְוִיחֵנוּ וְהַרְוַח לָנוּ יְיָ אֱלֹהֵינוּ מְהֵרָה מִכָּל צָרוֹתֵינוּ. וְנָא אַל תַּצְרִיכֵנוּ יְיָ אֱלֹהֵינוּ, לֹא לִידֵי מַתְּנַת בָּשָׂר וָדָם וְלֹא לִידֵי הַלְוָאָתָם, כִּי אִם לְיָדְךָ הַמְּלֵאָה הַפְּתוּחָה הַקְּדוֹשָׁה וְהָרְחָבָה, שֶׁלֹּא נֵבוֹשׁ וְלֹא נִכָּלֵם לְעוֹלָם וָעֶד.

On the Sabbath say:

(Be it Thy will, Lord our God, to strengthen us with Thy precepts and especially by the precept concerning the seventh day, this great and holy Sabbath. For this day is great and holy before Thee, that we may rest thereon in love, according to Thy gracious precept. By Thy grace, Lord our God, grant us repose, that there may be no trouble nor sorrow nor lamentation upon our

(רְצֵה וְהַחֲלִיצֵנוּ יְיָ אֱלֹהֵינוּ בְּמִצְוֹתֶיךָ וּבְמִצְוַת יוֹם הַשְּׁבִיעִי הַשַּׁבָּת הַגָּדוֹל וְהַקָּדוֹשׁ הַזֶּה. כִּי יוֹם זֶה גָּדוֹל וְקָדוֹשׁ הוּא לְפָנֶיךָ לִשְׁבָּת בּוֹ וְלָנוּחַ בּוֹ בְּאַהֲבָה כְּמִצְוַת רְצוֹנֶךָ. וּבִרְצוֹנְךָ הָנִיחַ לָנוּ יְיָ אֱלֹהֵינוּ שֶׁלֹּא תְהֵא צָרָה וְיָגוֹן וַאֲנָחָה בְּיוֹם מְנוּחָתֵנוּ. וְהַרְאֵנוּ יְיָ

אֱלֹהֵינוּ בְּנֶחָמַת צִיּוֹן עִירֶךָ וּבְבִנְיַן יְרוּשָׁלַיִם עִיר קָדְשֶׁךָ, כִּי אַתָּה הוּא בַּעַל הַיְשׁוּעוֹת וּבַעַל הַנֶּחָמוֹת.)

day of rest, and cause us to see the consolation of Zion, Thy city, and the building of Jerusalem, Thy holy city, for Thou art He who is Lord of redemption and Lord of consolation.)

אֱלֹהֵינוּ וֵאלֹהֵי אֲבוֹתֵינוּ, יַעֲלֶה וְיָבֹא וְיַגִּיעַ וְיֵרָאֶה וְיֵרָצֶה וְיִשָּׁמַע וְיִפָּקֵד וְיִזָּכֵר זִכְרוֹנֵנוּ וּפִקְדוֹנֵנוּ וְזִכְרוֹן אֲבוֹתֵינוּ וְזִכְרוֹן מָשִׁיחַ בֶּן דָּוִד עַבְדֶּךָ, וְזִכְרוֹן יְרוּשָׁלַיִם עִיר קָדְשֶׁךָ וְזִכְרוֹן כָּל עַמְּךָ בֵּית יִשְׂרָאֵל לְפָנֶיךָ לִפְלֵיטָה לְטוֹבָה, לְחֵן וּלְחֶסֶד וּלְרַחֲמִים לְחַיִּים וּלְשָׁלוֹם בְּיוֹם חַג הַמַּצּוֹת הַזֶּה. זָכְרֵנוּ יְיָ אֱלֹהֵינוּ בּוֹ לְטוֹבָה, וּפָקְדֵנוּ בוֹ לִבְרָכָה, וְהוֹשִׁיעֵנוּ בוֹ לְחַיִּים טוֹבִים. וּבִדְבַר יְשׁוּעָה וְרַחֲמִים חוּס וְחָנֵּנוּ, וְרַחֵם עָלֵינוּ וְהוֹשִׁיעֵנוּ, כִּי אֵלֶיךָ עֵינֵינוּ כִּי אֵל מֶלֶךְ חַנּוּן וְרַחוּם אָתָּה.

Our God and God of our fathers, may there ascend, and come, and arrive, and be seen, and accepted, and heard, and visited, and remembered; our remembrance, and our recollection, and the remembrance of our fathers, and the remembrance of the annointed Messiah, son of David Thy servant, and the remembrance of Jerusalem, Thy holy city, and the remembrance of the whole of Thy people, the house of Israel; for deliverence, and for good, and for grace, and for loving-kindness,and for mercy, and for life, and for peace, before Thee, upon this day, the Feast of Matzah. Remember us thereon, Lord our God, for good, and visit us thereon for a blessing, and save us thereon for life. And through tidings of redemption and mercy, pity us and show us grace, and be merciful unto us and redeem us, for to Thee are our eyes turned, for Thou art a gracious and merciful God and King.

וּבְנֵה יְרוּשָׁלַיִם עִיר הַקֹּדֶשׁ בִּמְהֵרָה בְיָמֵינוּ. בָּרוּךְ אַתָּה יְיָ בּוֹנֵה בְרַחֲמָיו יְרוּשָׁלָיִם, אָמֵן.

And build up Jerusalem the holy city speedily in our days.

בָּרוּךְ אַתָּה יְיָ אֱלֹהֵינוּ מֶלֶךְ הָעוֹלָם, הָאֵל אָבִינוּ מַלְכֵּנוּ אַדִּירֵנוּ בּוֹרְאֵנוּ גּוֹאֲלֵנוּ יוֹצְרֵנוּ קְדוֹשֵׁנוּ קְדוֹשׁ יַעֲקֹב, רוֹעֵנוּ רוֹעֵה יִשְׂרָאֵל, הַמֶּלֶךְ הַטּוֹב וְהַמֵּטִיב לַכֹּל, שֶׁבְּכָל יוֹם וָיוֹם הוּא הֵטִיב הוּא מֵטִיב הוּא יֵיטִיב לָנוּ. הוּא גְמָלָנוּ, הוּא גוֹמְלֵנוּ, הוּא יִגְמְלֵנוּ לָעַד, לְחֵן וּלְחֶסֶד וּלְרַחֲמִים וּלְרֶוַח הַצָּלָה וְהַצְלָחָה בְּרָכָה וִישׁוּעָה נֶחָמָה פַּרְנָסָה וְכַלְכָּלָה, וְרַחֲמִים וְחַיִּים וְשָׁלוֹם וְכָל טוֹב, וּמִכָּל טוּב לְעוֹלָם אַל יְחַסְּרֵנוּ.

Blessed art Thou, O Lord, who in His mercy rebuildeth Jerusalem. Amen.

Blessed art Thou, Lord our God, King of the universe, O God, our Father, our King, our Mighty One, our Creator, our Redeemer, our Maker, our Holy One, the Holy One of Jacob, our Shepherd, the Shepherd of Israel, the good King, who doth good to all, who upon every day did good, doth good, and will do good unto us. He hath bestowed, He doth bestow, He will bestow benefits upon us always, for grace, lovingkindness, mercy and deliverence, protection, prosperity, blessing, salvation, comfort, support, sustenance, mercy, life, peace and all good. And all good may He never let us lack!

The Leader puts down the wine cup.

הָרַחֲמָן הוּא יִמְלֹךְ עָלֵינוּ לְעוֹלָם וָעֶד.

May the Merciful One reign over us for ever and ever.

הָרַחֲמָן הוּא יִתְבָּרַךְ בַּשָּׁמַיִם וּבָאָרֶץ.

May the Merciful One be blessed in heaven and earth.

הָרַחֲמָן הוּא יִשְׁתַּבַּח לְדוֹר דּוֹרִים וְיִתְפָּאַר בָּנוּ לָעַד וּלְנֵצַח נְצָחִים, וְיִתְהַדַּר בָּנוּ לָעַד וּלְעוֹלְמֵי עוֹלָמִים.

May the Merciful One be praised for all generations, and may He be glorified through us for all ages, and exalted through us for ever and for all eternity.

הָרַחֲמָן הוּא יְפַרְנְסֵנוּ בְּכָבוֹד.

May the Merciful One grant us a livelihood with honor.

הָרַחֲמָן הוּא יִשְׁבּוֹר עֻלֵּנוּ מֵעַל צַוָּארֵנוּ, וְהוּא יוֹלִיכֵנוּ קוֹמְמִיּוּת לְאַרְצֵנוּ.

May the Merciful One break the yoke off our neck and may He lead us upright to our land.

הָרַחֲמָן הוּא יִשְׁלַח בְּרָכָה מְרֻבָּה בַּבַּיִת הַזֶּה וְעַל שֻׁלְחָן זֶה שֶׁאָכַלְנוּ עָלָיו.

May the Merciful One send an ample blessing to this house, and upon this table at which we have eaten.

הָרַחֲמָן הוּא יִשְׁלַח לָנוּ אֶת אֵלִיָּהוּ הַנָּבִיא, זָכוּר לַטּוֹב, וִיבַשֶּׂר לָנוּ בְּשׂוֹרוֹת טוֹבוֹת יְשׁוּעוֹת וְנֶחָמוֹת.

May the Merciful One send us Elijah the prophet, of blessed memory, to bring us good tiding, salvation and comfort.

The master of the house says:

הָרַחֲמָן הוּא יְבָרֵךְ אוֹתִי (וְאֶת אִשְׁתִּי וְאֶת זַרְעִי) וְאֶת כָּל אֲשֶׁר לִי,

May the Merciful One bless me, my wife and children and all that I possess;

A child at the parents' table says:

הָרַחֲמָן הוּא יְבָרֵךְ אֶת אָבִי מוֹרִי בַּעַל הַבַּיִת הַזֶּה וְאֶת אִמִּי מוֹרָתִי בַּעֲלַת הַבַּיִת הַזֶּה, אוֹתָם וְאֶת בֵּיתָם וְאֶת זַרְעָם וְאֶת כָּל אֲשֶׁר לָהֶם,

May the Merciful One bless my honored father and my honored mother, they, their house, their family and all belonging to them;

A guest says:

הָרַחֲמָן הוּא יְבָרֵךְ אֶת בַּעַל הַבַּיִת הַזֶּה וְאֶת בַּעֲלַת הַבַּיִת הַזֶּה, אוֹתָם

May the Merciful One bless the master of this house and the mistress of this house, they, their

וְאֶת בֵּיתָם וְאֶת זַרְעָם וְאֶת כָּל אֲשֶׁר לָהֶם,

אוֹתָנוּ וְאֶת כָּל אֲשֶׁר לָנוּ, כְּמוֹ שֶׁנִּתְבָּרְכוּ אֲבוֹתֵינוּ אַבְרָהָם יִצְחָק וְיַעֲקֹב „בַּכֹּל" „מִכֹּל" „כֹּל", כֵּן יְבָרֵךְ אוֹתָנוּ כֻּלָּנוּ יַחַד בִּבְרָכָה שְׁלֵמָה וְנֹאמַר אָמֵן.

house, their family and all belonging to them; us and all that is ours. As our fathers Abraham, Isaac and Jacob were blessed, with all, by all, in all, so may he bless us all together with a perfect blessing, and let us say, Amen.

בַּמָּרוֹם יְלַמְּדוּ עֲלֵיהֶם וְעָלֵינוּ זְכוּת שֶׁתְּהֵא לְמִשְׁמֶרֶת שָׁלוֹם, וְנִשָּׂא בְרָכָה מֵאֵת יְיָ וּצְדָקָה מֵאֱלֹהֵי יִשְׁעֵנוּ וְנִמְצָא חֵן וְשֵׂכֶל טוֹב בְּעֵינֵי אֱלֹהִים וְאָדָם.

In heaven, may merit be pleaded for us, that we may have everlasting peace. And may we receive a blessing from the Lord, and righteousness from the God of our salvation, so that we may find grace and understanding in the eyes of God and man.

On the Sabbath say:

(הָרַחֲמָן הוּא יַנְחִילֵנוּ יוֹם שֶׁכֻּלּוֹ שַׁבָּת וּמְנוּחָה לְחַיֵּי הָעוֹלָמִים.)

(May the Merciful One give us as an inheritance a day which is all Sabbath and rest, in life everlasting.)

הָרַחֲמָן הוּא יַנְחִילֵנוּ יוֹם שֶׁכֻּלּוֹ טוֹב.

May the Merciful One give us as an inheritance a day which is all good.

הָרַחֲמָן הוּא יְזַכֵּנוּ לִימוֹת הַמָּשִׁיחַ וּלְחַיֵּי הָעוֹלָם הַבָּא.

May the Merciful One make us worthy of the days of the Messiah and the life of the world to come.

„מִגְדּוֹל יְשׁוּעוֹת מַלְכּוֹ וְעֹשֶׂה חֶסֶד לִמְשִׁיחוֹ לְדָוִד וּלְזַרְעוֹ עַד עוֹלָם".

"A tower of salvation is He to His king; and showeth mercy to His anointed, to David and to his seed, for evermore" (II Sam. 22:51). He who maketh peace in

עֹשֶׂה שָׁלוֹם בִּמְרוֹמָיו הוּא יַעֲשֶׂה שָׁלוֹם עָלֵינוּ וְעַל כָּל יִשְׂרָאֵל וְאִמְרוּ אָמֵן.

heavens, may He make peace for us and for all Israel; and say ye, Amen.

„יְראוּ אֶת יְיָ קְדֹשָׁיו כִּי אֵין מַחְסוֹר לִירֵאָיו. כְּפִירִים רָשׁוּ וְרָעֵבוּ וְדֹרְשֵׁי יְיָ לֹא יַחְסְרוּ כָל טוֹב". „הוֹדוּ לַייָ כִּי טוֹב כִּי לְעוֹלָם חַסְדּוֹ". „פּוֹתֵחַ אֶת יָדֶךָ וּמַשְׂבִּיעַ לְכָל חַי רָצוֹן". „בָּרוּךְ הַגֶּבֶר אֲשֶׁר יִבְטַח בַּייָ וְהָיָה יְיָ מִבְטַחוֹ". „נַעַר הָיִיתִי גַּם זָקַנְתִּי וְלֹא רָאִיתִי צַדִּיק נֶעֱזָב וְזַרְעוֹ מְבַקֶּשׁ לָחֶם". יְיָ עֹז לְעַמּוֹ יִתֵּן יְיָ יְבָרֵךְ אֶת עַמּוֹ בַשָּׁלוֹם.

"O fear the Lord, ye His holy ones, for there is no want to them that fear Him. The young lions do lack and suffer hunger; but they that seek the Lord want not any good thing" (Ps. 34:10–11). "O give thanks unto the Lord, for He is good, for His mercy endureth for ever" (Ps. 118:1). "Thou openest Thy hand, and satisfiest every living thing with favor" (Ps. 145:16). "Blessed is the man that trusteth in the Lord, and whose trust the Lord is" (Jer. 17:7). "I have been young, and now am old; yet have I not seen the righteous forsaken, nor his seed begging bread" (Ps. 37:25). "The Lord will give strength unto His people; the Lord will bless His people with peace" (Ps. 29:11).

The wine cups are raised. The Leader and company say the following blessing aloud:

הִנְנִי מוּכָן וּמְזֻמָּן לְקַיֵּם מִצְוַת כּוֹס שְׁלִישִׁי מֵאַרְבַּע כּוֹסוֹת לְשֵׁם יִחוּד קוּדְשָׁא בְּרִיךְ הוּא וּשְׁכִינְתֵּיהּ עַל יְדֵי הַהוּא טָמִיר וְנֶעְלָם בְּשֵׁם כָּל יִשְׂרָאֵל.

I am ready and prepared to perform the commandment of the third of the four cups, to honor the Holy One, blessed be He and His Divine Presence, through the hidden and secret Guardian, on behalf of all Israel.

בָּרוּךְ אַתָּה יְיָ אֱלֹהֵינוּ מֶלֶךְ הָעוֹלָם, בּוֹרֵא פְּרִי הַגָּפֶן.

Blessed art Thou, Lord our God, King of the universe, Creator of the fruit of the vine.

Drink more than half the wine in the cup within four minutes. Males drink while reclining on the left. Remove the small piece of matzah from the table.

Hallel: *Praise* הַלֵּל

The wine goblets are filled for the fourth cup (some fill this cup before the next paragraph). The extra cup that was placed in the middle of the table, called the Cup of Elijah, is now filled. One of the company goes to open the front door. All rise (some pronounce the greeting *Barukh Habah,* Welcome). The Leader and company recite the following:

„שְׁפֹךְ חֲמָתְךָ אֶל הַגּוֹיִם אֲשֶׁר לֹא יְדָעוּךָ וְעַל מַמְלָכוֹת אֲשֶׁר בְּשִׁמְךָ לֹא קָרָאוּ. כִּי אָכַל אֶת יַעֲקֹב וְאֶת נָוֵהוּ הֵשַׁמּוּ״. „שְׁפָךְ עֲלֵיהֶם זַעְמְךָ וַחֲרוֹן אַפְּךָ יַשִּׂיגֵם״. „תִּרְדֹּף בְּאַף וְתַשְׁמִידֵם מִתַּחַת שְׁמֵי יְיָ״.

"Pour out Thy wrath upon the nations that know Thee not, and upon the kingdoms that call not upon Thy Name. For they have devoured Jacob and laid waste his habitation" (Ps. 79:6–7). "Pour out Thine indignation upon them, and let the fierceness of Thine anger overtake them" (Ps. 69:25). "Thou wilt pursue them in anger, and destroy them from under the heavens of the Lord" (Lam. 3:66).

The door is closed and everyone is seated. The *Hallel* continues to joyful, melodious tunes.

לֹא לָנוּ יְיָ לֹא לָנוּ כִּי לְשִׁמְךָ תֵּן כָּבוֹד עַל חַסְדְּךָ עַל אֲמִתֶּךָ. לָמָּה יֹאמְרוּ הַגּוֹיִם: אַיֵּה נָא אֱלֹהֵיהֶם? וֵאלֹהֵינוּ בַשָּׁמָיִם, כֹּל אֲשֶׁר חָפֵץ עָשָׂה. עֲצַבֵּיהֶם כֶּסֶף וְזָהָב, מַעֲשֵׂה יְדֵי אָדָם. פֶּה לָהֶם וְלֹא יְדַבֵּרוּ, עֵינַיִם לָהֶם וְלֹא יִרְאוּ, אָזְנַיִם לָהֶם

Not unto us, O Lord, not unto us, but unto Thy Name give glory, for Thy mercy, and for Thy truth's sake. Wherefore should the nations say, "Where is now their God?" But our God is in the heavens; whatsoever pleased Him He hath done. Their idols are silver and gold, the work of men's hands. They have mouths, but

וְלֹא יִשְׁמָעוּ, אַף לָהֶם וְלֹא יְרִיחוּן. יְדֵיהֶם וְלֹא יְמִישׁוּן, רַגְלֵיהֶם וְלֹא יְהַלֵּכוּ, לֹא יֶהְגּוּ בִּגְרוֹנָם. כְּמוֹהֶם יִהְיוּ עֹשֵׂיהֶם, כֹּל אֲשֶׁר בֹּטֵחַ בָּהֶם. יִשְׂרָאֵל בְּטַח בַּייָ, עֶזְרָם וּמָגִנָּם הוּא. בֵּית אַהֲרֹן בִּטְחוּ בַייָ, עֶזְרָם וּמָגִנָּם הוּא, יִרְאֵי יְיָ בִּטְחוּ בַייָ, עֶזְרָם וּמָגִנָּם הוּא.

יְיָ זְכָרָנוּ יְבָרֵךְ, יְבָרֵךְ אֶת בֵּית יִשְׂרָאֵל, יְבָרֵךְ אֶת בֵּית אַהֲרֹן. יְבָרֵךְ יִרְאֵי יְיָ, הַקְּטַנִּים עִם הַגְּדֹלִים. יֹסֵף יְיָ עֲלֵיכֶם, עֲלֵיכֶם וְעַל בְּנֵיכֶם. בְּרוּכִים אַתֶּם לַייָ, עֹשֵׂה שָׁמַיִם וָאָרֶץ. הַשָּׁמַיִם שָׁמַיִם לַייָ, וְהָאָרֶץ נָתַן לִבְנֵי אָדָם. לֹא הַמֵּתִים יְהַלְלוּ יָהּ וְלֹא כָּל יֹרְדֵי דוּמָה, וַאֲנַחְנוּ נְבָרֵךְ יָהּ, מֵעַתָּה וְעַד עוֹלָם; הַלְלוּיָהּ.

אָהַבְתִּי כִּי יִשְׁמַע יְיָ אֶת קוֹלִי תַּחֲנוּנָי. כִּי הִטָּה אָזְנוֹ לִי, וּבְיָמַי אֶקְרָא. אֲפָפוּנִי חֶבְלֵי מָוֶת וּמְצָרֵי

they speak not; eyes have they, but they see not. They have ears, but they hear not; noses have they, but they smell not. They have hands, but they handle not; feet have they, but they walk not; neither speak they with their throat. They that make them shall be like unto them; yea, every one that trusteth in them. O Israel, trust thou in the Lord! He is their help and their shield! O house of Aaron, trust ye in the Lord! He is their help and their shield! Ye that fear the Lord, trust in the Lord! He is their help and their shield. (Ps. 115:1–11)

The Lord hath been mindful of us; He will bless, He will bless the house of Israel; He will bless the house of Aaron. He will bless them that fear the Lord, both small and great. The Lord increase you more and more, you and your children. Blessed be ye of the Lord, who made heaven and earth. The heavens are the heavens of the Lord; but the earth hath He given to the children of men. The dead praise not the Lord, neither any that go down into silence; but we will bless the Lord from this time forth and forever. Hallelujah. (Ps. 115:12–18)

I love that the Lord should hear my voice and my supplications.

שְׁאוֹל מְצָאוּנִי, צָרָה וְיָגוֹן אֶמְצָא. וּבְשֵׁם יְיָ אֶקְרָא, אָנָּה יְיָ מַלְּטָה נַפְשִׁי. חַנּוּן יְיָ וְצַדִּיק וֵאלֹהֵינוּ מְרַחֵם. שֹׁמֵר פְּתָאִים יְיָ, דַּלּוֹתִי וְלִי יְהוֹשִׁיעַ. שׁוּבִי נַפְשִׁי לִמְנוּחָיְכִי, כִּי יְיָ גָּמַל עָלָיְכִי. כִּי חִלַּצְתָּ נַפְשִׁי מִמָּוֶת, אֶת עֵינִי מִן דִּמְעָה אֶת רַגְלִי מִדֶּחִי. אֶתְהַלֵּךְ לִפְנֵי יְיָ בְּאַרְצוֹת הַחַיִּים. הֶאֱמַנְתִּי כִּי אֲדַבֵּר, אֲנִי עָנִיתִי מְאֹד. אֲנִי אָמַרְתִּי בְחָפְזִי כָּל הָאָדָם כֹּזֵב.

מָה אָשִׁיב לַייָ, כָּל תַּגְמוּלוֹהִי עָלָי? כּוֹס יְשׁוּעוֹת אֶשָּׂא וּבְשֵׁם יְיָ אֶקְרָא. נְדָרַי לַייָ אֲשַׁלֵּם נֶגְדָה נָּא לְכָל עַמּוֹ. יָקָר בְּעֵינֵי יְיָ הַמָּוְתָה לַחֲסִידָיו. אָנָּה יְיָ כִּי אֲנִי עַבְדֶּךָ, אֲנִי עַבְדְּךָ בֶּן אֲמָתֶךָ, פִּתַּחְתָּ לְמוֹסֵרָי. לְךָ אֶזְבַּח זֶבַח תּוֹדָה, וּבְשֵׁם יְיָ אֶקְרָא. נְדָרַי לַייָ אֲשַׁלֵּם נֶגְדָה נָּא לְכָל עַמּוֹ. בְּחַצְרוֹת בֵּית יְיָ, בְּתוֹכֵכִי יְרוּשָׁלָיִם; הַלְלוּיָהּ.

Because He hath inclined His ear unto me, therefore will I call upon Him all my days. The cords of death compassed me, and the straits of the netherworld got hold upon me; I found trouble and sorrow. But I called upon the name of the Lord: "I beseech Thee, O Lord, deliver my soul." Gracious is the Lord, and righteous; yea, our God is compassionate. The Lord preserveth the simple; I was brought low, and He saved me. Return, O my soul, unto thy rest; for the Lord hath dealt bountifully with thee. For Thou hast delivered my soul from death, mine eyes from tears, and my feet from stumbling. I shall walk before the Lord in the lands of the living. I trusted even when I spoke: "I am greatly afflicted." I said in my haste: "All men are liars" (Ps. 116:1–11).

How can I repay unto the Lord all His bountiful dealings toward me? I will lift up the cup of salvation, and call upon the name of the Lord. My vows will I pay unto the Lord, yea, in the presence of all His people. Precious in the sight of the Lord is the death of His saints. I beseech Thee, O Lord, for I am Thy servant; I am Thy servant, the son of Thy handmaid; Thou hast loosed my bands. I will

הַלְלוּ אֶת יְיָ כָּל גּוֹיִם, שַׁבְּחוּהוּ כָּל הָאֻמִּים. כִּי גָבַר עָלֵינוּ חַסְדּוֹ, וֶאֱמֶת יְיָ לְעוֹלָם; הַלְלוּיָהּ.

offer to Thee the sacrifice of thanksgiving, and will call upon the name of the Lord. I will pay my vows unto the Lord, yea, in the presence of all His people; in the courts of the Lord's house, in the midst of thee, O Jerusalem. Hallelujah. (Ps. 116:12–19)

O praise the Lord, all ye nations; laud Him, all ye peoples. For His mercy is great toward us; and the truth of the Lord endureth for ever. Hallelujah. (Ps. 117)

When there are at least three persons present at the Seder, the Leader says each of the following four verses aloud and the rest of the company responds by repeating the first verse as a refrain.

הוֹדוּ לַייָ כִּי טוֹב כִּי לְעוֹלָם חַסְדּוֹ.

יֹאמַר נָא יִשְׂרָאֵל כִּי לְעוֹלָם חַסְדּוֹ.

יֹאמְרוּ נָא בֵית אַהֲרֹן
כִּי לְעוֹלָם חַסְדּוֹ.

יֹאמְרוּ נָא יִרְאֵי יְיָ כִּי לְעוֹלָם חַסְדּוֹ.

O give thanks unto the Lord, for He is good, for His mercy endureth for ever.

So let Israel now say, for His mercy endureth for ever.

So let the house of Aaron now say, for His mercy endureth for ever.

So let them now that fear the Lord say, for His mercy endureth for ever. (Ps. 118:1–4)

מִן הַמֵּצַר קָרָאתִי יָּהּ, עָנָנִי בַמֶּרְחַב יָהּ. יְיָ לִי לֹא אִירָא, מַה יַּעֲשֶׂה לִי

Out of my straits I called upon the Lord; He answered me with great enlargement. The Lord is for me; I will not fear; what can man do unto me? The Lord is for me as my helper; and I shall gaze upon them that hate me. It is better to take refuge in the Lord. than to trust in man. It is

אָדָם? יְיָ לִי בְּעֹזְרָי, וַאֲנִי אֶרְאֶה
בְשֹׂנְאָי. טוֹב לַחֲסוֹת בַּייָ מִבְּטֹחַ
בָּאָדָם. טוֹב לַחֲסוֹת בַּייָ מִבְּטֹחַ
בִּנְדִיבִים. כָּל גּוֹיִם סְבָבוּנִי, בְּשֵׁם יְיָ
כִּי אֲמִילַם. סַבּוּנִי גַם סְבָבוּנִי, בְּשֵׁם
יְיָ כִּי אֲמִילַם. סַבּוּנִי כִדְבֹרִים,
דֹּעֲכוּ כְּאֵשׁ קוֹצִים, בְּשֵׁם יְיָ כִּי
אֲמִילַם. דָּחֹה דְחִיתַנִי לִנְפֹּל וַייָ
עֲזָרָנִי. עָזִּי וְזִמְרָת יָהּ, וַיְהִי לִי
לִישׁוּעָה. קוֹל רִנָּה וִישׁוּעָה,
בְּאָהֳלֵי צַדִּיקִים, יְמִין יְיָ עֹשָׂה חָיִל.
יְמִין יְיָ רוֹמֵמָה, יְמִין יְיָ עֹשָׂה חָיִל.
לֹא אָמוּת כִּי אֶחְיֶה, וַאֲסַפֵּר מַעֲשֵׂי
יָהּ. יַסֹּר יִסְּרַנִּי יָּהּ, וְלַמָּוֶת לֹא
נְתָנָנִי. פִּתְחוּ לִי שַׁעֲרֵי צֶדֶק, אָבֹא
בָם אוֹדֶה יָהּ. זֶה הַשַּׁעַר לַייָ,
צַדִּיקִים יָבֹאוּ בוֹ.

better to take refuge in the Lord than to trust in princes. All nations compass me about; verily, in the name of the Lord I will cut them off. They compass me about, yea, they compass me about; verily, in the name of the Lord I will cut them off. They compass me about like bees; they are quenched as the fire of thorns; verily, in the name of the Lord I will cut them off. Thou didst thrust sore at me that I might fall; but the Lord helped me. The Lord is my strength and song; and He is become my salvation. The voice of rejoicing and salvation is in the tents of the righteous; the right hand of the Lord doeth valiantly. The right hand of the Lord is exalted; the right hand of the Lord doeth valiantly. I shall not die, but live, and declare the works of the Lord. The Lord hath chastened me sore; but He hath not given me over unto death. Open to me the gates of righteousness; I will enter into them, I will give thanks unto the Lord. This is the gate of the Lord; the righteous shall enter into it. (Ps. 118:5–20)

Each of the next four verses is chanted twice.

אוֹדְךָ כִּי עֲנִיתָנִי, וַתְּהִי לִי
לִישׁוּעָה.

I will give thanks unto Thee, for Thou hast answered me, and

אֶבֶן מָאֲסוּ הַבּוֹנִים הָיְתָה לְרֹאשׁ פִּנָּה.

art become my salvation. The stone which the builders rejected is become the chief cornerstone.

מֵאֵת יְיָ הָיְתָה זֹּאת, הִיא נִפְלָאת בְּעֵינֵינוּ.

This is the Lord's doing; it is marvellous in our eyes.

זֶה הַיּוֹם עָשָׂה יְיָ נָגִילָה וְנִשְׂמְחָה בוֹ.

This is the day which the Lord hath made; we will rejoice and be glad in it. (Ps. 118:21–24)

When there are at least three persons present at the Seder, the Leader says each of the following four verses aloud and the rest of the company repeats each verse after him. The Leader may, if he wishes, allow a child to lead this prayer.

אָנָּא יְיָ הוֹשִׁיעָה נָּא.

We beseech Thee, O Lord, save now!

אָנָּא יְיָ הוֹשִׁיעָה נָּא.

We beseech Thee, O Lord, save now!

אָנָּא יְיָ הַצְלִיחָה נָא.

We beseech Thee, O Lord, make us now to prosper.

אָנָּא יְיָ הַצְלִיחָה נָא.

We beseech Thee, O Lord, make us now to prosper. (Ps. 118:25)

Each of the next four verses is chanted twice.

בָּרוּךְ הַבָּא בְּשֵׁם יְיָ, בֵּרַכְנוּכֶם מִבֵּית יְיָ.

Blessed be he that cometh in the name of the Lord; we bless you out of the house of the Lord.

אֵל יְיָ וַיָּאֶר לָנוּ, אִסְרוּ חַג בַּעֲבֹתִים עַד קַרְנוֹת הַמִּזְבֵּחַ.

The Lord is God, and hath given us light; order the festival procession with boughs, even unto the horns of the altar.

אֵלִי אַתָּה וְאוֹדֶךָּ, אֱלֹהַי אֲרוֹמְמֶךָּ.

הוֹדוּ לַייָ כִּי טוֹב, כִּי לְעוֹלָם חַסְדּוֹ.

Thou art my God, and I will give thanks unto

Thee; Thou art my God, I will exalt Thee.

O give thanks unto the Lord, for He is good, for His mercy endureth for ever. (Ps. 118:26:29)

All Thy works praise Thee, Lord our God; and Thy pious ones, the just who do Thy will, and all the house of Israel shall thank and bless and praise and glorify and exalt and revere and sanctify and ascribe sovereignty to Thy Name, our King, in song. For it is good to give thanks unto Thee, and becoming to sing praises to Thy Name; for from everlasting unto everlasting Thou art God.

O give thanks unto the Lord, for He is good, for His mercy endureth for ever.

O give thanks unto the God of gods, for His mercy endureth for ever.

O give thanks unto the Lord of lords, for His mercy endureth for ever.

To Him who alone doeth great wonders, for His mercy endureth for ever.

To Him that by understanding made the heavens, for His mercy endureth for ever.

To Him that spread forth the earth above the waters, for His mercy endureth for ever.

To Him that made great lights, for His mercy endureth for ever.

יְהַלְלוּךָ יְיָ אֱלֹהֵינוּ כָּל מַעֲשֶׂיךָ.
וַחֲסִידֶיךָ צַדִּיקִים עוֹשֵׂי רְצוֹנֶךָ,
וְכָל עַמְּךָ בֵּית יִשְׂרָאֵל, בְּרִנָּה יוֹדוּ
וִיבָרְכוּ וִישַׁבְּחוּ וִיפָאֲרוּ וִירוֹמְמוּ
וְיַעֲרִיצוּ וְיַקְדִּישׁוּ וְיַמְלִיכוּ אֶת
שִׁמְךָ מַלְכֵּנוּ. כִּי לְךָ טוֹב לְהוֹדוֹת
וּלְשִׁמְךָ נָאֶה לְזַמֵּר כִּי מֵעוֹלָם וְעַד
עוֹלָם אַתָּה אֵל.

הוֹדוּ לַייָ כִּי טוֹב כִּי לְעוֹלָם חַסְדּוֹ.
הוֹדוּ לֵאלֹהֵי הָאֱלֹהִים
כִּי לְעוֹלָם חַסְדּוֹ.
הוֹדוּ לַאֲדֹנֵי הָאֲדֹנִים
כִּי לְעוֹלָם חַסְדּוֹ.
לְעֹשֵׂה נִפְלָאוֹת גְּדֹלוֹת לְבַדּוֹ
כִּי לְעוֹלָם חַסְדּוֹ.
לְעֹשֵׂה הַשָּׁמַיִם בִּתְבוּנָה
כִּי לְעוֹלָם חַסְדּוֹ.
לְרוֹקַע הָאָרֶץ עַל הַמָּיִם
כִּי לְעוֹלָם חַסְדּוֹ.
לְעֹשֵׂה אוֹרִים גְּדֹלִים
כִּי לְעוֹלָם חַסְדּוֹ.
אֶת הַשֶּׁמֶשׁ לְמֶמְשֶׁלֶת בַּיּוֹם
כִּי לְעוֹלָם חַסְדּוֹ.

אֶת הַיָּרֵחַ וְכוֹכָבִים לְמֶמְשְׁלוֹת בַּלָּיְלָה כִּי לְעוֹלָם חַסְדּוֹ.

לְמַכֵּה מִצְרַיִם בִּבְכוֹרֵיהֶם.
כִּי לְעוֹלָם חַסְדּוֹ.

וַיּוֹצֵא יִשְׂרָאֵל מִתּוֹכָם
כִּי לְעוֹלָם חַסְדּוֹ.

בְּיָד חֲזָקָה וּבִזְרוֹעַ נְטוּיָה
כִּי לְעוֹלָם חַסְדּוֹ.

לְגֹזֵר יַם סוּף לִגְזָרִים
כִּי לְעוֹלָם חַסְדּוֹ.

וְהֶעֱבִיר יִשְׂרָאֵל בְּתוֹכוֹ
כִּי לְעוֹלָם חַסְדּוֹ.

וְנִעֵר פַּרְעֹה וְחֵילוֹ בְיַם סוּף
כִּי לְעוֹלָם חַסְדּוֹ.

לְמוֹלִיךְ עַמּוֹ בַּמִּדְבָּר
כִּי לְעוֹלָם חַסְדּוֹ.

לְמַכֵּה מְלָכִים גְּדֹלִים
כִּי לְעוֹלָם חַסְדּוֹ.

וַיַּהֲרֹג מְלָכִים אַדִּירִים
כִּי לְעוֹלָם חַסְדּוֹ.

לְסִיחוֹן מֶלֶךְ הָאֱמֹרִי
כִּי לְעוֹלָם חַסְדּוֹ.

וּלְעוֹג מֶלֶךְ הַבָּשָׁן
כִּי לְעוֹלָם חַסְדּוֹ.

The sun to rule by day, for His mercy endureth for ever.

The moon and stars to rule by night, for His mercy endureth for ever.

To Him that smote Egypt in their first-born, for His mercy endureth for ever.

And brought out Israel from among them, for His mercy endureth for ever.

With a strong hand, and with an outstretched arm, for His mercy endureth for ever.

To Him who divided the Red Sea in sunder, for His mercy endureth for ever.

And made Israel to pass through the midst of it, for His mercy endureth for ever.

But overthrew Pharaoh and his host in the Red Sea, for His mercy endureth for ever.

To Him that led His people through the wilderness, for His mercy endureth for ever.

To Him that smote great kings; for His mercy endureth for ever.

And slew mighty kings, for His mercy endureth for ever.

Sihon, king of the Amorites, for His mercy endureth for ever.

And Og, king of Bashan, for His mercy endureth for ever.

And gave their land for a heritage, for His mercy endureth for ever.

וְנָתַן אַרְצָם לְנַחֲלָה
כִּי לְעוֹלָם חַסְדּוֹ.
נַחֲלָה לְיִשְׂרָאֵל עַבְדּוֹ
כִּי לְעוֹלָם חַסְדּוֹ.
שֶׁבְּשִׁפְלֵנוּ זָכַר לָנוּ
כִּי לְעוֹלָם חַסְדּוֹ.
וַיִּפְרְקֵנוּ מִצָּרֵינוּ כִּי לְעוֹלָם חַסְדּוֹ.
נֹתֵן לֶחֶם לְכָל בָּשָׂר
כִּי לְעוֹלָם חַסְדּוֹ.
הוֹדוּ לְאֵל הַשָּׁמָיִם
כִּי לְעוֹלָם חַסְדּוֹ.

נִשְׁמַת כָּל חַי תְּבָרֵךְ אֶת שִׁמְךָ יְיָ אֱלֹהֵינוּ, וְרוּחַ כָּל בָּשָׂר תְּפָאֵר וּתְרוֹמֵם זִכְרְךָ מַלְכֵּנוּ תָּמִיד. מִן הָעוֹלָם וְעַד הָעוֹלָם אַתָּה אֵל, וּמִבַּלְעָדֶיךָ אֵין לָנוּ מֶלֶךְ גּוֹאֵל וּמוֹשִׁיעַ, פּוֹדֶה וּמַצִּיל וּמְפַרְנֵס וּמְרַחֵם בְּכָל עֵת צָרָה וְצוּקָה, אֵין לָנוּ מֶלֶךְ אֶלָּא אָתָּה. אֱלֹהֵי הָרִאשׁוֹנִים וְהָאַחֲרוֹנִים, אֱלוֹהַּ כָּל בְּרִיּוֹת. אֲדוֹן כָּל תּוֹלָדוֹת, הַמְהֻלָּל בְּרֹב הַתִּשְׁבָּחוֹת, הַמְנַהֵג עוֹלָמוֹ בְּחֶסֶד וּבְרִיּוֹתָיו בְּרַחֲמִים. וַיְיָ לֹא יָנוּם וְלֹא יִישָׁן, הַמְעוֹרֵר יְשֵׁנִים,

Even a heritage unto Israel, His servant, for His mercy endureth for ever.

Who remembered us in our low estate, for His mercy endureth for ever.

And hath delivered us from our adversaries, for His mercy endureth for ever.

Who giveth food to all flesh, for His mercy endureth for ever.

O give thanks unto the God of heaven, for His mercy endureth for ever. (Ps. 136)

The breath of all that lives shall praise Thy Name, Lord our God, and the spirit of all flesh shall glorify and exalt Thy remembrance, O our King. Continually, from everlasting to everlasting, Thou art God, and beside Thee we have no King who redeemeth and saveth, delivereth and protecteth, sustaineth and pitieth in all time of trouble and stress; we have no King but Thee. Thou art God of the first and of the last; God of all creatures, Lord of all generations, who is lauded with many praises, and who guideth His world with loving-kindness and His creatures with mercy. For the Lord neither slumbereth nor sleepeth; He awakeneth those that sleep and arouseth those that slumber, giveth

speech to the dumb, looseneth the bound, supporteth the falling, and raiseth up the bowed. To Thee alone do we give thanks.

Though our mouths were filled with song as the sea, and our tongues with joy as its multitude of waves, and our lips with praise as the expanse of the firmament; though our eyes were radiant as the sun and the moon, and our hands were outspread as the wings of the eagles of heaven, and our feet were fleet as the hinds'; we should yet be inadequate to thank Thee, O Lord our God, and God of our Fathers, for one in a thousand of the many thousands of thousands and myriads of myriads of loving-kindnesses that Thou hast bestowed on our fathers and on us.

From Egypt didst Thou deliver us, Lord our God, and from the house of bondage didst Thou release us; in famine didst Thou feed us, and in plenty didst Thou sustain us; from the sword didst Thou deliver us, and from pestilence didst Thou protect us, and from sore and grievous sickness didst Thou withdraw us. Thus far Thy mercies have helped us, and Thy loving-kindness have not deserted us: O, forsake us not, O Lord, our God, for ever! Wherefore, the limbs which

וְהַמֵּקִיץ נִרְדָּמִים, וְהַמֵּשִׂיחַ
אִלְּמִים, וְהַמַּתִּיר אֲסוּרִים, וְהַסּוֹמֵךְ
נוֹפְלִים, וְהַזּוֹקֵף כְּפוּפִים, לְךָ לְבַדְּךָ
אֲנַחְנוּ מוֹדִים.

אִלּוּ פִינוּ מָלֵא שִׁירָה כַּיָּם, וּלְשׁוֹנֵנוּ
רִנָּה כַּהֲמוֹן גַּלָּיו, וְשִׂפְתוֹתֵינוּ שֶׁבַח
כְּמֶרְחֲבֵי רָקִיעַ, וְעֵינֵינוּ מְאִירוֹת
כַּשֶּׁמֶשׁ וְכַיָּרֵחַ, וְיָדֵינוּ פְרוּשׂוֹת
כְּנִשְׁרֵי שָׁמָיִם, וְרַגְלֵינוּ קַלּוֹת
כָּאַיָּלוֹת, אֵין אֲנַחְנוּ מַסְפִּיקִים
לְהוֹדוֹת לְךָ, יְיָ אֱלֹהֵינוּ וֵאלֹהֵי
אֲבוֹתֵינוּ, וּלְבָרֵךְ אֶת שְׁמֶךָ, עַל
אַחַת מֵאָלֶף אֶלֶף אַלְפֵי אֲלָפִים
וְרִבֵּי רְבָבוֹת פְּעָמִים, הַטּוֹבוֹת
שֶׁעָשִׂיתָ עִם אֲבוֹתֵינוּ וְעִמָּנוּ.

מִמִּצְרַיִם גְּאַלְתָּנוּ, יְיָ אֱלֹהֵינוּ,
וּמִבֵּית עֲבָדִים פְּדִיתָנוּ, בְּרָעָב
זַנְתָּנוּ, וּבְשָׂבָע כִּלְכַּלְתָּנוּ, מֵחֶרֶב
הִצַּלְתָּנוּ, וּמִדֶּבֶר מִלַּטְתָּנוּ, וּמֵחֳלָיִם
רָעִים וְנֶאֱמָנִים דִּלִּיתָנוּ. עַד הֵנָּה
עֲזָרוּנוּ רַחֲמֶיךָ, וְלֹא עֲזָבוּנוּ
חֲסָדֶיךָ, וְאַל תִּטְּשֵׁנוּ יְיָ אֱלֹהֵינוּ,

לָנֶצַח. עַל כֵּן, אֵבָרִים שֶׁפִּלַּגְתָּ בָּנוּ, וְרוּחַ וּנְשָׁמָה שֶׁנָּפַחְתָּ בְּאַפֵּינוּ, וְלָשׁוֹן אֲשֶׁר שַׂמְתָּ בְּפִינוּ, הֵן הֵם יוֹדוּ וִיבָרְכוּ וִישַׁבְּחוּ וִיפָאֲרוּ וִירוֹמְמוּ וְיַעֲרִיצוּ וְיַקְדִּישׁוּ וְיַמְלִיכוּ אֶת שִׁמְךָ מַלְכֵּנוּ, כִּי כָל פֶּה לְךָ יוֹדֶה, וְכָל לָשׁוֹן לְךָ תִשָּׁבַע, וְכָל בֶּרֶךְ לְךָ תִכְרַע, וְכָל קוֹמָה לְפָנֶיךָ תִשְׁתַּחֲוֶה, וְכָל לְבָבוֹת יִירָאוּךָ, וְכָל קֶרֶב וּכְלָיוֹת יְזַמְּרוּ לִשְׁמֶךָ. כַּדָּבָר שֶׁכָּתוּב: כָּל עַצְמוֹתַי תֹּאמַרְנָה יְיָ מִי כָמוֹךָ, מַצִּיל עָנִי מֵחָזָק מִמֶּנּוּ, וְעָנִי וְאֶבְיוֹן מִגּוֹזְלוֹ. מִי יִדְמֶה לָּךְ וּמִי יִשְׁוֶה לָּךְ וּמִי יַעֲרָךְ לָךְ. הָאֵל הַגָּדוֹל הַגִּבּוֹר וְהַנּוֹרָא, אֵל עֶלְיוֹן קֹנֵה שָׁמַיִם וָאָרֶץ. נְהַלֶּלְךָ וּנְשַׁבֵּחֲךָ וּנְפָאֶרְךָ וּנְבָרֵךְ אֶת שֵׁם קָדְשֶׁךָ, כָּאָמוּר: „לְדָוִד, בָּרְכִי נַפְשִׁי אֶת יְיָ, וְכָל קְרָבַי אֶת שֵׁם קָדְשׁוֹ".

הָאֵל בְּתַעֲצֻמוֹת עֻזֶּךָ, הַגָּדוֹל בִּכְבוֹד שְׁמֶךָ, הַגִּבּוֹר לָנֶצַח וְהַנּוֹרָא בְּנוֹרְאוֹתֶיךָ, הַמֶּלֶךְ הַיּוֹשֵׁב עַל כִּסֵּא רָם וְנִשָּׂא.

Thou hast formed in us, and the breath and spirit which thou hast blown into our nostrils, and the tongue which Thou hast placed in our mouths—lo! they shall thank, bless, praise, glorify, extol, reverence, hallow, and ascribe sovereignty to Thy Name, O our King! For to Thee every mouth shall give thanks, to Thee every tongue shall swear, to Thee every knee shall bend, and before Thee every stature shall bow down; Thee every heart shall fear, and unto Thy Name shall all men's inmost being sing praise; according to that which is written: "All my bones shall say: O Lord, who is like unto Thee? which delivereth the poor from him that is too strong for him, yea, the poor and the needy from him that spoileth him?" (Ps. 35:10). Who is like unto Thee? who is equal to Thee? who can be compared unto Thee? Thou great, mighty, and tremendous God, most high God, possessor of heaven and earth! We will praise Thee, laud Thee, glorify Thee, and bless Thy holy Name: as David said: "Bless the Lord, O my soul; and all that is within me, bless His holy Name" (Ps. 103:1).

O God! in the might of Thy power, great in the glory of Thy Name,

mighty for ever, tremendous by Thy tremendous acts! O King, who sitteth upon a high and lofty throne!

He that abideth eternally, exalted and holy is His Name. It is written: "Rejoice in the Lord, O ye righteous, for praise is comely for the upright" (Ps. 33:1). In the mouth of the upright shalt Thou be praised; with the words of the righteous shalt Thou be blessed; by the tongue of the pious shalt Thou be extolled; and in the inmost being of the holy shalt Thou be hallowed. And in the assemblies of the multitudes of Thy people, the house of Israel, shall Thy Name be glorified in song, O our King, in every generation. For such is the duty of all creatures, before Thee, Lord our God, and God of our fathers, to thank, praise, laud, glorify, extol, reverence, bless, exalt and adore, above all the words of the songs and praises of David, the son of Jesse, Thine anointed servant.

Be Thy Name praised for ever, O our King; God and King, great and hallowed in Heaven and on earth. For unto Thee are becoming, Lord our God, and God of our fathers, song and praise, adoration and psalmody, strength and dominion; victory, greatness, and might; praise and glory;

שׁוֹכֵן עַד, מָרוֹם וְקָדוֹשׁ שְׁמוֹ. וְכָתוּב: „רַנְּנוּ צַדִּיקִים בַּייָ, לַיְשָׁרִים נָאוָה תְהִלָּה". בְּפִי יְשָׁרִים תִּתְהַלָּל, וּבְדִבְרֵי צַדִּיקִים תִּתְבָּרַךְ, וּבִלְשׁוֹן חֲסִידִים תִּתְרוֹמָם, וּבְקֶרֶב קְדוֹשִׁים תִּתְקַדָּשׁ. וּבְמַקְהֲלוֹת רִבְבוֹת עַמְּךָ בֵּית יִשְׂרָאֵל, בְּרִנָּה יִתְפָּאַר שִׁמְךָ מַלְכֵּנוּ בְּכָל דּוֹר וָדוֹר. שֶׁכֵּן חוֹבַת כָּל הַיְצוּרִים לְפָנֶיךָ, יְיָ אֱלֹהֵינוּ, וֵאלֹהֵי אֲבוֹתֵינוּ לְהוֹדוֹת, לְהַלֵּל, לְשַׁבֵּחַ, לְפָאֵר, לְרוֹמֵם, לְהַדֵּר, לְבָרֵךְ, לְעַלֵּה, וּלְקַלֵּס עַל כָּל דִּבְרֵי שִׁירוֹת וְתִשְׁבְּחוֹת דָּוִד בֶּן יִשַׁי, עַבְדְּךָ מְשִׁיחֶךָ.

יִשְׁתַּבַּח שִׁמְךָ לָעַד מַלְכֵּנוּ, הָאֵל הַמֶּלֶךְ הַגָּדוֹל וְהַקָּדוֹשׁ בַּשָּׁמַיִם וּבָאָרֶץ, כִּי לְךָ נָאֶה יְיָ אֱלֹהֵינוּ וֵאלֹהֵי אֲבוֹתֵינוּ, שִׁיר וּשְׁבָחָה, הַלֵּל וְזִמְרָה, עֹז וּמֶמְשָׁלָה, נֶצַח, גְּדֻלָּה וּגְבוּרָה, תְּהִלָּה וְתִפְאֶרֶת, קְדֻשָּׁה וּמַלְכוּת, בְּרָכוֹת וְהוֹדָאוֹת מֵעַתָּה וְעַד עוֹלָם. בָּרוּךְ אַתָּה יְיָ

holiness and sovereignty; blessings and thanksgiving, from henceforth and for ever. Blessed art Thou, Lord God and King, great in praises, God of thanksgivings, Lord of wonders, who delightest in songs of praise, King and God, Life of all worlds!

אֵל מֶלֶךְ גָּדוֹל בַּתִּשְׁבָּחוֹת, אֵל הַהוֹדָאוֹת, אֲדוֹן הַנִּפְלָאוֹת, הַבּוֹחֵר בְּשִׁירֵי זִמְרָה, מֶלֶךְ אֵל חֵי הָעוֹלָמִים.

The Leader and company raise their wine cups for the fourth cup. All recite the blessing aloud.

I am ready and prepared to perform the commandment of the fourth of the four cups, to honor the Holy One, blessed be He and His Divine Presence, through the hidden and secret Guardian, on behalf of all Israel.

הִנְנִי מוּכָן וּמְזֻמָּן לְקַיֵּם מִצְוַת כּוֹס רְבִיעִי מֵאַרְבַּע כּוֹסוֹת לְשֵׁם יִחוּד קוּדְשָׁא בְּרִיךְ הוּא וּשְׁכִינְתֵּיהּ עַל יְדֵי הַהוּא טָמִיר וְנֶעְלָם בְּשֵׁם כָּל יִשְׂרָאֵל.

Blessed art Thou, Lord our God, King of the universe, Creator of the fruit of the vine.

בָּרוּךְ אַתָּה יְיָ אֱלֹהֵינוּ מֶלֶךְ הָעוֹלָם, בּוֹרֵא, פְּרִי הַגָּפֶן.

Drink the entire contents of the cup within four minutes. Males must recline on the left. After finishing, the Leader and the entire company recite the following final blessing, adding the words in parenthesis on Friday night.

Blessed art Thou, Lord our God, King of the Universe, for the vine and for the fruit of the vine, and for the pleasant, goodly, and ample land which Thou hast willed to give as an inheritance to our Fathers, to eat of its fruit and be satisfied with its goodness. Have mercy, O Lord, our God, upon Israel, Thy people, and

בָּרוּךְ אַתָּה יְיָ אֱלֹהֵינוּ מֶלֶךְ הָעוֹלָם, עַל הַגֶּפֶן וְעַל פְּרִי הַגֶּפֶן, וְעַל תְּנוּבַת הַשָּׂדֶה, וְעַל אֶרֶץ חֶמְדָּה טוֹבָה וּרְחָבָה, שֶׁרָצִיתָ וְהִנְחַלְתָּ לַאֲבוֹתֵינוּ, לֶאֱכֹל מִפִּרְיָהּ וְלִשְׂבֹּעַ מִטּוּבָהּ. רַחֵם נָא, יְיָ אֱלֹהֵינוּ, עַל יִשְׂרָאֵל עַמֶּךָ, וְעַל

יְרוּשָׁלַיִם עִירֶךָ, וְעַל צִיּוֹן מִשְׁכַּן
כְּבוֹדֶךָ, וְעַל מִזְבְּחֶךָ וְעַל הֵיכָלֶךָ.
וּבְנֵה יְרוּשָׁלַיִם עִיר הַקֹּדֶשׁ
בִּמְהֵרָה בְיָמֵינוּ, וְהַעֲלֵנוּ לְתוֹכָהּ,
וְשַׂמְּחֵנוּ בְּבִנְיָנָהּ, וְנֹאכַל מִפִּרְיָהּ,
וְנִשְׂבַּע מִטּוּבָהּ, וּנְבָרֶכְךָ עָלֶיהָ
בִּקְדֻשָּׁה וּבְטָהֳרָה. (בשבת וּרְצֵה
וְהַחֲלִיצֵנוּ בְּיוֹם הַשַּׁבָּת הַזֶּה.)
וְשַׂמְּחֵנוּ בְּיוֹם חַג הַמַּצּוֹת הַזֶּה, כִּי
אַתָּה יְיָ, טוֹב וּמֵטִיב לַכֹּל, וְנוֹדֶה
לְּךָ עַל הָאָרֶץ וְעַל פְּרִי הַגָּפֶן. בָּרוּךְ
אַתָּה יְיָ, עַל הָאָרֶץ וְעַל פְּרִי הַגָּפֶן.

upon Jerusalem, Thy city, and upon Zion, the abode of Thy glory and upon Thine altar and upon Thy shrine. Build Thou again Jerusalem the Holy City speedily in our days; bring us up into its midst and cause us to rejoice in its establishment, so that we may eat of its fruit and be satisfied with its goodness and bless Thee for it in holiness and purity. (Be it Thy Will to strengthen us upon this Sabbath day) and make us to rejoice upon this Feast of Matzah. For Thou, O Lord, art good, and doest good to all: and we shall thank Thee for the land and for the fruit of the vine. Blessed art Thou, O Lord, for the land and for the fruit of the vine.

One may not eat any food or drink any liquid except water for the rest of the evening. The rest of the *Haggadah*, usually led by the children, is sung to the various tunes written for the occasion. Anyone may offer *divrei Torah*. The Seder must end before daybreak.

Nirtzah: *Acceptance Prayer* נִרְצָה

חֲסַל סִדּוּר פֶּסַח כְּהִלְכָתוֹ, כְּכָל
מִשְׁפָּטוֹ וְחֻקָּתוֹ, כַּאֲשֶׁר זָכִינוּ
לְסַדֵּר אוֹתוֹ, כֵּן נִזְכֶּה לַעֲשׂוֹתוֹ. זָךְ

Accomplished is the order of the Passover according to its precept, to all its law and its custom. Even as we have had the merit to order it, So may we have the

שׁוֹכֵן מְעוֹנָה, קוֹמֵם קְהַל עֲדַת מִי
מָנָה. בְּקָרוֹב נַהֵל נִטְעֵי כַנָּה,
פְּדוּיִים לְצִיּוֹן בְּרִנָּה.

merit to fulfill it. Thou Pure One, who dwellest on high! Redress the congregation that is without number! Speedily lead Thou the offshoots of the stock Thou hast planted, redeemed, to Zion in song.

לְשָׁנָה הַבָּאָה בִּירוּשָׁלָיִם.

NEXT YEAR IN JERUSALEM.

On the second night of Passover, counting the *Omer* begins.

הִנְנִי מוּכָן וּמְזֻמָּן לְקַיֵּם מִצְוַת עֲשֵׂה שֶׁל סְפִירַת הָעֹמֶר כְּמוֹ שֶׁכָּתוּב בַּתּוֹרָה: וּסְפַרְתֶּם לָכֶם מִמָּחֳרַת הַשַּׁבָּת מִיּוֹם הֲבִיאֲכֶם אֶת עֹמֶר הַתְּנוּפָה, שֶׁבַע שַׁבָּתוֹת תְּמִימוֹת תִּהְיֶינָה, עַד מִמָּחֳרַת הַשַּׁבָּת הַשְּׁבִיעִית תִּסְפְּרוּ חֲמִשִּׁים יוֹם.

I am ready and prepared to fulfill the positive commandment of the counting of the Omer as it is written in the Torah: "And ye shall count unto you from the morrow after the day of rest that ye brought the sheaf of the waving; seven weeks shall there be complete; even unto the morrow after the seventh week shall ye number fifty days."

בָּרוּךְ אַתָּה יְיָ אֱלֹהֵינוּ מֶלֶךְ
הָעוֹלָם, אֲשֶׁר קִדְּשָׁנוּ בְּמִצְוֹתָיו
וְצִוָּנוּ עַל סְפִירַת הָעֹמֶר.

Blessed art Thou, Lord our God, King of the universe, who hast sanctified us by Thy commandments, and hast commanded us concerning the counting of the Omer.

הַיּוֹם יוֹם אֶחָד לָעֹמֶר.

This is the first day of the Omer.

On the first Seder night say:

And It Happened in the Middle of the Night

וּבְכֵן וַיְהִי בַּחֲצִי הַלַּיְלָה.
אָז רוֹב נִסִּים הִפְלֵאתָ בַּלַּיְלָה,
בְּרֹאשׁ אַשְׁמוּרוֹת זֶה הַלַּיְלָה.
גֵּר צֶדֶק נִצַּחְתּוֹ כְּנֶחֱלַק לוֹ לַיְלָה,
וַיְהִי בַּחֲצִי הַלַּיְלָה.

Of old, Thou didst perform most miracles at night; at the beginning of the watches of this night. The righteous proselyte prevailed when he broke up his host at night.

And it happened in the middle of the night.

דַּנְתָּ מֶלֶךְ גְּרָר בַּחֲלוֹם הַלַּיְלָה,
הִפְחַדְתָּ אֲרַמִּי בְּאֶמֶשׁ לַיְלָה,
וַיָּשַׂר יִשְׂרָאֵל לָאֵל וַיּוּכַל לוֹ לַיְלָה,
וַיְהִי בַּחֲצִי הַלַּיְלָה.

Thou didst judge the king of Gerar in a dream of night; the Syrian was struck with terror yester-night, and Israel strove with God, and yet prevailed at night.
And it happened in the middle of the night.

זֶרַע בְּכוֹרֵי פַתְרוֹס מָחַצְתָּ בַּחֲצִי הַלַּיְלָה,
חֵילָם לֹא מָצְאוּ בְּקוּמָם בַּלַּיְלָה,
טִיסַת נְגִיד חֲרֹשֶׁת סִלִּיתָ בְּכוֹכְבֵי לַיְלָה,
וַיְהִי בַּחֲצִי הַלַּיְלָה.

The first-born seed of Pathros didst thou crush in dead of night. Their substance they found not when they rose at night. The battalions of Harosheth's captain didst sweep away through the stars of night.
And it happened in the middle of the night.

יָעַץ מְחָרֵף לְנוֹפֵף אִוּוּי הוֹבַשְׁתָּ פְגָרָיו בַּלַּיְלָה,
כָּרַע בֵּל וּמַצָּבוֹ בְּאִישׁוֹן לַיְלָה,
לְאִישׁ חֲמוּדוֹת נִגְלָה רָז חֲזוֹת לַיְלָה.
וַיְהִי בַּחֲצִי הַלַּיְלָה.

The impious thought to scatter My chosen. Thou didst shame his dead by night. Bel and his pillar were prostrate at night. The man of delight was told the key of mysteries of night.
And it happened in the middle of the night.

מִשְׁתַּכֵּר בִּכְלֵי קֹדֶשׁ נֶהֱרַג בּוֹ בַּלַּיְלָה,
נוֹשַׁע מִבּוֹר אֲרָיוֹת פּוֹתֵר בִּעֲתוּתֵי לַיְלָה,
שִׂנְאָה נָטַר אֲגָגִי וְכָתַב סְפָרִים בַּלַּיְלָה,
וַיְהִי בַּחֲצִי הַלַּיְלָה.

He who was drunken in the sacred vessels—he was slain that night; when he who had escaped the lions' den revealed the awesome dreams of night. The Agagite cherished hatred, and missives wrote at night.
And it happened in the middle of the night.

עוֹרַרְתָּ נִצְחֲךָ עָלָיו בְּנֶדֶד שְׁנַת לַיְלָה,
פּוּרָה תִדְרוֹךְ לְשׁוֹמֵר מַה מִּלַּיְלָה,
צָרַח כַּשּׁוֹמֵר וְשָׂח אָתָא בֹקֶר וְגַם לָיְלָה,
וַיְהִי בַּחֲצִי הַלַּיְלָה.

Thou didst arouse Thy victory on him, when sleep fled at night. The wine-press Thou shalt tread for him who asks the watchman, What of night? Like a watchman shall He answer, saying: "Morning's come, and, too, the night."
And it happened in the middle of the night.

קָרֵב יוֹם אֲשֶׁר הוּא לֹא יוֹם וְלֹא לַיְלָה,
רָם הוֹדַע כִּי לְךָ יוֹם אַף לְךָ לַיְלָה,
שׁוֹמְרִים הַפְקֵד לְעִירְךָ כָּל הַיּוֹם וְכָל הַלַּיְלָה,
תָּאִיר כְּאוֹר יוֹם חֶשְׁכַת לַיְלָה,
וַיְהִי בַּחֲצִי הַלַּיְלָה.

Bring near the day, which is not day nor night! All-High! Make known that Thine is day and Thine is night! Set guards about Thy city, all the day and all the night. Make Thou light as the day the dark of night!
And it happened in the middle of the night.

On the second Seder night say:

וּבְכֵן וַאֲמַרְתֶּם זֶבַח פֶּסַח.
אֹמֶץ גְּבוּרוֹתֶיךָ הִפְלֵאתָ בַּפֶּסַח,
בְּרֹאשׁ כָּל מוֹעֲדוֹת נִשֵּׂאתָ פֶּסַח,
גִּלִּיתָ לְאֶזְרָחִי חֲצוֹת לֵיל פֶּסַח,
וַאֲמַרְתֶּם זֶבַח פֶּסַח.

And Ye Shall Say: Tis the Offering of the Passover.

The strength of Thy might was wondrously displayed on Passover. Above all feasts didst Thou raise up the Passover. To the Ezrahite Thou didst reveal the midnight marvels of the Passover.
And ye shall say: Tis the offering of the Passover.

דְּלָתָיו דָּפַקְתָּ כְּחֹם הַיּוֹם בַּפֶּסַח,
הִסְעִיד נוֹצְצִים עֻגוֹת מַצּוֹת בַּפֶּסַח,
וְאֶל הַבָּקָר רָץ זֵכֶר לְשׁוֹר עֵרֶךְ

Upon his doors didst knock at noontide heat on Passover. He feasted angels with unleavened

cakes on Passover. And to the herd he ran; so do we read the Lesson of the Ox on Passover.

And ye shall say: Tis the offering of the Passover.

The furious Sodomites Thou didst consume in fire on Passover. Lot, saved from them, baked unleavened bread towards the end of Passover. Thou didst sweep clean the land of Moph and Noph when Thou didst near on Passover.

And ye shall say: Tis the offering of the Passover.

Lord! Thou didst smite each first-born's head on Passover. Omnipotent! Thy first-born didst Thou spare on Passover. Not suffering a destroyer to pass my doors on Passover.

And ye shall say: Tis the offering of the Passover.

Strong Jericho was straitly closed towards the time of Passover. Midian was destroyed by a cake of barley, the offering of the Passover. The mighty ones of Pul and Lud were burned up in a conflagration on the Passover.

And ye shall say: Tis the offering of the Passover.

Destined was he to stay in Nob, until there came the time of Passover. A Hand wrote Babylon's fate upon the wall on Passover. The watch is set: the table spread—on Passover.

פֶּסַח,

וַאֲמַרְתֶּם זֶבַח פֶּסַח.

זוֹעֲמוּ סְדוֹמִים וְלֹהֲטוּ בָּאֵשׁ בַּפֶּסַח,
חֻלַּץ לוֹט מֵהֶם וּמַצּוֹת אָפָה בְּקֵץ פֶּסַח,
טִאטֵאתָ אַדְמַת מֹף וְנֹף בְּעָבְרְךָ בַּפֶּסַח,

וַאֲמַרְתֶּם זֶבַח פֶּסַח.

יָהּ רֹאשׁ כָּל אוֹן מָחַצְתָּ בְּלֵיל שִׁמּוּר פֶּסַח,
כַּבִּיר עַל בֵּן בְּכוֹר פָּסַחְתָּ בְּדַם פֶּסַח,
לְבִלְתִּי תֵּת מַשְׁחִית לָבֹא בִּפְתָחַי בַּפֶּסַח.

וַאֲמַרְתֶּם זֶבַח פֶּסַח.

מְסֻגֶּרֶת סֻגָּרָה בְּעִתּוֹתֵי פֶּסַח,
נִשְׁמְדָה מִדְיָן בִּצְלִיל שְׂעוֹרֵי עֹמֶר פֶּסַח,
שֹׂרְפוּ מִשְׁמַנֵּי פּוּל וְלוּד בִּיקַד יְקוֹד פֶּסַח,

וַאֲמַרְתֶּם זֶבַח פֶּסַח.

עוֹד הַיּוֹם בְּנֹב לַעֲמֹד עַד גָּעָה עוֹנַת פֶּסַח,

פַּס יָד כָּתְבָה לְקַעֲקֵעַ צוּל בַּפֶּסַח,
צָפֹה הַצָּפִית עָרוֹךְ הַשֻּׁלְחָן בַּפֶּסַח,
וַאֲמַרְתֶּם זֶבַח פֶּסַח.
קָהָל כִּנְּסָה הֲדַסָּה צוֹם לְשַׁלֵּשׁ בַּפֶּסַח,
רֹאשׁ מִבֵּית רָשָׁע מָחַצְתָּ בְּעֵץ חֲמִשִּׁים בַּפֶּסַח,
שְׁתֵּי אֵלֶּה רֶגַע תָּבִיא לְעוּצִית בַּפֶּסַח,
תָּעֹז יָדְךָ תָּרוּם יְמִינְךָ כְּלֵיל הִתְקַדֵּשׁ חַג פֶּסַח,
וַאֲמַרְתֶּם זֶבַח פֶּסַח.

And ye shall say: Tis the offering of the Passover.

Hadassah gathered all, for three-fold fast on Passover. Thou didst smite the chief of the evil house on Passover. These twain shalt Thou together bring for Edom on the Passover. Thy hand shall be strong: Thy right arm uplifted as on the night of sanctification of the Passover.

And ye shall say: Tis the offering of the Passover.

כִּי לוֹ נָאֶה. כִּי לוֹ יָאֶה

Ki Lo Naeh

אַדִּיר בִּמְלוּכָה, בָּחוּר כַּהֲלָכָה, גְּדוּדָיו יֹאמְרוּ לוֹ: לְךָ וּלְךָ, לְךָ כִּי לְךָ, לְךָ אַף לְךָ, לְךָ יְיָ הַמַּמְלָכָה. כִּי לוֹ נָאֶה, כִּי לוֹ יָאֶה.

דָּגוּל בִּמְלוּכָה, הָדוּר כַּהֲלָכָה, וָתִיקָיו יֹאמְרוּ לוֹ: לְךָ וּלְךָ, לְךָ כִּי לְךָ, לְךָ אַף לְךָ, לְךָ יְיָ הַמַּמְלָכָה. כִּי לוֹ נָאֶה, כִּי לוֹ יָאֶה.

זַכַּאי בִּמְלוּכָה, חָסִין כַּהֲלָכָה, טַפְסְרָיו יֹאמְרוּ לוֹ: לְךָ וּלְךָ, לְךָ כִּי

Mighty in kingship, chosen of right! To Him say His armies: "To Thee and to Thee, to Thee yea to Thee, to Thee true to Thee, to Thee Lord, is the sovereignty.
To Him is it becoming, to Him shall it be comely!"

Foremost in kingship, glorious of right! To Him say His trusty: "To Thee and to Thee, to Thee yea to Thee, to Thee true to Thee, to Thee, Lord, is the sovereignty.
To Him is it becoming, to Him shall it be comely!"

All-pure in kingship, powerful of right! To Him say His courtiers: "To Thee and to Thee, to Thee yea to Thee, to Thee true to Thee, to

Thee, Lord, is the sovereignty.
To Him is it becoming, to Him shall it be comely!"

Single in kingship, mighty of right! To Him say His wise ones: "To Thee and to Thee, to Thee yea to Thee, to Thee true to Thee, to Thee, Lord, is the sovereignty.
To Him is it becoming, to Him shall it be comely!"

Exalted in kingship, revered of right! To Him say those around Him: "To Thee and to Thee, to Thee yea to Thee, to Thee true to Thee, to Thee, Lord, is the sovereignty.
To Him is it becoming, to Him shall it be comely!"

Gentle in kingship, redeeming of right! To Him say His righteous: "To Thee and to Thee, to Thee yea to Thee, to Thee true to Thee, to Thee, Lord, is the sovereignty.
To Him is it becoming, to Him shall it be comely!"

Holy in kingship, merciful of right! To Him say His myriads: "To Thee and to Thee, to Thee yea to Thee, to Thee true to Thee, to Thee, Lord, is the sovereignty.
To Him is it becoming, to Him shall it be comely!"

Excellent in kingship, sustaining of right! To

לְךָ, לְךָ אַף לְךָ, לְךָ יְיָ הַמַּמְלָכָה. כִּי
לוֹ נָאֶה, כִּי לוֹ יָאֶה.

יָחִיד בִּמְלוּכָה, כַּבִּיר כַּהֲלָכָה,
לִמּוּדָיו יֹאמְרוּ לוֹ: לְךָ וּלְךָ, לְךָ כִּי
לְךָ, לְךָ אַף לְךָ, לְךָ יְיָ הַמַּמְלָכָה. כִּי
לוֹ נָאֶה, כִּי לוֹ יָאֶה.

מָרוֹם בִּמְלוּכָה, נוֹרָא כַּהֲלָכָה,
סְבִיבָיו יֹאמְרוּ לוֹ: לְךָ וּלְךָ, לְךָ כִּי
לְךָ, לְךָ אַף לְךָ, לְךָ יְיָ הַמַּמְלָכָה. כִּי
לוֹ נָאֶה, כִּי לוֹ יָאֶה.

עָנָיו בִּמְלוּכָה, פּוֹדֶה כַּהֲלָכָה,
צַדִּיקָיו יֹאמְרוּ לוֹ: לְךָ וּלְךָ, לְךָ כִּי
לְךָ, לְךָ אַף לְךָ, לְךָ יְיָ הַמַּמְלָכָה. כִּי
לוֹ נָאֶה, כִּי לוֹ יָאֶה.

קָדוֹשׁ בִּמְלוּכָה, רַחוּם כַּהֲלָכָה,
שִׁנְאַנָּיו יֹאמְרוּ לוֹ: לְךָ וּלְךָ, לְךָ כִּי
לְךָ, לְךָ אַף לְךָ, לְךָ יְיָ הַמַּמְלָכָה. כִּי
לוֹ נָאֶה, כִּי לוֹ יָאֶה.

תַּקִּיף בִּמְלוּכָה, תּוֹמֵךְ כַּהֲלָכָה,
תְּמִימָיו יֹאמְרוּ לוֹ: לְךָ וּלְךָ, לְךָ כִּי

Him say His perfect: "To Thee and to Thee, to Thee yea to Thee, to Thee true to Thee, to Thee, Lord, is the sovereignty.
To Him is it becoming, to Him shall it be comely!"

Addir Hu

Strong is He! May He build His temple speedily! Rapidly, rapidly, in our days speedily! O God build, O God build;
build Thy temple speedily!

Choice is He, Great is He, Foremost He! May He build His temple speedily! Rapidly, rapidly, in our days speedily! O God build, O God build;
build Thy temple speedily!

Glorious He, Trusty He, Guileless He! May He build His temple speedily! Rapidly, rapidly, in our days speedily! O God build, O God build;
build Thy temple speedily!

Righteous He, Pure is He, One is He! May He build His temple speedily! Rapidly, rapidly, in our days speedily! O God build O God, build;
build Thy temple speedily!

Mighty He, Wise is He, King is He! May He build His temple speedily! Rapidly, rapidly, in our days speedily! O God build, O God build;

לְךָ, לְךָ אַף לְךָ, לְךָ יְיָ הַמַּמְלָכָה. כִּי לוֹ נָאֶה, כִּי לוֹ יָאֶה.

אַדִּיר הוּא, יִבְנֶה בֵיתוֹ בְּקָרוֹב, בִּמְהֵרָה בִּמְהֵרָה בְּיָמֵינוּ בְּקָרוֹב. אֵל בְּנֵה, אֵל בְּנֵה, בְּנֵה בֵיתְךָ בְּקָרוֹב.

בָּחוּר הוּא, גָּדוֹל הוּא, דָּגוּל הוּא, יִבְנֶה בֵיתוֹ בְּקָרוֹב, בִּמְהֵרָה בִּמְהֵרָה בְּיָמֵינוּ בְּקָרוֹב. אֵל בְּנֵה, אֵל בְּנֵה, בְּנֵה בֵיתְךָ בְּקָרוֹב.

הָדוּר הוּא, וָתִיק הוּא, זַכַּאי הוּא, יִבְנֶה בֵיתוֹ בְּקָרוֹב, בִּמְהֵרָה בִּמְהֵרָה בְּיָמֵינוּ בְּקָרוֹב. אֵל בְּנֵה, אֵל בְּנֵה, בְּנֵה בֵיתְךָ בְּקָרוֹב.

חָסִיד הוּא, טָהוֹר הוּא, יָחִיד הוּא, יִבְנֶה בֵיתוֹ בְּקָרוֹב, בִּמְהֵרָה בִּמְהֵרָה בְּיָמֵינוּ בְּקָרוֹב. אֵל בְּנֵה, אֵל בְּנֵה, בְּנֵה בֵיתְךָ בְּקָרוֹב.

כַּבִּיר הוּא, לָמוּד הוּא, מֶלֶךְ הוּא, יִבְנֶה בֵיתוֹ בְּקָרוֹב, בִּמְהֵרָה בִּמְהֵרָה בְּיָמֵינוּ בְּקָרוֹב. אֵל בְּנֵה, אֵל בְּנֵה, בְּנֵה בֵיתְךָ בְּקָרוֹב.

נוֹרָא הוּא, סַגִּיב הוּא, עִזּוּז הוּא, יִבְנֶה בֵּיתוֹ בְּקָרוֹב, בִּמְהֵרָה בִּמְהֵרָה בְּיָמֵינוּ בְּקָרוֹב. אֵל בְּנֵה, אֵל בְּנֵה, בְּנֵה בֵיתְךָ בְּקָרוֹב.

פּוֹדֶה הוּא, צַדִּיק הוּא, קָדוֹשׁ הוּא, יִבְנֶה בֵּיתוֹ בְּקָרוֹב, בִּמְהֵרָה בִּמְהֵרָה בְּיָמֵינוּ בְּקָרוֹב. אֵל בְּנֵה, אֵל בְּנֵה, בְּנֵה בֵיתְךָ בְּקָרוֹב.

רַחוּם הוּא, שַׁדַּי הוּא, תַּקִּיף הוּא, יִבְנֶה בֵּיתוֹ בְּקָרוֹב, בִּמְהֵרָה בִּמְהֵרָה בְּיָמֵינוּ בְּקָרוֹב. אֵל בְּנֵה, אֵל בְּנֵה, בְּנֵה בֵיתְךָ בְּקָרוֹב.

build Thy temple speedily!

Awe-inspiring He, Exalted He, Powerful He! May He build His temple speedily! Rapidly, rapidly, in our days speedily! O God build, O God build; build Thy temple speedily!

Redeeming He, Good is He, Holy He! May He build His temple speedily! Rapidly, rapidly, in our days speedily! O God build, O God build; build Thy temple speedily!

Merciful He, Almighty He, Lord is He! May He build His temple speedily! Rapidly, rapidly, in our days speedily! O God build, O God build; build Thy temple speedily!

Eḥad Mi Yodea

אֶחָד מִי יוֹדֵעַ? — אֶחָד אֲנִי יוֹדֵעַ: אֶחָד אֱלֹהֵינוּ שֶׁבַּשָּׁמַיִם וּבָאָרֶץ.

שְׁנַיִם מִי יוֹדֵעַ? — שְׁנַיִם אֲנִי יוֹדֵעַ: שְׁנֵי לֻחוֹת הַבְּרִית, אֶחָד אֱלֹהֵינוּ שֶׁבַּשָּׁמַיִם וּבָאָרֶץ.

שְׁלֹשָׁה מִי יוֹדֵעַ? — שְׁלֹשָׁה אֲנִי יוֹדֵעַ:

Who knows *one?* One I know! One is our God in heaven and on earth.

Who knows *two?* Two I know! Two are the tables of covenant; one is our God in heaven and on earth.

Who knows *three?* Three I know! Three are the fathers; two are the tables of covenant; one

שְׁלֹשָׁה אָבוֹת, שְׁנֵי לֻחוֹת הַבְּרִית, אֶחָד אֱלֹהֵינוּ שֶׁבַּשָּׁמַיִם וּבָאָרֶץ.

is our God in heaven and on earth.

אַרְבַּע מִי יוֹדֵעַ? — אַרְבַּע אֲנִי יוֹדֵעַ:
אַרְבַּע אִמָּהוֹת, שְׁלֹשָׁה אָבוֹת, שְׁנֵי לֻחוֹת הַבְּרִית, אֶחָד אֱלֹהֵינוּ שֶׁבַּשָּׁמַיִם וּבָאָרֶץ.

Who knows *four?* Four I know! Four are the mothers; three are the fathers; two are the tables of covenant; one is our God in heaven and on earth.

חֲמִשָּׁה מִי יוֹדֵעַ? — חֲמִשָּׁה אֲנִי יוֹדֵעַ:
חֲמִשָּׁה חוּמְשֵׁי תוֹרָה, אַרְבַּע אִמָּהוֹת, שְׁלֹשָׁה אָבוֹת, שְׁנֵי לֻחוֹת הַבְּרִית, אֶחָד אֱלֹהֵינוּ שֶׁבַּשָּׁמַיִם וּבָאָרֶץ.

Who knows *five?* Five I know! Five are the books of the Torah; four are the mothers; three are the fathers; two are the tables of covenant; one is our God in heaven and on earth.

שִׁשָּׁה מִי יוֹדֵעַ? — שִׁשָּׁה אֲנִי יוֹדֵעַ:
שִׁשָּׁה סִדְרֵי מִשְׁנָה, חֲמִשָּׁה חוּמְשֵׁי תוֹרָה, אַרְבַּע אִמָּהוֹת, שְׁלֹשָׁה אָבוֹת, שְׁנֵי לֻחוֹת הַבְּרִית, אֶחָד אֱלֹהֵינוּ שֶׁבַּשָּׁמַיִם וּבָאָרֶץ.

Who knows *six?* Six I know! Six are the orders of the Mishnah; five are the books of the Torah; four are the mothers; three are the fathers; two are the tables of covenant; one is our God in heaven and on earth.

שִׁבְעָה מִי יוֹדֵעַ? — שִׁבְעָה אֲנִי יוֹדֵעַ:
שִׁבְעָה יְמֵי שַׁבַּתָּא, שִׁשָּׁה סִדְרֵי

Who knows *seven?* Seven I know! Seven are the days of the week; six are the orders of the Mishnah; five are the books of the Torah; four are the mothers; three are the fathers; two are the tables of covenant; one is our God in heaven and on earth.

מִשְׁנָה, חֲמִשָּׁה חוּמְשֵׁי תוֹרָה, אַרְבַּע אִמָּהוֹת, שְׁלֹשָׁה אָבוֹת, שְׁנֵי לֻחוֹת הַבְּרִית, אֶחָד אֱלֹהֵינוּ שֶׁבַּשָּׁמַיִם וּבָאָרֶץ.

Who knows *eight?* Eight I know! Eight are the days of circumcision; seven are the days of the week; six are the orders of the Mishnah; five are the books of the Torah; four are the mothers; three are the fathers; two are the tables of covenant; one is our God in heaven and on earth.

שְׁמוֹנָה מִי יוֹדֵעַ? — שְׁמוֹנָה אֲנִי יוֹדֵעַ:

שְׁמוֹנָה יְמֵי מִילָה, שִׁבְעָה יְמֵי שַׁבַּתָּא, שִׁשָּׁה סִדְרֵי מִשְׁנָה, חֲמִשָּׁה חוּמְשֵׁי תוֹרָה, אַרְבַּע אִמָּהוֹת, שְׁלֹשָׁה אָבוֹת, שְׁנֵי לֻחוֹת הַבְּרִית, אֶחָד אֱלֹהֵינוּ שֶׁבַּשָּׁמַיִם וּבָאָרֶץ.

Who knows *nine?* Nine I know! Nine are the months of pregnancy; eight are the days of circumcision; seven are the days of the week; six are the orders of the Mishnah; five are the books of the Torah; four are the mothers; three are the fathers; two are the tables of covenant; one is our God in heaven and on earth.

תִּשְׁעָה מִי יוֹדֵעַ? — תִּשְׁעָה אֲנִי יוֹדֵעַ:

תִּשְׁעָה יַרְחֵי לֵדָה, שְׁמוֹנָה יְמֵי מִילָה, שִׁבְעָה יְמֵי שַׁבַּתָּא, שִׁשָּׁה סִדְרֵי מִשְׁנָה, חֲמִשָּׁה חוּמְשֵׁי תוֹרָה, אַרְבַּע אִמָּהוֹת, שְׁלֹשָׁה אָבוֹת, שְׁנֵי לֻחוֹת הַבְּרִית, אֶחָד אֱלֹהֵינוּ שֶׁבַּשָּׁמַיִם וּבָאָרֶץ.

Who knows *ten?* Ten I know! Ten are the commandments; nine are the months of pregnancy; eight are the days of circumcision; seven are the days of the week; six are the orders of the Mishnah; five are the books of the Torah; four are the mothers; three are the fathers; two are the tables of covenant; one is our God in heaven and on earth.

עֲשָׂרָה מִי יוֹדֵעַ? — עֲשָׂרָה אֲנִי יוֹדֵעַ,

עֲשָׂרָה דִּבְּרַיָּא, תִּשְׁעָה יַרְחֵי לֵדָה, שְׁמוֹנָה יְמֵי מִילָה, שִׁבְעָה יְמֵי

שַׁבַּתָּא, שִׁשָּׁה סִדְרֵי מִשְׁנָה, חֲמִשָּׁה
חוּמְשֵׁי תוֹרָה, אַרְבַּע אִמָּהוֹת,
שְׁלֹשָׁה אָבוֹת, שְׁנֵי לֻחוֹת הַבְּרִית,
אֶחָד אֱלֹהֵינוּ שֶׁבַּשָּׁמַיִם וּבָאָרֶץ.

Who knows *eleven?* Eleven I know! Eleven are the stars; ten are the commandments; nine are the months of pregnancy; eight are the days of circumcision; seven are the days of the week; six are the orders of the Mishnah; five are the books of the Torah; four are the mothers; three are the fathers; two are the tables of covenant; one is our God in heaven and on earth.

אַחַד עָשָׂר מִי יוֹדֵעַ? — אַחַד עָשָׂר
אֲנִי יוֹדֵעַ:
אַחַד עָשָׂר כּוֹכְבַיָּא, עֲשָׂרָה דִּבְּרַיָּא,
תִּשְׁעָה יַרְחֵי לֵדָה, שְׁמוֹנָה יְמֵי
מִילָה, שִׁבְעָה יְמֵי שַׁבַּתָּא, שִׁשָּׁה
סִדְרֵי מִשְׁנָה, חֲמִשָּׁה חוּמְשֵׁי
תוֹרָה, אַרְבַּע אִמָּהוֹת, שְׁלֹשָׁה
אָבוֹת, שְׁנֵי לֻחוֹת הַבְּרִית, אֶחָד
אֱלֹהֵינוּ שֶׁבַּשָּׁמַיִם וּבָאָרֶץ.

Who knows *twelve?* Twelve I know! Twelve are the tribes; eleven are the stars; ten are the commandments; nine are the months of pregnancy; eight are the days of circumcision; seven are the days of the week; six are the orders of the Mishnah; five are the books of the Torah; four are the mothers; three are the fathers; two are the tables of covenant; one is our God in heaven and on earth.

שְׁנֵים עָשָׂר מִי יוֹדֵעַ? — שְׁנֵים
עָשָׂר אֲנִי יוֹדֵעַ:
שְׁנֵים עָשָׂר שִׁבְטַיָּא, אַחַד עָשָׂר
כּוֹכְבַיָּא, עֲשָׂרָה דִּבְּרַיָּא, תִּשְׁעָה
יַרְחֵי לֵדָה, שְׁמוֹנָה יְמֵי מִילָה,
שִׁבְעָה יְמֵי שַׁבַּתָּא, שִׁשָּׁה סִדְרֵי
מִשְׁנָה, חֲמִשָּׁה חוּמְשֵׁי תוֹרָה,
אַרְבַּע אִמָּהוֹת, שְׁלֹשָׁה אָבוֹת, שְׁנֵי
לֻחוֹת הַבְּרִית, אֶחָד אֱלֹהֵינוּ
שֶׁבַּשָּׁמַיִם וּבָאָרֶץ.

Who knows *thirteen?* Thirteen I know! Thirteen are the Attributes of God; twelve are the tribes; eleven are the stars; ten are the commandments; nine are the

שְׁלֹשָׁה עָשָׂר מִי יוֹדֵעַ? — שְׁלֹשָׁה עָשָׂר אֲנִי יוֹדֵעַ:
שְׁלֹשָׁה עָשָׂר מִדַּיָּא, שְׁנֵים עָשָׂר שִׁבְטַיָּא, אַחַד עָשָׂר כּוֹכְבַיָּא, עֲשָׂרָה דִבְּרַיָּא, תִּשְׁעָה יַרְחֵי לֵדָה, שְׁמוֹנָה יְמֵי מִילָה, שִׁבְעָה יְמֵי שַׁבַּתָּא, שִׁשָּׁה סִדְרֵי מִשְׁנָה, חֲמִשָּׁה חוּמְשֵׁי תוֹרָה, אַרְבַּע אִמָּהוֹת, שְׁלֹשָׁה אָבוֹת, שְׁנֵי לֻחוֹת הַבְּרִית, אֶחָד אֱלֹהֵינוּ שֶׁבַּשָּׁמַיִם וּבָאָרֶץ.

months of pregnancy; eight are the days of circumcision; seven are the days of the week; six are the orders of the Mishnah; five are the books of the Torah; four are the mothers; three are the fathers; two are the tables of covenant; one is our God in heaven and on earth.

Ḥad Gadya

חַד גַּדְיָא, חַד גַּדְיָא,
דִּזְבַן אַבָּא בִּתְרֵי זוּזֵי. חַד גַּדְיָא, חַד גַּדְיָא.

One kid, an only kid, that father bought for two zuzim.
One kid, an only kid.

וְאָתָא שׁוּנְרָא, וְאָכְלָה לְגַדְיָא, דִּזְבַן אַבָּא בִּתְרֵי זוּזֵי. חַד גַּדְיָא, חַד גַּדְיָא.

Then came a cat and ate the kid, that father bought for two zuzim.
One kid, an only kid.

וְאָתָא כַלְבָּא, וְנָשַׁךְ לְשׁוּנְרָא, דְּאָכְלָה לְגַדְיָא, דִּזְבַן אַבָּא בִּתְרֵי זוּזֵי. חַד גַּדְיָא, חַד גַּדְיָא.

Then came a dog and bit the cat, that ate the kid, that father bought for two zuzim.
One kid, an only kid.

וְאָתָא חוּטְרָא, וְהִכָּה לְכַלְבָּא, דְּנָשַׁךְ לְשׁוּנְרָא, דְּאָכְלָה לְגַדְיָא, דִּזְבַן אַבָּא בִּתְרֵי זוּזֵי. חַד גַּדְיָא, חַד גַּדְיָא.

Then came a stick and beat the dog, that bit the cat, that ate the kid, that father bought for two zuzim.
One kid, an only kid.

וְאָתָא נוּרָא, וְשָׂרַף לְחוּטְרָא, דְּהִכָּה לְכַלְבָּא, דְּנָשַׁךְ לְשׁוּנְרָא, דְּאָכְלָה לְגַדְיָא, דִּזְבַן אַבָּא בִּתְרֵי זוּזֵי. חַד גַּדְיָא, חַד גַּדְיָא.

Then came the fire and burned the stick, that beat the dog, that bit the cat, that ate the kid, that father bought for two zuzim.
One kid, an only kid.

וְאָתָא מַיָּא, וְכָבָה לְנוּרָא, דְּשָׂרַף לְחוּטְרָא, דְּהִכָּה לְכַלְבָּא, דְּנָשַׁךְ לְשׁוּנְרָא, דְּאָכְלָה לְגַדְיָא, דִּזְבַן אַבָּא בִּתְרֵי זוּזֵי. חַד גַּדְיָא, חַד גַּדְיָא.

Then water came and quenched the fire, that burned the stick, that beat the dog, that bit the cat, that ate the kid, that father bought for two zuzim.
One kid, an only kid.

וְאָתָא תוֹרָא, וְשָׁתָה לְמַיָּא, דְּכָבָה לְנוּרָא, דְּשָׂרַף לְחוּטְרָא, דְּהִכָּה לְכַלְבָּא, דְּנָשַׁךְ לְשׁוּנְרָא, דְּאָכְלָה לְגַדְיָא, דִּזְבַן אַבָּא בִּתְרֵי זוּזֵי. חַד גַּדְיָא, חַד גַּדְיָא.

Then came an ox and drank the water, that quenched the fire, that burned the stick, that beat the dog, that bit the cat, that ate the kid, that father bought for two zuzim.
One kid, an only kid.

וְאָתָא הַשּׁוֹחֵט, וְשָׁחַט לְתוֹרָא, דְּשָׁתָה לְמַיָּא, דְּכָבָה לְנוּרָא, דְּשָׂרַף לְחוּטְרָא, דְּהִכָּה לְכַלְבָּא, דְּנָשַׁךְ לְשׁוּנְרָא, דְּאָכְלָה לְגַדְיָא, דִּזְבַן אַבָּא בִּתְרֵי זוּזֵי. חַד גַּדְיָא, חַד גַּדְיָא.

Then came the slaughterer and slaughtered the ox, that drank the water, that quenched the fire, that burned the stick, that beat the dog, that bit the cat, that ate the kid, that father bought for two zuzim.
One kid, an only kid.

Then came the Angel of Death and slew the slaughterer, that slaughtered the ox, that drank the water, that quenched the fire, that burned the stick, that beat the dog, that bit the cat, that ate the kid, that father bought for two zuzim. One kid, an only kid.

וְאָתָא מַלְאַךְ הַמָּוֶת, וְשָׁחַט לְשׁוֹחֵט, דְּשָׁחַט לְתוֹרָא, דְּשָׁתָה לְמַיָּא, דְּכָבָה לְנוּרָא, דְּשָׂרַף לְחוּטְרָא, דְּהִכָּה לְכַלְבָּא, דְּנָשַׁךְ לְשׁוּנְרָא, דְּאָכְלָה לְגַדְיָא, דִּזְבַן אַבָּא בִּתְרֵי זוּזֵי. חַד גַּדְיָא, חַד גַּדְיָא.

Then came the Holy One, Blessed be He and smote the Angel of Death, that slew the slaughterer, that slaughtered the ox, that drank the water, that quenched the fire, that burned the stick, that beat the dog, that bit the cat, that ate the kid, that father bought for two zuzim. One kid, an only kid.

וְאָתָא הַקָּדוֹשׁ בָּרוּךְ הוּא, וְשָׁחַט לְמַלְאַךְ הַמָּוֶת, דְּשָׁחַט לְשׁוֹחֵט, דְּשָׁחַט לְתוֹרָא, דְּשָׁתָה לְמַיָּא, דְּכָבָה לְנוּרָא, דְּשָׂרַף לְחוּטְרָא, דְּהִכָּה לְכַלְבָּא, דְּנָשַׁךְ לְשׁוּנְרָא, דְּאָכְלָה לְגַדְיָא, דִּזְבַן אַבָּא בִּתְרֵי זוּזֵי. חַד גַּדְיָא, חַד גַּדְיָא.